NORTH**YORK**

NORTH YORK

REALIZING THE DREAM

Corporate Profiles by William A. Evans

Produced in Cooperation with the
City of North York,
Department of Property and Economic Development

Windsor Publications (Canada) Ltd.
Burlington, Ontario

Windsor Publications (Canada) Ltd.
—Book Division

Managing Editor: Karen Story
Design Director: Alexander D'Anca

Staff for *North York: Realizing the Dream*
Senior Editor: Pamela Schroeder
Photo Editor: Larry Molmud
Copy Editor: Maryanne L. Kibodeaux
Assistant Copy Editor: Suzanne Kelley
Coordinator, Corporate Profiles: Gladys
    McKnight
Editor, Corporate Profiles: Brenda Berryhill
Senior Production Editor, Corporate Profiles:
    Phyllis Gray
Editorial Assistants: Didier Beauvoir, Thelma
    Fleischer, Kim Kievman, Rebecca Kropp,
    Michael Nugwynne, Kathy B. Peyser,
    Pat Pittman, Theresa Solis
Sales Manager, Corporate Profiles: Paul Pender
Sales Representatives, Corporate Profiles:
    Maria Pender, Hughes Winfield
Designer: Thomas Prager
Layout Artist: Robaire Ream
Layout Artist, Corporate Profiles: Bonnie Felt

Windsor Publications (Canada) Ltd.
Elliot Martin, Chairman of the Board
James L. Fish III, Chief Operating Officer

The Don Valley Parkway and Highway 401 inter-change can be seen in this aerial view. Photo by Derek Trask/The StockMarket

CONTENTS

Part 1
North York: Shaping Its Destiny   10

CONTENTS

FOREWORD

Nowhere is the human spirit stronger than in the City of North York. I find the title of our *Realizing the Dream* book most appropriate.

Our city is built on dreams. The vision began with our earliest pioneer settlers who saw the promise of a new beginning in the North York farmland of yesteryear. The pioneers' dream of prosperity and progress was a foundation on which to build. Today our citizens, businesses and industries have worked to realize this dream and have helped to create one of Canada's most exciting and dynamic cities by following the path of ideas and innovation forged by our pioneers.

A city is more than buildings, bricks and mortar. People are what make a city truly great. And the City of North York is the greatest "people place" around. Our lush parks, excellent shopping, recreation, fine dining facilities, hotels and interesting sites attract visitors like bees to clover.

The homes in our well-kept North York communities are the nation's most desirable to live in. They are consistently on the real estate industry's bestseller list and are gaining in value faster than any other Canadian city's. When you look at all of our North York advantages, it's easy to see why we are the popular choice of hundreds of thousands of residents.

We are centrally located in the heart of Metropolitan Toronto, linked by wide arterial roads, major highways, and clean, speedy subways and efficient public transit. Our schools, community colleges, and universities offer a complete range of educational services. Places of worship feed the spiritual lives of every religious denomination.

North York's services and amenities are second to none. Our modern library system has maintained an unbeatable standard of excellence. Some of Canada's busiest libraries are found within North York's boundaries. They loan more than books. Records, videos, tapes, works of art and toys, a vast multilingual collection, and an array of materials for physically disabled people are among the items available.

As for culture and the arts, the City of North York is rich with art galleries, theatres, cinemas, museums, and musical groups, including our acclaimed symphony orchestra and concert band, our chamber orchestra, award-winning choirs, and performing groups such as our steel drum band.

The focal point of our city is what I refer to as North York's Miracle on Yonge Street—a $4-billion downtown that's being constructed in our city centre, complete with a civic square and major performing arts centre. Millions of square feet of retail establishments, offices, and residences are sprouting up seemingly overnight.

But it took many years of planning in partnership with our citizens. Area ratepayer groups participated fully in the forging of our downtown plan and gave it their complete support. Outside of North York, it is rare to see so keen a level of cooperative planning between local government and its citizenry.

We have immense pride in our city and in all that we have accomplished in a relatively short time. It is nothing short of miraculous that we are creating a downtown after we built the city and that this barrage of construction activity is happening all at one time, spurring us on from one success to the next.

The City of North York is quickly becoming the main magnet for commerce in Metropolitan Toronto. Our shiny new miracle of a downtown has prompted major corporate head office relocations and a flood of new business activity, and has spawned an unprecedented demand for our office space.

When completed, our downtown will generate full-time jobs for 60,000 employees, homes for more than 30,000 new residents, and $100 million annually in business and realty taxes. We're in great shape. We are becoming recession-proof.

Having served as Mayor of the City of North York since 1972, I have watched our city grow and bloom with promise at every stage. Once a small suburban township, we are flourishing now—a major force to be reckoned with in the world marketplace. Strong, aggressive, and progressive: this is North York.

Thanks to the cooperation of our diverse citizenry, our builders, commercial and industrial interests, service providers, and agencies in the City of North York, we have realized a dream that will assure our solid foothold in the future.

Mel Lastman

North York:
Shaping Its
Destiny

CHAPTER 1

Claiming a Home

The pioneer settlers who claimed a home in the wilderness could hardly have imagined the North York of today—a gleaming, vibrant city that symbolizes modern Canada.

The oldest remaining school in North York is the Zion School, constructed in 1869. Shown here near the turn of the century, it has since been restored and today functions as a living museum, with traditional classroom sessions offered to visiting schoolchildren. Courtesy, North York Historical Society

by Helga V. Loverseed

With a population of more than 560,000, North York is one of the largest cities in Canada. Bustling, modern, and industrious, North York is part of Metropolitan Toronto, which will soon be home to over 3 million people. North York is bordered on the west by the Humber River and on the east by Victoria Park Avenue, which separates it from Scarborough. Steeles Avenue delineates its northern border. Several streets divide it from the south and the rest of Metro—six municipalities in all.

A sprawling, vibrant city, North York is replete with dynamic neighborhoods, luxury condominiums, and gleaming office towers. And it's large. It sprawls over 69.44 square miles and encompasses a wider area and a greater population than any Ontario municipality except Toronto, from which it was originally carved. At one time, both were part of the large York Township, but in 1922 citizens of the northern district broke away to form the Township of North York. In 1967 North York became a borough. On February 14, 1979, it attained city status.

At that time city politicians and developers started to create an ultra-modern downtown core. This "Downtown, Uptown" as it is called (to distinguish it from Toronto's downtown) lines both sides of Yonge Street, North York's main artery, which more than anything else defines this thriving urban centre. Born out of decades of pioneer toil, North York symbolizes modern Canada as it stands on the threshold of the future—the exciting twenty-first century.

Looking at North York today, it seems astonishing that a mere three centuries ago the area was a wilderness inhabited only by Indians. They, like the European settlers who followed and helped to further their demise, were drawn by the bounty of the land. North York's forests were rich with game. The Humber River and its tributary, Black Creek, yielded fresh water and countless salmon and trout.

The Indians most commonly found in North York were Hurons, agricultural nomads who cultivated crops such as squash, beans, and pumpkins. Their custom was to set up camp for a couple of seasons, then move to another spot as local game or soil became exhausted.

Three such encampments have been found along Black Creek. The one on the west side of Jane Street, north of Wilson Avenue, is typical of the Indian villages which flourished in Ontario between 1400 and 1650. Its centre core, spread over five acres, was protected by a double palisade. Outside were hundreds of acres of cultivated land.

The most striking feature of such villages was the longhouse—a rustic dwelling built from a frame of saplings, covered with layers of bark. Such communal houses were large. At least 20 feet wide and 20 feet high, they were often over 200 feet long. Fireplaces were built in the middle with only an opening in the roof to serve as a chimney. Such homes were dark, smoky, and unsanitary—a far cry from the luxurious mansions that now grace North York's side streets.

The longhouses were also bitterly cold in winter, but they seemed to serve their purpose, as did the early log homes of the pioneers, which in many cases were little more than hovels. The Indians were a hardy race—that is, until the Europeans arrived and introduced such killers as liquor and disease—and they had furs to keep them warm. Here, as elsewhere in Upper Canada (as Ontario used to be known), the Indians traded pelts with French merchants and their *coureurs de bois*.

The fur traders of the mighty North-West Company, chief rival of the even mightier Hudson's Bay Company (which later took North-West over), sailed along Lake Ontario, then travelled by flat-bottomed boat up the Don River, which crosses North York. The boats were then mounted on wheels and hauled through the wilderness to Lake Simcoe—a tremendous achievement considering that even

now, on modern highways, it takes well over an hour to drive there.

But then this was an era of challenge. Hardship and larger-than-life accomplishments were second nature to fur traders. By the beginning of the nineteenth century, large-scale European settlement of Southern Ontario had begun and the fur traders moved north, further into the wilderness.

In 1787 Lord Dorchester bought some 500 square miles of territory from the Indians for £1,700—a paltry sum even for those times. Known as the Toronto Purchase, in fact it ran from Lake Ontario almost to Lake Simcoe, and included what is now North York. In time a military garrison was set up in Toronto, whose Indian name was changed to York in honor of the Duke of York. (It was subsequently renamed Toronto.) The farms around the Home District, to the north of York, grew into York Township.

North York essentially resulted from the establishment of that military garrison. As York grew, North York followed. To a certain extent its growth is still linked to that of Toronto—North York is, after all, only one of several interlocking cities that make up Metro—but it has also forged its own unique identity.

But in the beginning, York was the most important centre in this part of Upper Canada. It was founded by

John Graves Simcoe, right, is shown in this 1773 William Pars painting with John Burridge Cholwick, seated, and Archdeacon Andrew, left. Considered the founder of York, Simcoe's greatest achievement was the building of Yonge Street, today the world's longest thoroughfare. Courtesy, Metropolitan Toronto Library

Elizabeth Postuma Simcoe, wife of John Graves Simcoe, builder of Yonge Street, documented her travels into the interior with her husband with drawings and observations. Courtesy, Metropolitan Toronto Library

Lieutenant-Governor John Graves Simcoe, who arrived from England with his family on July 30, 1793. Simcoe stayed a scant three years, but he was to prove a most effective administrator. His wife, Elizabeth, also played a part: an avid diarist, she documented their travels to the interior with drawings and pungent observations.

Simcoe's most celebrated achievement was the building of Yonge Street. Yonge Street (also known as Highway ll), which runs 1,148 miles from Lake Ontario to the Minnesota border, is the world's longest thoroughfare as well as the main street of myriad communities throughout Ontario; 4.4 miles run straight through North York.

In Simcoe's day, of course, Yonge Street was little more than a dirt track. Simcoe built it because he decided that in order for the British to keep military and commercial control of Upper Canada, they would have to establish a safe and easy passage between Lake Ontario and Georgian Bay via Lake Simcoe (named in honor of Simcoe's father) and the Severn River.

With a handful of the Queen's Rangers, his famed soldier-engineers, he set off north to Penatanguishene to explore the possibilities of establishing such a route. They came back along the Don Trail, a tried and tested Indian track, and Simcoe decided that this should form the foundation of his military road.

As was the custom among colonial rulers, Simcoe named Yonge Street after a prominent British politician. Sir George Yonge was then Secretary of War. Work on the road started in the spring of 1794 at Holland Landing. By May more than a hundred 200-acre lots had been laid out on either side, as far as Eglinton Avenue, North York's southern boundary.

Yonge Street was improved and widened through the years, but for a long time it was a stump-laden track, impassable in inclement weather and a hazard to man and beast. It was particularly bad at Hogg's Hollow, a deep ravine at the south end of North York. Nevertheless, Simcoe's road quickly opened up the hinterland.

Settlers poured into Upper Canada, and Simcoe, realizing that manpower was vital for a fledgling colony, encouraged them every step of the way. To attract pioneers, the government offered generous land grants. Army officers and upper-class families were particularly favored (a system that was to lead to the establishment of the much-hated Family Compact a generation later). Influential entrepreneurs grabbed entire townships, and ruthless middlemen selling useless bush moved in on unsuspecting newcomers.

Soldiers could get as much as 5,000 free acres apiece. "Ordinary" settlers, such as impoverished working-class immigrants and Loyalists from

The namesake of the vital thoroughfare of North York was prominent British politician Sir George Yonge, who was then Secretary of War. Courtesy, Metropolitan Toronto Library

This swing bridge connected the two Hogg farms separated by the Don River. Mrs. Helen Hogg and son Alvin are shown crossing it in 1901. Courtesy, North York Historical Society

south of the border, received only 200 acres. Still, to people who had only a handful of money and few assets, the lure of free land was enough enticement.

To qualify for a land grant, settlers had to build a dwelling of at least 16 feet by 20 feet and occupy it within one year. Five acres out of every 100 had to be cleared and fenced and half of the road in front of the house made accessible. Clearing the wilderness was an immense challenge. Huge, ancient trees had to be felled to create space—an enormous job, since the axes used at that time were little more than hatchets. It often took a decade for stumps to become rotten enough to be yanked out of the ground by oxen or horses. In the meantime, these patches of land dotted with felled trees served as fields, where the settlers planted potatoes, turnips, and pumpkins.

North York's first houses were shanties or crude log cabins. Most had mud floors (planked floors came much later), roofs covered with bark, and small wall openings instead of windows. Glass was in short supply in the early days. The only way to keep warm was to hang heavy coverings over the doors and openings, and stuff the log walls with rags and clay.

Susanna Moodie, one of Canada's first novelists and the author of *Roughing it in the Bush*, published in 1852, didn't mince words when it came to describing these early homes. They were, she sniffed, ". . . dens of dirt and misery, which would in many instances be shamed by an English pig-sty."

Only the most monied settlers had proper furniture. Most made their own—simple, utilitarian tables, chairs, and beds, fashioned from rough-hewn planks.

North York's settlers were, perhaps, more fortunate than most. The Humber and Don rivers provided power for lumber mills and gristmills—essential to a burgeoning pioneer community—and the land proved workable and fertile. When the market opened at York in 1803, North York's pioneers were already supplying it with pork, beef, oatmeal, and potatoes. In fact, wheat was so plentiful that it was exported to England and America.

The city's first White resident is believed to have been Thomas Mercer. An Irishman who came to North York in 1794 by way of Pennsylvania, he settled in York Mills, bringing with him his family and worldly belongings in a wagon, with a cow tethered behind. Cornelius Anderson, a Scot disbanded from the British forces after the Revolutionary War, also settled in York Mills. He trudged here all the way from New Brunswick, which even today is a good three days' journey by car.

Jacob and Elizabeth Kummer arrived around the same time. Their name (anglicized to Cummer) lives on in Cummer Avenue. Another reminder of this era is the frame house at 90 Burndale Avenue, built by pioneer Joseph Shepard in 1812.

The area where the Kummers put down roots was known, appropriately, as Kummer's Settlement. (Its name was changed to Willowdale, the name in use today, when David Gibson petitioned the government for a post office.) Shortly after their arrival, Elizabeth Kummer gave birth to a son, John, believed to be the first White child born in North York.

Jacob Kummer, like most pioneers, was knowledgeable about animal husbandry, and it wasn't long before he had a thriving farm at the northwest corner of Yonge and Finch. A Lutheran who became a Methodist when he came to Canada, Kummer also started a Sunday school in his log house in 1816. In 1834 he donated half an acre on the east side of Yonge for a church.

Churches were among the first buildings to be established in North York. Not only houses of worship, they served as schools and social centres as well. But early church gatherings often took place in private homes such as Kummer's. North York's first services were held in Seneca Ketchum's log house on Yonge Street. Ketchum had wanted to enter the ministry, but he settled instead for a farm between Lawrence Avenue and York Mills.

In 1816, the Shepard family donated land to build an Anglican church on Old Yonge Street. The cornerstone of St. John's, as the church was called, was laid in mid-September. Since this was only the second Anglican church in the Home District, the opening was attended by dignitaries such as

Sir Francis Gore was Lieutenant-Governor of Upper Canada from 1806 to 1817. He was present at the opening of St. John's Episcopalian Church. Courtesy, Metropolitan Toronto Library

The Reverend John Strachan became Toronto's first bishop and one of the leaders of the Family Compact. Courtesy, Metropolitan Toronto Library

decent, and what was much better, they were filled with an attentive congregation. As you see very few inhabitants on your way out, I could not conceive where all these people came from; and it was pleasing to hear the voice of prayer and thanksgiving rising up from the wilderness, I hope in sweet memorial, before the Lord. The people were clean and neatly dressed, and interested in the service.

The fact that folk were "neatly dressed," as Strachan put it, was largely due to their own labors. Pioneer families wove their own cloth with linen thread from flax they grew themselves. They also butchered, salted, and smoked their own meat; fermented cider; baked bread; made candles and soap; and preserved all manner of fruit and vegetables.

In North York, woolen mills, gristmills, and sawmills sprang up around Black Creek, the Humber River, and the Don River. Samuel Heron opened the first mill in 1804 at the intersection of York Mills and Yonge Street where the west Don flowed through a ravine. Seven years later he added a distillery, which turned out 18 gallons of whiskey per day.

On the other side of Yonge (under the present-day Highway 401 viaduct), Thomas Arnold constructed a sawmill. Later he built a gristmill. In 1824, a Scottish emigrant named James Hogg bought the Arnold property, added a distillery, and named it York Mills.

Several buildings made up the Hogg complex. As well as the mills, there was a general store which housed North York's first postal station. Hogg and his son-in-law, John Anderson, also opened an inn. Called Anderson's Tavern, it burned down in 1855, but was replaced by the Jolly Miller, still a popular pub.

Two workmen's cottages built by carpenter Robert Gray on land sold to him by three of Hogg's sons are also still in existence. Recently moved from their original site to the northwest side of Yonge Street and York Mills, the cottages are now part of a French restaurant found in the new Yonge Corporate Centre.

Lieutenant-Governor Francis Gore and the Reverend John Strachan. (Strachan became Toronto's first bishop and one of the leaders of the hated Family Compact, the tightly knit group of officials who dominated provincial government in the early 1800s.) In the spring of 1817, after "uncommon exertions" by local families, the frame church was opened.

James Strachan, brother of the reverend, visited from Edinburgh in 1819 and described it thus:

The church is too low for its length, but it is very comfortably fitted up. The dimensions are 60 feet by 30: the pews are very

As early as 1806 Samuel Snider and his family, who arrived in North York after a two-month trek, settled at the edge of Black Creek, south of Finch. Here the Sniders constructed a barn, blacksmith shop, and smokehouse. By 1851 they had a sawmill and a second home overlooking the mill pond. Four years later Conrad Gram (like Snider, a Pennsylvania German) settled north of Finch and west of Dufferin. His second house still stands.

In 1820 Eli Beman operated a sawmill at Bayview and Lawrence. For the past 60 years this ravine has been spanned by a high bridge, but one can still see the small bridge and road which marked the earlier crossing of the valley. Mills were later operated on the same site by tanner Jacob Lawrence and William McDougall, a lawyer/publisher who became a politician and one of the Fathers of Confederation.

Alexander Milne, a Scottish-born weaver from Long Island, arrived at the southwest corner of Leslie and Lawrence streets (today's Edwards' Gardens) in 1827. He soon erected a sawmill and woolen mill and advertised that wheat, oats, barley, and corn

William McDougall, a lawyer/publisher who operated a mill at Bayview and Lawrence, later became an influential politician and one of the Fathers of Confederation. Courtesy, Metropolitan Toronto Library

When Anderson's Tavern burned down in 1855, it was replaced by the Jolly Miller, still a popular pub. Courtesy, North York Historical Society

Facing page: Alexander Milne, shown here with wife Harriet Margaret Heron Milne, erected a sawmill and woolen mill at what is today Edwards' Gardens, and advertised that wheat, oats, barley, and corn would be taken in payment for his goods and services. Courtesy, North York Historical Society

Small commercial operations like Alexander Milne's woolen mill inevitably went on to become thriving businesses and were the foundation on which North York's success has been built. Courtesy, North York Historical Society

would be taken in payment for his products. (At that time, barter was more common than cash transactions.)

These small commercial concerns, built initially to serve the immediate needs of settlers, inevitably became thriving businesses and the foundation on which North York's prosperity has been built. Along with the mills (the last ceased operation only in 1926) came general stores, inns, blacksmiths, brick makers, shingle makers, potteries, shoemakers, distilleries, and tanner-

ies. By the mid-1800s, there was a tannery at each concession along Yonge: Lawrence, York Mills, Sheppard, and Finch.

Schools followed. The first one in North York was built at Newtonbrook in 1801. Like most buildings at that time, it was crudely fashioned from logs. By all accounts, these one-room schoolhouses were woefully inadequate, especially during the winter. They had wood stoves, but were still chilly and damp. It was hard to concen-

trate on education when the ink froze in the bottles.

The first schools were built close to the road so that children wouldn't get lost in the woods or fall prey to wild animals. And the children often had to walk for miles. Not surprisingly, playing hooky was a regular occurrence. In any case, in this pioneer society little importance was given to schooling; there was too much work to be done, and children were a much-needed labor force. The emphasis on the "three Rs" as a passport to better things didn't come until much later, when North York had moved from being a self-sufficient pioneer society to one where agriculture and small business were the backbone of the community.

The first teachers had scant education themselves and were often chosen simply for their ability to keep order. Students were taught by rote from the few books that were available, and had to sit in class from 9 a.m. to 4 p.m., every day except Sunday. No doubt it was difficult for the students to adapt to such a narrow, rigid schedule. Pioneer youngsters were used to working at an early age, and were happiest running free in the open air. According to the log book from SS #23 school, the regimen was too much for one restless lad. Stanley Smith, it records, came to school one day armed with an axe, which he promptly used to chop down the steps!

The oldest remaining school in North York (and one of only two remaining in Metro) is the Zion School, near the corner of Finch and Leslie avenues, a one-room brick building constructed in 1869 to replace an earlier log schoolhouse. Zion School served the people of L'Amaroux for over 80 years. After school hours, it became a community centre, hosting meetings, dances, and concerts. It was closed in 1955, rendered obsolete by the advent of modern central schools. But it has recently been restored and furnished to portray a turn-of-the-century rural school. It is managed by the North York Historical Board and once again its doors are open to local children. Elementary school classes,

under the direction of a schoolmistress, re-enact a typical school day in 1910, complete with period desks, slates, and the rigid discipline of days gone by.

Places of entertainment, such as inns and public meeting halls, were also simple places compared to those of today. Having fun centred around the church or one's home. All kinds of bees—spelling bees, quilting bees, husking bees, logging bees, and barn-raising bees—were popular. These large assemblies not only provided the necessary manpower to complete various tasks, but were also lively social gatherings.

Community bees gave people the chance to get together and catch up on news. Men swapped stories and information about crops and animals. Women chatted about family matters and the problems of living in the bush.

For them, a bee was a heaven-sent opportunity to escape the round of boredom and drudgery that was their lot. Women were often stuck in the wilderness for months on end, while the men went off to hunt, or into town.

Not surprisingly, drunkenness was common at these affairs—as it often was during the pioneer era (the main reason why the temperance movement took such a strong hold during the mid-1800s). And there were coaching inns and taverns everywhere, especially along Yonge Street. According to contemporary reports, there was roughly one tavern per mile between Toronto and Barrie. In North York there were two inns where Yonge Street meets Sheppard Avenue, run by Thomas Hill and John Everson. When Everson moved to Lawrence Avenue, his inn was replaced by the Golden Lion Hotel.

The Golden Lion was "a large square frame building with verandahs running along the east and south sides . . . Over the door was an oak lion with a putty main. To the south were the large stables and on the north side at the intersection were the driving sheds that would hold a dozen horses and vehicles . . . "

The Golden Lion quickly became a favorite place for locals to hang out. A popular ditty of the early 1820s ran:

Here am I
On my way to Zion
I find my sons
in the Golden Lion

In a delicious twist of irony, the inn was bought in the early 1900s by the Reverend T.W. Pickett. A Methodist

The Golden Lion Hotel, long a favorite gathering place for locals, was purchased in the early 1900s by Reverend T.W. Pickett, a Methodist preacher who held Sunday school classes in what had once been the bar. Courtesy, North York Historical Society

preacher, he held Sunday school classes in what was once the bar.

Inns such as the Golden Lion attracted all manner of people—community leaders, settlers anxious to air their grievances, salesmen trying to make a fast buck, and farmers moving produce to and from the market in Toronto.

Inevitably, taverns also became forums for political rallies. Later some became administrative offices for local government. The Golden Lion served as York Township's council office until it was torn down in 1928. The hot issue of the 1830s was the Family Compact; opposition to it led to the Rebellion of 1837. Montgomery's Tavern, at Yonge and Eglinton, was the focal point for much of the action.

The Family Compact was the name given to the colonial rulers of Upper Canada—the governor, lieutenant-governors and Church of England clergy, who ran British North America (as Canada was then called). Members of a privileged class, they routinely handed out plum jobs to their family and friends and granted favorable business contracts to their political allies.

There were local councils and an elected House of Assembly, but they had no real power. The election system was patently unfair. York Township residents consistently elected reform-minded members such as Jesse Ketchum and David Gibson, in the hope that they might bring about changes, but they were only permitted to choose two representatives—even though York Township's population was greater than those of the five or six neighboring counties. Moreover, the governor of Upper Canada was answerable not to the people but to a colonial minister in London, who generally knew little about life in the country for which he was responsible.

Despite the objections of the settlers, the colonial rulers were impervious to these glaring inequities. They apparently hadn't learned a lesson from the Revolutionary War in the United States, which had so recently wrenched 13 colonies from Mother England. They counted on the hope that

Canadians would continue to be loyal to the Crown and ignore the republican movement south of the border. Many of the new settlers, however, had left Britain precisely because of unfair political practices and class inequality. Few were prepared to accept an arrogant, self-interested government.

As had happened in the United States, the settlers started to criticize the Mother Country. At first the protests were muted, but as time went by people began to air their grievances more openly. Outspoken and demanding leaders emerged—notably David Gibson and William Lyon Mackenzie.

Gibson, a Scotsman, built a house just north of the Shepards' in 1829 and was the first settler in North York to be a member of a profession. A surveyor by trade, he quickly became involved in public life and was twice elected to the House of Assembly.

Mackenzie, a fellow Scot, was Toronto's first mayor. A publisher, and a man of passion and political zeal, his prime aim in life was to undermine the influence of the Family Compact. Through his newspaper, the *Colonial Advocate*, he reviled its members, berating them for their bank scams, land-grabbing, and patronage practices. At public rallies he openly defied the colonial rulers, extolling the virtues of the American system of government—anathema to the true-blue Tories to whom king and country were the ultimate symbols of power.

The first open discussion of revolt was heard in North York on June 30, 1837. Fuelled by the revolutionary rantings of Mackenzie, a group of disgruntled settlers met to declare by public resolution that constitutional resistance to oppression had failed, and that all Reformers should now arm themselves in defence of their rights.

In secret, blacksmiths started forging simple weapons. Men practised military drills, and "pigeon shoots," a front for rifle practice, were held at taverns around North York. In August, Mackenzie published what was in essence a declaration of independence, following the American model and giving support to revolutionary forces in

David Gibson, along with other notable settlers like William Mackenzie, was an outspoken and demanding leader who aired his grievances openly. Gibson was the first settler in North York to be a member of a profession; he was a surveyor. Courtesy, North York Historical Society

Lower Canada (Quebec). Sir Francis Bond Head, the governor, responded in a typically high-handed manner by dismissing Mackenzie's talk of revolution as "childish." In fact, he was so sure of the government's superiority that he actually sent his troops to Lower Canada to quell unrest there, leaving York dangerously undefended.

This was just the opportunity Mackenzie had been waiting for. He quickly plotted to capture Government House. With the help of his supporters, now some 3,000 strong, he planned to imprison the governor and force him to acknowledge the political rights so long denied the Reformers (as those seeking change were called). To carry off his coup, Mackenzie sought the advice of Colonel Anthony Van Egmond, a retired officer who had fought at the Battle of Waterloo. His forces were to be led by Captain Anthony Anderson of Lloydtown and Samuel Lount of Holland Landing. They were

to reconnoiter at Montgomery's Tavern, then march from there to York.

But right from the start, the Rebellion was fraught with errors on both sides. Although government forces finally quelled the unrest, that was due more to chance than to good planning.

The government had on its side Colonel James Fitzgibbon, a hero of the War of 1812. Hearing of the rebels' intentions, he tried to rally Sir Francis and the Loyalists of York to prepare for an uprising, but the governor rebuffed him, reiterating, in his usual superior manner, his belief that the Reformers' complaints weren't serious. Luckily for the government, Fitzgibbon, an experienced military man, pressed on anyway.

Things quickly began to heat up. On Monday, December 4, Dr. John Rolph, a rebel who was slated to head the provisional government, heard that a warrant for Mackenzie's arrest was out, and sent word to David Gibson at

Dempsey's Store was built by Joseph Shepard II, who fought with William Lyon Mackenzie at the Battle of Montgomery Tavern. Courtesy, North York Historical Society

Facing page: Sir Francis Bond Head, Lieutenant-Governor of Upper Canada from 1835 to 1838, dismissed William Lyon Mackenzie's talk of revolution as "childish." Courtesy, Metropolitan Toronto Library

Lansing. Mackenzie was in the bush gathering support, so Gibson ordered Samuel Lount to come down from Holland Landing. Lount was promptly stopped and arrested near Richmond Hill, and released on the promise that he would go home. After lying low for a while, Lount and his 50 followers continued their journey to Montgomery's Tavern.

Colonel Robert Moodie, a retired army officer on the government side, was dispatched to York with two associates to warn Sir Francis of the rebels' intentions. They got as far as Eglinton, where Moodie was challenged by the rebels and shot to death. One of his companions escaped and ran towards York. The rebellion was fast getting out of hand.

Meanwhile, Mackenzie, with Joseph Shepard's son (also named Joseph), Captain Anderson, and some others, rode towards town. At Gallows Hill, just south of present-day St. Clair Avenue, they encountered Alderman John Powell and Archibald McDonald.

In the haphazard way that had marked this rebellion from the start, Mackenzie didn't bother to search Powell for arms. Unfortunately, Powell was carrying a pistol and shot Anderson dead.

By Tuesday Sir Francis finally realized that the rebels were serious and, through mediators, offered Mackenzie and his followers a verbal amnesty, provided they would immediately disperse. Mackenzie would have none of it, insisting that in order to take a peace initiative seriously he would have to see it in writing. His intransigence enraged the governor and ended any chance of a settlement.

At this point Mackenzie still had the upper hand, but instead of attacking York immediately, he returned to North York. This was to prove the rebels' downfall. By now Loyalist forces were pouring into York from around the province. By 6 p.m. the rebels, carrying only pikes and axe handles, started down Yonge Street where they were quickly outnumbered by the armed militia.

But even this encounter was fraught with errors. Sheriff William Jarvis and his men met the rebels at Maitland Street and opened fire, killing two men. The rebels, for their part, answered the fire; then the front line dropped to the ground to allow those behind to get a clear view. This was a common military manoeuvre, but the men at the rear, misunderstanding what had happened, thought their companions had been killed and retreated to North York.

By Wednesday, Dr. Rolph had fled to the United States. Sir Francis, accompanied by 1,200 troops, marched north to attend the funeral of Colonel Moodie and, on the way, attacked Montgomery's Tavern. Only a few volleys were exchanged, but a cannonball that whizzed through the building sent the few remaining rebels fleeing around the countryside. Sir Francis ordered his men to torch the building and the home of David Gibson.

Mackenzie, one of those who fled, managed to get a fresh horse at the Golden Lion. Four days later he rode into Niagara and escaped to the United

Sheriff William Jarvis, at left, is shown with his two sons, William and Colborne; it is not known which is which. Jarvis confronted rebels at Maitland, shooting and killing two men. Courtesy, Metropolitan Toronto Library

This steam shovel crew is laying track for the building of the CNR in the Don Mills area. Courtesy, North York Historical Society

States. Gibson hid in an Oshawa farm for weeks, then crossed Lake Ontario in an open boat and finally made it to Lockport. Lount was captured trying to cross Lake Erie and was subsequently hanged. Colonel Van Egmond, found hiding under a bed in Shepard's home, was tossed into jail and quickly died of pneumonia.

So ended the most colorful event in North York's history, one that was to have wide repercussions for Upper Canada. The incompetent Sir Francis Bond Head resigned, and within a few years Lord Durham's report paved the way for "responsible" government in Ontario and Quebec.

Queen Victoria eventually pardoned the rebels. Joseph Shepard came back to North York, where he built a large brick building at the corner of Yonge and Sheppard that is still in use as the Dempsey Brothers' store. David Gibson also returned, and constructed a handsome brick home to replace the one destroyed in the Rebellion. Today it's a "living history" museum with costumed guides. When Gibson built it, an acre of land with Yonge Street frontage sold for around $30. Today an acre in this part of the city routinely sells for more than $10 million. Clearly, North York has come a long way in a mere century and a half.

CHAPTER 2

Building a Community

North York's early residents shaped the city's destiny by melding many communities into one and framing a true metropolis with an identity all its own.

This was the North York Police force in 1947. Today, the force has three district divisional headquarters and employs more than 800 officers. Courtesy, Metropolitan Police Museum

Joseph Shepard's shop, at the northwest corner of Yonge Street and Sheppard Avenue West, was built about 1860. The shop was owned by R.B. Brown from 1888 to 1921, then by the Dempsey Brothers. Today it is a thoroughly modern hardware store. Courtesy, Metropolitan Toronto Library

by Helga V. Loverseed with Sheila White

With the 1837 Rebellion over, the people of York Township settled down to the business of building a community. The foundations of North York's social services and its commercial base were laid in the mid- to late 1800s. As the nineteenth century drew to a close, the pioneers, who had at first produced only for their own needs, became more business-oriented farmers and manufacturers.

It was, of course, a long time before North York became a single entity. In the 1800s the city was still a collection of villages and hamlets scattered throughout York Township: Lansing (Yonge and Sheppard), Morgan's Corners, Kummer's Settlement (later Willowdale), Newtonbrook, Reading Mills, Eglinton (Bathurst to Bayview, north of Lawrence), Don Mills, Oriole (Sheppard and Leslie), Fisherville, Kaiserville, Flynntown, L'Amaroux, Fairbank (Dufferin Street and Vaughan Road), Downsview, Elia (from Sheppard Avenue to Steeles, between Dufferin and Jane), and Emery (later Humber Summit). Situated at Islington and Steeles Avenue, Emery marked the northern corner of what was to become the city of North York.

Most of these communities have long since vanished, swallowed up by the roads and subdivisions built after World War II. Some, such as Don Mills and Downsview, although within the city boundaries, are still known by their original names. Others are remembered only in the name of a local school or library.

Each of these communities had its own fascinating beginnings, and some highlights should be noted, if only because the communities and their hardworking inhabitants made North York what it is today.

Lansing, which was at the corner of Yonge and Sheppard, is now part of North York's gleaming "Downtown, Uptown"—a forest of shopping malls and glistening office towers. The one remaining building from its pioneering heyday is Dempsey Brothers Limited, the brick store built by Joseph Shepard in 1860.

Then, as now, the corner of Yonge and Sheppard was a business centre and meeting place for local residents. Joseph Shepard's shop was one of those typical nineteenth-century general stores with a large, pot-bellied stove where people would gather to chat and catch up on the gossip. According to contemporary records, Shepard sold all kinds of merchandise—tools, implements, rope, nails, gunpowder, wool, bolts of cotton, and 100-pound cheeses.

In 1866 a post office was added. Shortly after, an agricultural implements maker, a carpenter, a cobbler, and a harness-maker moved into what quickly became a busy intersection. The store was sold in 1921 to the Dempsey Brothers. It is now on prime land slated for redevelopment.

Newtonbrook is best known for producing one of Canada's most famous native sons—politician Lester B. Pearson. His father, Edwin Arthur Pearson, was a circuit minister who held services at the parsonage near Hendon Avenue. Lester B. was born there, in 1897. In 1957, after his adroit handling of the Suez Canal affair, Pearson won the Nobel Peace Prize, and in 1963 he became Prime Minister of Canada.

Don Mills was, as its name suggests, the site of several mills which remained in business until the early 1900s. The mills were on the Don River (named after the Don in Yorkshire, England), which flowed through the area between Bayview and Victoria Park avenues, from Eglinton Avenue to York Mills Road. Sadly, the river has slowed to a trickle and is now badly polluted. But there are areas of parkland along its banks where residents can stroll or picnic.

In 1914 David Dunlap, a millionaire who made a fortune from silver and gold mines in northern Ontario, bought most of the valley to establish a research farm. No expense was spared, and his prizewinning livestock and experimental equipment drew visitors from around the world. Dubbed "a model for the universe," Dunlap's farm was by all accounts a remarkable place: pigs were given a bath twice a week, then rubbed with olive oil to keep their skins sleek and supple; stable hands mucked out the stables with

This is the Bayview Avenue Bridge, over the Don River, north of Lawrence Avenue East, as it appeared in the early 1900s. Courtesy, Metropolitan Toronto Library

Lester B. Pearson, Canada's foremost diplomat, was born on a farm in Newtonbrook. In 1957, after his handling of the Suez Canal affair, he was awarded the Nobel Peace Prize. Courtesy, Metropolitan Toronto Library

solid brass pitchforks; and the cows were vacuum cleaned and milked by men with manicured hands who wore white suits while they worked.

Later, Don Mills was to be associated with another millionaire, industrialist E.P. Taylor. Taylor and a group of his associates were responsible for laying out the Don Mills subdivision, Canada's first "planned community" and a protoype for others throughout North America.

Oriole (Sheppard and Leslie) spawned two politicians—William Mulholland, who twice served on York

Township's council, and George S. Henry, who became Premier of Ontario in 1930. Its earliest residents included the Shepard brothers, Michael and Thomas, who after being pardoned for their part in the 1837 Rebellion returned to North York to build mills. By the time George Henry was born, in 1898, several farms had been established in the area. He himself bred prize Holstein cattle.

Downsview, today the home of the Boeing-owned De Havilland aircraft plant and a Canadian Armed Forces Base, was also prime farming land. Mathias Sanders settled on Lawrence Avenue west of Dufferin as early as 1801, but was killed in the 1813 American invasion of York when the powder magazine was blown up by the defending commander. His son took over the farm in 1824, and the family remained in the area until well into the twentieth century.

In 1804 John Denison owned two lots south of Lawrence and west of Keele. His son, George Taylor Denison, supported the government in the 1837 Rebellion and was responsible for founding "Denison's Horse," a volunteer militia that became the famed Governor-General's Body Guard.

Downsview's best-known nineteenth-century resident was Sir Sandford Fleming, the inventor of standard time. An immigrant from Scotland and a civil engineer, Fleming's long and distinguished career as a railway builder in the Maritimes, Quebec, and Ontario included surveying the Canadian Pacific Railway routes through the Rocky Mountains. His invention—a universal day with the world divided into 24 time zones—greatly simplified communications and navigation systems on ships and, later, airplanes.

In 1856 Fleming, trying to sell land north of Lawrence Avenue between Keele and Dufferin, proved to be not so good a salesman as he was an inventor. His advertising sounded promising: ". . . The taxes charged on the property are those of the Township of York, amounting to a mere trifle when compared with those paid in Toronto . . ." But his business scheme failed.

Fisherville, named after Jacob Fisher who settled here in 1797, grew up around a mill site on the west Don,

A turn-of-the-century view of the Jolly Miller Tavern, then known as David Birrell's Hotel, also includes the Hogg Brothers' shop. Courtesy, Metropolitan Toronto Library/Pen and ink drawing by B. Gloster

The proud owner of a four-seater Ford drives down Keele Street. Courtesy, North York Historical Society

just east of Dufferin. In 1915 Colonel Albert Gooderham, then president of the Ontario Red Cross, purchased the site and donated it, along with an additional 58 acres, to the University of Toronto. The site became Connaught Medical Research Laboratories, one of the greatest successes of which was the mass production of insulin.

The laboratories made a big name for themselves during World War I,

when wounded soldiers created a huge demand for anti-tetanus vaccines. Insulin was discovered in 1921, by Sir Frederick Grant Banting and Charles Herbert Best. Using extract from the pancreatic tissue of dogs, they were the first to produce the life-saving substance in a pure enough form to be injected into diabetes sufferers.

Today the Connaught Laboratories are world leaders in the production of vaccines, antibiotics, and penicillin. Now a subsidiary of CDC Life Sciences, they employ 1,300 scientists and lab technicians in Canada and the United States.

World War I brought many changes to the lives of people in York Township. Men of York Township went off to the battlefields of France, while the women organized patriotic dances and rallies to collect money, food, and clothes for the troops overseas. Farmers grew large quantities of flax, needed for making airplane wings. (Because of the primitive state of aviation technology at that time, aircraft wings had to be made of a light fabric in order to have enough lift.) The Canadian Aeroplanes plant on Dufferin Street, which manufactured such wings for the Curtiss JN-4s (commonly called "Jennies"), did a roaring trade. Each plane needed several sets of wings because pilots were continually crashing.

Production peaked when Belgium and Northern France, for years major flax-growing areas, were captured by Germany. Linen manufacturers faced a tremendous shortage of raw material, and the farmers of York Township gladly took up the slack. By 1918 the flax industry had become so important to the local economy that the citizens of York Township staged a Flax Festival. The local branch of the Canadian

Canadian Defence Production Minister C.D. Howe inspects the De Havilland plant in 1954. Courtesy, Toronto Telegram Collection, York University Archives

Red Cross raised $1,700 to send to Nance, a war-torn village in France.

Pilots belonging to the Royal Flying Corps (neither the Royal Air Force nor the Royal Canadian Air Force existed at this point) trained in the Armor Heights area. The airfield ran from Bathurst east to what became Avenue Road, and north of Wilson Avenue on what was then the Wellington Mulholland farm.

With the young and inexperienced pilots, crashes were a regular occurrence. Ed Snow, who lives on Bogert Avenue, recalls the days of pilot training: ". . . my brother Bert and I used to walk there to watch the excitement. Planes kept crashing all over the place. Farmers became accustomed to finding stunned or injured fliers wandering in the fields and air force trucks arriving to haul away wrecked planes."

Such training sessions, fraught though they were with disasters, were nothing compared to the real thing. The European conflict was to prove a long and bloody one. But the Allies won, despite primitive equipment and overwhelming odds.

With the war over, the economy of York Township grew at a steady pace. Turn-of-the-century inventions such as electricity, the telephone, and the automobile made themselves felt. Agriculture was still the mainstay of the local economy, but people started to commute back and forth to work in the fast-developing metropolis of Toronto.

Travelling between North York and Toronto was more feasible than before, because roads were slowly improving. In 1910 George S. Henry, a wealthy dairy farmer and Reeve of York Township, had introduced uniform quality control for highway construction. Six years later he received

These three De Havilland workers seem justly proud of the Dragon model behind them. Courtesy, Toronto Telegram Collection, York University Archives

legislative approval for a three-way cost-sharing plan: the county of York, Toronto, and the province of Ontario now paid jointly for the building of roads. A common practice today, it was in the early 1900s an innovative idea. An astute politician, Henry became Premier of Ontario in 1930.

A more efficient system of road maintenance was also introduced in the 1920s by a labor statute requiring farmers to work three days per year improving the roads of the Township. The back roads were little more than dirt tracks, and even Yonge Street was still a muddy two-lane road with wooden sidewalks. The farmers, helped by veterans from the war, started covering them with cinders and crushed rocks—a great improvement, especially in wet weather.

A radial railway linked York Township with Toronto. At first the line, owned by the Metropolitan Street Railway Company of Toronto, ran only as far as Hogg's Hollow, which was the Toronto/North York boundary. In 1904 the line was taken over by the Toronto and York Railway Company, which extended service through North York as far north as Jackson's Point on Lake Simcoe.

The Thornhill Streetcar (#61) was one of the Toronto and York Radial Railway cars on the Metropolitan Line. By the mid-1920s, the three radial lines were running at a deficit of more than half a million dollars. The Toronto Transit Commission took over in 1927 and established a bus service. Courtesy, Metropolitan Toronto Library

George S. Henry served as Minister of Public Works and Highways (1923-1931) and as Premier of Ontario (1930-1934). He is credited for building hundreds of kilometres of new roads in the province. Courtesy, Metropolitan Toronto Library

The railway later became a money loser, but in 1930 North York co-purchased a portion of the company with Vaughan, Richmond Hill, and Markham. North Yonge Railways was inaugurated on July 17, 1930, and for the next 19 years it served commuters well, just as today commuters are served by the TTC (Toronto Transit Commission).

As travel between Toronto and North York became easier, Torontonians started casting their eyes north to the rural communities. York Township was a collection of small, neighborly villages with enough space to build large homes, develop businesses, and raise families. To folks tiring of the bustling city, it had a very strong appeal.

York Township was still run by Toronto's town council, which neglected the outlying communities in favor of its own interests. Preoccupied with urban affairs such as improved sidewalks, streets, lighting, waterworks, and sewers, Toronto's government often ignored the needs of the rural dwellers.

Those who lived in the north were outnumbered by Torontonians and had little political clout. When it came to voting, they were outnumbered twelve to one. In 1919 Toronto had 75,000 inhabitants. The northern area of York Township had only 6,000, most of them farmers. North Yorkers comprised a mere 8 percent of the population but they paid 23 percent of the taxes—an unfair situation, to say the least.

Not surprisingly, the citizens of northern York Township soon got fed up with this grossly inequitable situation. In 1921 the farmers banded together to apply for "independence" from Toronto. Under the leadership of Roy Risebrough, an employee of the

This work crew took time off from working on the Bayview Street Bridge to pose for this picture in 1929. Courtesy, North York Historical Society

Ontario Department of Agriculture, they decided to break away from the town and form a new North York Township, so they could better manage their own affairs.

Risebrough, a congenial and easy-going farmer who lived at the corner of Cummer and Bayview avenues, seemed an unlikely fellow to lead a revolution. But he proved an able negotiator. He was also one of the few people who owned a car at that time. With his hand-cranked Model T Ford he was able to drive from farm to farm, collecting signatures for a petition to be put before the Ontario Legislature. The farmers presented their case to E.C. Drury, pre-mier of the province. After a year of deliberation, the private bill became law. The Township of North York was born on June 13, 1922.

The first five-man council, all farmers, was elected on August 12. R.F. Hicks, a dairy farmer whose property was on the west side of Bathurst Street, north of Finch Avenue, became North York's first Reeve. One year later, Roy Risebrough was appointed the township's first police chief, a post he was to hold for the next 34 years.

Throughout the twenties and thirties, only a handful of men—Risebrough, Robert Wilson, Percy Smithson, and John Harrison—were re-

E.C. Drury was Ontario's first Minister of Agriculture. He was also president and co-founder of the United Farmers of Ontario. Drury was drafted as Premier of the newly formed government in 1919. Courtesy, Metropolitan Toronto Library

43

Right: Police Chief Roy Risebrough retired in 1957 after 35 years of service. When he joined the force in 1922, North York had only 6,000 residents. As the town's only constable, Risebrough also served as school attendance officer and milk inspector. Courtesy, Metropolitan Police Museum

Facing page, top: The North York Municipal Offices on the corner of Yonge Street and Empress Avenue were built in 1923. This building housed the municipal offices until 1956, when it became headquarters for North York Hydro. Courtesy, Metropolitan Toronto Library

Facing page, bottom: This is a vintage North York Hydro Electric Commission truck. Today, the NYHEC maintains a huge fleet of vehicles to provide service to its many thousands of customers. It is the second largest hydro system in Ontario. Courtesy, North York Historical Society

sponsible for keeping law and order. North York was still a sleepy, friendly community where everybody knew their neighbors' business. There was little major crime. Most misdemeanors were confined to drunkenness, chicken thievery, and occasional cattle rustling.

Teenage pranksters were the bane of Risebrough's life. Their favorite trick was to move the privies which graced the backyards of farms and houses. They played it so often that Risebrough and Hawkins could never catch all the culprits. But as Donald Copeland, a retired North Yorker who lives on Abitibi Avenue, recalls in an interview in the *Toronto Star*, the pranksters often got their comeuppance.

"Sometimes the trick backfired," said Copeland, "when an astute owner, before our arrival, moved it (his privy)

a few feet. In the dark it was not easy to see the open hole where the privy had stood earlier. Kids sometimes fell down them."

By 1957 North York's police force numbered almost 200. That year, it amalgamated with the rest of the Metropolitan Toronto Police Force. A new office was built in Sanderling Place in Don Mills. Today North York has three district divisional headquarters, which employ over 800 officers.

The creation of North York Township brought other benefits. A permanent town hall was built and public services such as fire protection, hydro, sewers, and water were introduced. In 1922 Dr. Carl Hill was appointed North York's first Medical Officer of Health. His department was put in charge of water and sewage control and the monitoring of food, diseases, and public health.

That same year, the North York Hydro Commission was established. Prior to that time, electricity was supplied by the Toronto and York Metropolitan Radial Railway Lines. Two years later, the first Hydro office was built at a cost of $3,650. This was little more than a warehouse for storing equipment, but in 1929 an office was constructed beside it.

North York Hydro has expanded enormously since then. In 1922 North York had only 13 streetlights. Today the city has over 30,000. The Hydro Commission has a huge fleet of cars and trucks to help it maintain service to its many thousands of customers, and it is now the second largest hydro system in Ontario.

On December 19, 1923, a brand new municipal building was opened on the corner of Yonge Street and Empress Avenue. Designed by architect

Murray Brown, who also designed North York's original corporate seal and its slogan, "Progress with Economy," it was constructed at a cost of $35,000.

The building of a new town hall was well overdue. Until its construction, council members had to conduct business in various buildings around town, such as the Willowdale School, the Golden Lion Hotel, and the apartments above the Harrington Block. One February morning in 1923 the Harrington Block caught fire. Residents tried to extinguish the conflagration by covering the roof of a neighboring building with wet blankets and by shovelling snow into the basement, but it was to no avail. North York's fire brigade, then in its infancy, was ill equipped to handle a blaze of that magnitude. Most of North York Township's early records were lost.

It was because of that fire that the new municipal building was erected so promptly, and in 1923 North York also got its first properly organized fire service. As in most small communities,

North York's first firemen were volunteers—businessmen and public-spirited citizens who were a far cry from today's professional firefighters. They used crude training methods and had only basic equipment, but it was a step in the right direction.

The first fire chief was William John Nelson. He was chosen mainly because he operated a garage—Nelson's Pioneer Garage at 4898 Yonge Street, just north of Sheppard Avenue—where he was able to house and maintain the fire department's sole truck, a Model T Ford.

By 1942 the need for a more efficient fire service became clear. North York was in the midst of a population explosion and people were moving to the suburbs in unprecedented numbers. That year, on January 1, a new brick fire station opened next door to the municipal building. The new fire force had two pumper trucks—a 1926 Reo and a 1936 Bickle—and five permanent employees. Volunteers still helped out, but by 1949 the permanent force had

Members of North York Fire Department pose with their new fire truck in 1943. Tired of wartime shortages, these men built the truck themselves in their spare time, piecing together parts from other machines. They are, left to right, Chief Ivan Nelson, W. Ballantyne, C. Symonds, F. Bennett, and C. Prowse. Courtesy, Toronto Telegram Collection, York University Archives

been extended to 21 members and the fire trucks were fitted with radios.

In 1952 a second fire station was built on Lawrence Avenue, just east of Bathurst Street. Two new stations opened in 1956. Since then more and more stations have been added as the need has arisen. Today the city has 17 fire stations with 665 employees. These men and women have the benefit of state-of-the-art equipment: computers, aerial trucks, rescue vehicles, and a mock subway station where emergency "rescues" can be staged.

The fire department has come a long way in 50 years, but the original fire station still stands, as does the municipal building. Two years ago the city sold them both to Menkes Developments Inc. The new owners intend to redevelop the site, but the old facades will be retained as part of a Heritage Walk.

With municipal services in place, the way was open for new housing and businesses. Many of North York's most successful commercial enterprises started up during this period. Nelson's Meat and Groceries, North York's oldest butcher shop, opened at 4983 Yonge Street in 1920; John and George McKenzie's Lumber Company and Sawmill was doing business on what is now the site of C-I-L's head office; and Dominion, the food chain found in several provinces, was established in Willowdale.

In 1926 North York got its first newspaper, *The Enterprise*. In 1941 it was bought by the Dempseys, who owned Dempsey Brothers' store. Later it was sold to the *Toronto Star*. A second newspaper, the *Don Mills Mirror*, was established in 1957 by Ken Larone, Russ Eastcott, and George Maclean. Today the *Mirror* is part of the huge Metroland Printing and Publishing empire controlled by *Torstar*.

A large, outdoor market with thirty stalls opened on June 19, 1926 to service local growers. (North York was known as a vegetable- and fruit-growing area until well into the 1940s.) Nicknamed the Tin Market because of

The crew of The Maple Leaf Fire Brigade of 1940 pose with their truck. The men are, left to right, Harold Shirely, Joe Hands, Frank Laver, Tom Marsh, Alfred Partridge, Brook Banks, and Jim Marsh. Courtesy, North York Historical Society

The Glen Echo Carhouse of the Toronto and York Radial Railway was sold in 1930 to the North York Township Market. The building was sold again in 1952 to an auto dealer. Courtesy, Metropolitan Toronto Library

its tin roof, it stood on Yonge Street at the Toronto city limits, south of York Mills Road, where a Loblaws store stands today. The market eventually outgrew its premises and was moved farther up Yonge, just south of Steeles Avenue. In its 1920s heyday it was a busy, bustling place. At its peak it employed over 80 farmers, and consumers came from miles around to purchase everything from fresh eggs to hooked rugs.

North York Township's business base was expanding. Statistics for 1922 show that property values that year were assessed at around $7.5 million (today the value is close to $2 billion). Not all of the new buildings were businesses. City dwellers, mostly from Toronto, were pouring into North York, attracted by its appealing living conditions and wide-open spaces. By 1926 North York's population had risen to 8,800, almost 3,000 more than when the Township of North York was established in 1922.

Many of these "new" North Yorkers moved to Bathurst Street and Avenue Road. War veterans and their families settled along Yonge Street. In-

evitably, speculators saw the chance to make a fast buck. Developers snapped up vast tracts of farmland and subdivided them into building lots. But many of these would-be entrepreneurs saw their dreams turn to dust. By the beginning of the 1930s, the Depression had Canada firmly in its hold.

One real estate developer who got caught in the squeeze was Bill Cox. He bought the Jolly Miller, by then a boarded-up tavern, and tried to run it as an elegant nightclub. According to a contemporary newspaper report, it opened to great fanfare on October 17, 1930: ". . . its dance floor is as smooth as a Paris night club, its music as modern as even a debutante could want. The food is delicious. The prices are reasonable." It should have been a success, but Cox's timing was wrong. These were tough economic times and the Jolly Miller closed within a year.

The Depression hit North York very hard. Jobs in Toronto were fast drying up and suburban workers were the first to be let go. Toronto was saved the cost of placing these workers on welfare, but it shifted the economic burden to North York. Soon one-third of the township's men were out of work.

Every council meeting was consumed with discussion of relief for the unemployed. Earl Bales, a member of one of North York's founding families and the township's Reeve from 1934 to 1941, recalls a "few sleepless nights" consulting with township clerk Herb Goode, treasurer Frank Brown, engineer Gordon Baker, and provincial supervisor Alf Gray, agonizing over what to do for beleaguered citizens.

Residents decried their plight angrily to council members. North York's annual taxes were a modest $33, but even those were too high for many people. To alleviate the problem, food vouchers were issued to poor families, and the township, under "make-work" schemes, hired men on welfare to do menial jobs, such as digging ditches and laying water mains. The wages were paltry, but to most people having even such ill-remunerated, back-breaking jobs was better than no job at all.

Fred Speer, who ran a grocery store at Avenue Road and Fairlawn Avenue, recalls what it was like for North Yorkers during the Depression years: "Twice a week, welfare recipients would line up with food vouchers, given in return for a day's work on some Township project."

And welfare recipients gathered daily at a garbage dump on the northeast corner of Lawrence and Avenue Road. They rummaged through the rubbish to salvage spoiled vegetables and fruit which they made into preserves for the long winter months.

Speer remembers that there was a chronic shortage of fuel. "One day a hydro crew installed several new Hydro poles on Avenue Road and left the old ones lying on a vacant lot at the corner of Fairlawn and Avenue Road. The next day, these 50-foot heavy poles were gone. Welfare people had come during the nights with crosscut saws, wheelbarrows and baby buggies, to cut up the poles and use them for good fuel in their furnaces and stoves . . . "

Public projects were put on hold. When St. George's Anglican Church on Yonge Street was built, there was only enough money to construct a basement. (The church was completed in 1950.) And councillors took a pay cut. In March 1933, Reeve George Elliott announced that councillors' wages would be reduced by 15 percent.

But such stopgap measures weren't enough to stave off insolvency. North York's "make-work" programs, coupled with the cost of relief, drove the township into bankruptcy. Like a lot of Ontario municipalities, North York was forced into operating under provincial supervision. From 1935 to 1941, all expenditures required provincial approval—a situation hard to imagine in the prosperous and wealthy North York of 1988.

But when prosperity returned after World War II, North York was one of the few municipalities to completely clear its debt. World War II brought hardship to many, but in economic terms it benefitted the country. Canada emerged from the conflict a wealthy and highly industrialized nation. The war created a demand for expertise and equipment (hundreds of the famous Mosquito aircraft were manufactured in Downsview by De Havilland Aircraft of Canada), and when it ended, industrial development shifted to the civilian sector.

In the 1950s and 1960s, Canada boomed. Scores of foreign companies rushed to invest in the vibrant, healthy economy. Speculators competed for a piece of the action, and immigrants, most from war-torn Europe, poured into the country. Nowhere was this more true than in North York. Immigrants were joined by war veterans and urban dwellers who, attracted by cheap land and low taxes, flocked to the suburbs.

There was a tremendous population explosion. North York quickly earned the distinction of having the highest birthrate in Canada. Schools couldn't cope with the influx of youngsters. Before new schools were built, pupils at Earl Haig High School were required to attend half-day only, to ease the overcrowding. In the war years, North York's population was 27,000.

By 1945 it had more than doubled. Five years later it had soared to 150,000. According to recent statistics, 95 percent of North York's inhabitants arrived after 1951.

The population explosion triggered a building boom in both the commercial and private sectors. The value of building permits in both sectors rose from approximately $9 million in 1946 to $129 million in 1958. Housing was cheap and readily available. Under the Veteran's Land Act (V.L.A.) introduced by the federal government, men who fought in World War II were able to purchase a half-acre lot with a bungalow for $6,000, or $18 per month. (Today, those same North York bungalows are selling for an average of $160,000.) Amortized over 25 years, the interest rate on the mortgage was a mere 3 percent per year.

Vacant lots were going for a song. North York Township had seized 4,000, abandoned by speculators during the Depression, and made them available to builders. Murphy Hall, a contractor in North York for 40 years, recently recalled that: ". . . in those days you could get a lot at Bathurst and Lawrence serviced with sewers for $12 a [front] foot . . . " Today, a front foot sells for $3,000 to $5,000.

Most of these lots were already serviced with sewers and water mains. At first developers paid the township for providing water mains and the like, but after a zoning by-law was passed in 1952 they had to ensure that essential services were part of their plans.

Although sewers and water mains could readily be put in place, North York had a serious problem with water supply. The city is landlocked. Its two reservoirs (at Bayview and Sheppard, and Bathurst and Wilson), and the filtration plant and pumping station at Leslie and Sheppard avenues, quickly became inadequate for the burgeoning population.

Water shortages were a fact of life. Rationing was introduced. People were

Frederick Henry Brigden, shown here in 1954 in the studio at his house on Cummer Avenue, was a member of the Royal Canadian Academy and the Ontario Society of Artists. Brigden was also a successful businessman, and his engraving company produced the Eaton's Mail-order Catalogue for several years. Courtesy, Metropolitan Toronto Library

The Earl Haig Secondary School is located at 100 Princess Avenue. The cornerstone for the collegiate institute was laid in 1929. Courtesy, North York Historical Society

restricted to watering their lawns once a week, and if they wanted to take a bath, they had to visit friends outside the township. At one stage there were even rumors that babies were being washed in soda water. To alleviate the shortages, the township started purchasing water from the neighboring municipalities of Scarborough and Etobicoke. The situation improved in 1954, when Bill 80 established Metro Toronto as a single entity. In 1957, at the urging of Reeve Verne Singer, the metropolitan government installed trunk mains that pumped water to North York from Lake Ontario.

The establishment of the Metropolitan government contributed greatly to North York's prosperity. By sharing the financial burden, the township was relieved of some of its major capital expenditures, and it benefitted enormously from the increased services—a reliable water supply, the installation of trunk sewers, arterial roads, sewage disposal, a good public transit system, and a large and efficient police force.

Developers as well as residents profitted from these new civic services. More than ever, North York became a desirable place to do business. Building contractors such as Lou Rice, Vincede Marco, Alex Grossman, the Del Zotto family, the Hurlburts, the Schikedanz brothers, Al and Harold Green, and numerous others went into a frenzy of activity. These families, many of whom are still active in the construction industry, formed the foundation of North York's prosperity, constructing offices and homes "built to last a century and a half."

One project which stood out above all the others was the Don Mills subdivision. This massive development, inaugurated in 1953, sprawled over 2,058 acres between the two forks of the Don River; it was Canada's first town to be planned completely on the drawing board. The brainchild of E.P. Taylor, then president of Argus Corporation and Canadian Breweries (O'-Keefe Breweries), it was a unique concept at the time: a self-contained community for 32,000 people, with its own industrial base, shopping centres, housing, and facilities for communal activities. Sixty percent of the land was designated for residential use. The balance was earmarked for industry.

The $200-million town was divided into neighborhood quadrants, each with its own school, church, park, and pedestrian walkways. Every neighborhood had access to a town "centre" with a landscaped shopping area and recreational amenities. Cul-de-sacs, T-junctions, and winding roads were built to stop cars from racing through the quiet streets. In order to stave off overdevelopment, a greenbelt of parkland was built around the community.

Don Mills featured a mix of housing styles, from townhouses to large family homes. Different builders were employed to ensure that the buildings wouldn't look too uniform, and houses were aimed at various income levels, priced from $12,000 to $50,000. Creative young architects such as John B. Parkin, Henry Fliess, Michael Bach,

The MacDonald-Cartier freeway was under construction in June 1954. Courtesy, Metropolitan Toronto Library

and Irving Grossman designed distinctive, innovative structures. By the early 1960s Don Mills had won numerous accolades, including 5 national and 18 regional Canadian Housing Design Awards.

But Don Mills also faced opposition. Building a new community in the middle of nowhere was an innovative concept, and sceptics warned that Don Mills was too far from Toronto to ever spawn successful industries. They were wrong. The Reichmann family, which runs Olympia and York Developments, believed in Don Mills and built office towers for Nestle, the Ontario Hospital Association, and Blue Cross. Today Olympia and York is a huge real estate conglomerate which is currently changing the faces of New York's Manhattan and London, England.

Other large corporations moved in, among them IBM, Philco, Ford, Barber Greene Canada Limited, Bata, Wrigley's, CBS Records Canada, and Imperial Oil, joined by the Four Seasons' Inn on the Park. Opened in 1964, it was the first in a chain of prestigious hotels now found around the world.

Don Mills was followed by other planned communities such as the Flemingdon Park Development, a multi-million dollar highrise complex on a 125-acre site, south of Eglinton Avenue and west of Don Mills Road.

The 1960s heralded the "mall-ing" of Canada. Small stores and strip plazas were replaced by large, regional shopping centres, and large retailers like Loblaws, Simpson's, Eatons, and Henry Morgan and Co. (later the Bay) moved into North York. During the next decade, numerous shopping centres opened around the township—the York Mills Shopping Centre (where Canada's first Shoppers Drug Mart was established), the Don Mills Shopping Centre, Northtown Shopping Centre, Towne and Countrye Square, Yorkdale Shopping Centre, and Fairview Mall, now in the throes of a massive expansion.

By 1967 North York had developed to the point where it was no longer considered to be merely a suburb of Toronto. When it achieved borough status that year, Mayor James Service said, "a suburb depends on the city for its livelihood, and North York's long past that."

Since then North York has developed into a recognized urban entity. On February 14 (Valentine's Day) of 1979, it became a city, hence its nickname, "The City With Heart." North York sold its old municipal buildings to the Province of Ontario for $7.2 million and moved into new government headquarters, the futuristic City Hall at 5100 Yonge Street. Two acres of adjacent land still belong to the City, and part of the site will be developed as a performing arts centre.

Yonge Street between Finch and Sheppard avenues—North York's "Downtown, Uptown"—has exploded in a frenzy of development. Olympia & York, Inducon Inc., Marathon Realty Company Limited, Tridel, Bramalea, Menkes Development, the Edgecombe Group, and York-Trillium are just some of the corporations currently building here. North York has become the home base for producers and sellers of goods in every sector of the economy, from auto parts to hamburgers. Magna International, Canada's leading auto components manufacturer, has 20 subsidiary companies here. McDonald's Restaurants, which in 1969 opened its first Canadian franchise at 3777 Keele Street, now has its national headquarters in North York.

Major companies have located in North York because of its central location and efficient communications and transportation networks. The city is well served by public transit, railway lines, and major, multi-lane expressways. The Don Valley Parkway, Highway 400, the Allen Road, and Yonge Street give access to the north and south.

But most of all, North York is a marvellous place to live, work, and play. It is a "people" city with good housing, excellent educational and health facilities, pleasant parks, and a lively cultural scene. Moreover, it has an identity quite separate from Toronto's. The metropolis to the south was once its raison d'être, but North York has long since spread its wings.

Construction at the site of the Yorkdale Shopping Centre, one of the many shopping complexes opening around the township, was just getting under way in 1964. Courtesy, Panda Photography/Toronto Telegram Collection, York University Archives

CHAPTER 3

Designing the New Downtown

North York's newly restructured "Downtown, Uptown" is a model of what a city centre can be. Today's downtown is a dynamic hub of commercial and residential development, recreation, culture, and the arts.

The newly restructured "Downtown, Uptown" area of North York, located 20 miles north of Lake Ontario in Metro Toronto, is beginning to rival major city centres in Canada and the U.S. Photo by Lorraine C. Parow/First Light

by Philip L. Johnson

Come on up to North York's downtown. That's what The City With Heart is saying. Indeed, this thriving community has opened up its heart to redevelopment on Yonge Street, its main north-and-south roadway. In a stretch that's little more than two miles long, from Sheppard Avenue in the south to Finch Avenue in the north, $1 billion in high-rise office, condominium, and commercial construction has gone up in the past few years, and another $2 billion is expected over the next seven years. There are cultural, leisure, and recreational facilities being built to complement several that already exist. In the area of education there is one of the finest post-secondary schools, Seneca College, which is currently expanding. This newly restructured "Downtown, Up-

town," located 20 miles north of Lake Ontario in Metro Toronto, is today beginning to rival major city centres anywhere in Canada and the U.S. Before the end of the century, the Yonge Street core will eventually house some 66,000 workers and 33,000 residents, containing about 36 million square feet of development.

This is the prediction of Mayor Mel Lastman, the shrewd and high-powered salesman who has guided the fortunes of North York as mayor for 16 years, one of the longest terms in Canada. Lastman is the envy of many Canadian mayors, having successfully attracted to North York several major corporations—Xerox, North American Life, and Petro Canada, to name a few—plus hotels, government entities, and several federal departments. Many of them have moved their corporate headquarters to North York, thus providing the city with huge assessment and tax benefits. Lastman's eyes light

A time exposure turns the lights of automobiles travelling the busy Highway 401 into rivers of light. Photo by John O'Brien

The North American Life Centre is the largest of the mammoth developments that have recently been added to the downtown core. Photo by Dawn Goss/First Light

The Petro Canada complex was just one of the many massive developments recently completed along Yonge Street. Here, a construction worker puts the finishing touches on a brick that will become part of the structure. Photo by Lorraine C. Parow/First Light

up and a smile crosses his face whenever this is mentioned. There is even a brand new Civic Square named after him. "We are definitely not pie in the sky," Lastman says. "The word is out—North York is THE place to locate."

In just a few short years, this city of 560,000 has witnessed the rise of such mammoth developments as the Madison Centre, with offices, stores, upscale nightspots, restaurants, and cinemas all located in one building on the west side of Yonge, just north of Sheppard; the Petro Canada complex on Yonge in the new City Centre (the centre, which is a showcase all in itself, is situated in the middle of the Yonge Street redevelopment); and the North American Life Centre, the office-retail project located farther north at Yonge and Finch. In that same space of time, the new and ultra-modern Central Library went up within the Civic Centre block, the $26-million North York Centre subway station opened in 1987, spurring growth around the square,

and the spectacular Douglas Snow (former parks commissioner) Aquatic Centre, a multi-use pool and recreation complex, was installed just behind City Hall in the City Centre.

This dramatic upward surge of the Yonge Street core (once a haven for low-rise buildings, but now sporting several 23-storey structures, giving it a true city skyline) is being aided by the existence of the Yonge Street subway line. With stations at the main Sheppard and Finch intersections, and a third at

Park Home Avenue in the Civic Square, the subway is providing much-needed public transportation to this new area of growth. Added to that is the widening of Yonge Street from six lanes to seven, and the close access from Yonge south of Sheppard to Highway 401, a major 12-lane route that crosses the north end of Metro Toronto. Also, North York owns several major parcels of undeveloped land, and there are numerous parking lots. A relatively new $4-million, 400-space mu-

One billion dollars in high-rise office, condominium, and office tower construction has been pumped into a two-mile stretch of Yonge Street. Another $2 billion is expected to be invested in the next seven years. Photo by Lorraine C. Parow/First Light

nicipal parking garage was built by a developer in the centre of the Yonge Street redevelopment, at no cost to the city.

In the residential sector, this new downtown has created renewed vitality for the city's real estate market. One real estate survey revealed that Willowdale, a community that takes in the Yonge Street core, was one of the hottest housing markets in Canada. For example, the average price of a home in Willowdale in March 1988 had increased in value to $275,000 from $240,000 a year ago, a 15 percent jump. Some of the homes that lined streets close to Yonge have been bought by developers and torn down (or will be demolished) to make way for the building boom. But the highrise condominiums that have risen in the area in the past few years are offering an alternative. Indeed, condos purchased in that time have increased dramatically in value, proving to be a good investment.

The Petro Canada Building is shown here, its already-looming structure intensified through the use of a wide-angle lens. Photo by Lorraine C. Parow/First Light

The library is the biggest example of Lastman's ability to get something for next to nothing. Instead of paying $20 million in taxpayers' money and interest charges, the mayor got the developers to build the library free, in exchange for a lease on the development rights to the lands.

Central Library, which celebrated its first birthday in June of 1988, was designed by award-winning architect Raymond Moriyama. The colorful and bright interior features a large atrium that rises six floors. Housed here are 1.6 million pieces of reading material, a fully stocked audio-visual centre, and a fully computerized system to facilitate fast processing and recording of books. The library also boasts a 200-seat theatre and can provide services in 27 languages. The library and the square are fully accessible to the handicapped.

Next to the library, there is an indoor retail area and a glass-roofed galleria sporting the most up-to-date shops and restaurants. On the subway level below the library is the North York Memorial Community Hall, with a huge, colorful, and picturesque War Memorial mural created by two North York artists. The City Centre even contains a tower with music that can be heard for miles, provided by Mel's Bells, as they're affectionately known. Located high in a 23-storey office building, the 14 large bells ring out regularly with familiar or pleasant tunes, seemingly setting the tone for all that is to come.

Once outside in the square, visitors and workers are treated to a large, aesthetically pleasing open-space area. It combines lush green and colorful landscaping among decorative structures, including garden rooms and a glassed-in portico that acts as an entrance on the south side. On the east side, just in from Yonge, there is a fountain which has a stream that slopes gently downwards into a giant reflecting pool. Youngsters can wade in the pool in the summer, and skaters can enjoy it when it's frozen over in the winter. For culture buffs, a 400-seat amphitheatre will be open for business

Maxwell's Mix is just one of the places to get a bite to eat in the downtown core, which features an eclectic mix of shops, offices, and eateries. Photo by Lorraine C. Parow/First Light

Facing page: The Petro Canada complex is located in the new City Centre on Yonge Street. Shown is a detail of "Mel's Bells" (named after the town's mayor) high atop a 23-storey office building. Photo by Lorraine C. Parow/First Light

The Mel Lastman Square of the City Centre is one of the mayor's proudest accomplishments. It will open with a flourish, highlighted by two days of almost continuous entertainment and events. In addition to housing the existing City Hall and board of education offices, the centre will hold the regional headquarters for Petro Canada and its 1,400 employees, the delightfully designed luxury Novotel Hotel, two towers containing more than 1.2 million square feet of office space, and the spacious Central Library.

The Xerox Tower, at the North American Life Centre, features one of Canada's largest senior centres. Photo by Glen Jones

garden enclosure gives newlyweds and tourists a perfect backdrop for photographs. For artists and craftspeople, there are spaces to display their work. And for a place to sit and enjoy all this, there are sidewalk cafés. Future plans call for a large glassed-in winter garden forming what will be the new south entrance to the square and City Centre. This structure will also be used by the public for gatherings and social events.

Just up the street from City Centre, on Yonge at Finch, is another edifice named after the mayor, Mel Lastman Place. Located in the Xerox Tower at the North American Life Centre, it houses one of Canada's largest senior centres, containing 17,500 square feet of space for up to 3,000 elder citizens. The $2.1-million facility offers a swimming pool, game and meeting rooms, lounge, shops, crafts rooms, and a dining room and kitchen for members to enjoy. Grants from North York and other levels of government covered half of the centre's cost, while the seniors themselves raised the other half.

In May of 1988, after many months of negotiations, the city announced that Ontario Hydro had purchased a 9.5-acre property just south of the City Centre (7 acres owned by the province and 2.5 by North York). Ontario Hydro would build new facilities to replace several of its old buildings in downtown Toronto. This site can accommodate upwards of 2 million square feet of office-retail construction on the seven acres. The 2.5 acres, acquired by Ontario Hydro from North York for density rights, was leased back to the city for a performing arts centre, without density, and gave North York $17 million and the majority of the money needed to finally build the centre.

The Performing Arts Centre is another jewel in the crown for Lastman. "It will be the most modern around," he says. Located in the heart of the downtown core, the centre will contain a theatre with about 1,500 seats, plus a 400-seat auditorium and related facilities. It will provide patrons with the best in stage shows, from Broadway hits to symphonies. But it was the Ontario Hydro transaction that

spring, summer, and fall. The facility will offer such events as festivals and concerts, multi-cultural celebrations, exhibitions of arts and crafts, theatrical productions, pageants, and fashion shows. There is also the possibility of a speaker's corner, such as the one in Britain's Hyde Park. And back indoors, overlooking all of this, are the city politicians' spacious new offices. (For 10 years, councillors had worked in windowless, somewhat small quarters in the interior of City Hall.) Elsewhere in the square, a gazebo with a

was key to bringing about the Performing Arts Centre.

Ken Stroud, North York's commissioner of property and economic development, says by 1991 Ontario Hydro will occupy a major portion of the site, and some 2,500 of its employees will eventually be located there. "This is the goal of every city in Canada—to get a corporate entity like this," Stroud says. The property is "the last piece of the puzzle, so to speak, on the west side of Yonge Street, completing the link (both development-wise and underground) from Sheppard Avenue to the Civic Centre." Its acquisition will accelerate

North York's downtown redevelopment by five years. It will also act as a catalyst for other developers to initiate their projects sooner than they might have and facilitate the downtown area's becoming viable both day and night.

Once built, Ontario Hydro will provide a major weather-protected underground walk-way link with the Madison office and condominium project to the south. People will then be able to walk and shop in comfort from Sheppard to the Civic Square. This underground system was started in the early 1970s. The first tunnel was built by the city from the Sheppard Centre on the east side of Yonge to the federal build-

The variety of buildings along the highly developed section of Yonge Street comprising the downtown core is a study in modern architecture. Photo by Lorraine C. Parow/First Light

Top: The extensive downtown highrise development in the North York core is the site of perhaps the largest corporate relocation in North America according to Ken Stroud, the city's commissioner of property and economic development. Photo by Lorraine C. Parow/First Light

Bottom: Yonge Street, essentially the core artery of North York, features a varied blend of modern and traditional architecture. Photo by Glen Jones

ing on the west side. As further construction has progressed north on Yonge Street's west side, developers have paid for the continuation of the tunnel system to their projects.

Above ground, North York is taking steps to protect pedestrians from the hazards of high-velocity winds on Yonge. In downtown Toronto, where several high-rise buildings have been constructed close to one another, a "canyon effect" has been created.

Winds are whipped up and sent rushing through the narrow streets and spaces between these buildings, knocking people over and causing injury. To prevent the canyon effect in the Yonge Street redevelopment area, wind tunnel studies for buildings over six storeys could be required as part of the rezoning process. Building designs could also be adapted to prevent such problems. For example, erecting podiums or protected walkways in front would deflect winds, or projects could be set far enough back from the street.

Next in line, according to Stroud, is the provision of cultural amenities. "This will be the hottest place in North America," he boasts. "Our downtown will be precedent setting—a most modern and all-embracing community, vibrant 24 hours a day." From Sheppard to Finch on Yonge, there are numerous restaurants and cafés that offer the best in international and Canadian cuisine, plus modern cinemas, and nightspots, pubs, and lounges featuring top entertainment and comfortable surroundings. For years movie buffs enjoyed the old Willow Theatre, where first-run films cost less than $3. In 1987 the small but comfortable Willow was torn down to make way for a new development. In its place a new and roomy European-style cinema, featuring extra-wide seats, is to be built. Just down the street, five new film houses are now in operation at the Cineplex theatre in the Madison Centre.

Other new ingredients helping to add even more life to Yonge Street are streetscaping and walk-ways. A $3-million, three- to five-year program is under way to landscape downtown streets. This involves the planting of trees and flowers, the installation of lights and benches, and the widening of sidewalks. Each new project on the east side of Yonge will likely have street-front outlets, patios, and indoor shops. On the west side, modern and exclusive retail stores will also be featured along with three systems of walk-ways—one similar to the east side; another that will feature an interior walk-way set back from the street, such as the one that exists in the Madison Centre; and a third consisting of inside walk-ways above and below the street level. Ultimately the enclosed walk-way system will provide pedestrian access from the developments immediately surrounding the Civic Square, linking both sides of Yonge at the subway station, south through the square to the Madison Centre, Federal Building and Sheppard Centre, on into the Sheppard subway, the bus terminal on the west side, and eventually into the surrounding developments. These linkages will help create added commercial and leisure activity in the area.

Local workers stroll past the very futuristic architecture at Madison Centre. Photo by Glen Jones

North York boasts a well-developed fire-fighting force to protect its burgeoning metropolitan developments. Photo by Lorraine C. Parow/First Light

One other spur to the current growth was the Ontario Municipal Board's approval of Amendment 277 to the city's official plan early in 1988. The amendment permits building heights up to 23 storeys (except on the site south of the Civic Square, which allows 29 storeys). It also splits the main development areas into Yonge-Sheppard in the south end, and Yonge-Finch in the north. The development potential for the south sector, from Highway 401 halfway to Finch, is 13.6 million square feet of residential and 13.4 million square feet of commercial-office-institutional development. The north half up to Finch and just beyond allows for 3.9 million square feet of residential and 4.2 million square feet of commercial building.

Amendment 277 also expands the redevelopment area around the Civic Square because of the existence of the Park Home subway station. Densities under Amendment 277 enable North York to deal with sewage capacity and transportation. The amendment also gives North York a blueprint for development over the next few years. But what lies beyond 277 raises some questions, and will ultimately require a further comprehensive review some years in the future. Nevertheless, many major Canadian developers are now working in the city. "It's great to watch all of [them] vying for a piece of the action . . . competing with each other to see who will build the most attractive buildings," Lastman says.

Yes, North York's future is rosy. But was anything like this spurt in growth envisioned by city fathers and planners in the past? In 1968 this city, then a borough, was a quiet community. Along Yonge, a number of low-rise commercial buildings dotted the street. And just behind them were pleasant residential neighborhoods. But the Yonge subway, which at that time ended at Eglinton Avenue far to the

Says Mayor Mel Lastman, "It's great to watch all of the major Canadian developers vying for a piece of the action . . . competing with each other to see who will build the most attractive building." Photo by Lorraine C. Parow/First Light

The crew of the North York Fire Department stands ready for action in front of Fire Station No. 1. Photo by John O'Brien

south, loomed large. It was poised for continuation up Yonge, well into North York. It was eventually decided that the subway would go as far as Finch, instead of Sheppard, because there was more parking space at Finch. Also, the buses on Yonge between Sheppard and Finch were already overcrowded.

To prepare for the subway and what it would bring, city politicians commissioned a study by Murray V. Jones and Associates and John B. Parkin Associates. This study recommended the construction of a 1,200-foot communications

tower near Yonge, south of present City Hall. Because of the higher elevation in North York, this tower would have been taller than the present CN Tower in downtown Toronto. It would have made the building of the CN Tower unnecessary. The North York tower went as far in the planning stage as public hearings, and it even had zoning approval. To this day the tower is still permitted by the zoning bylaw, according to Al O'Neill, deputy commissioner of the property and economic development department. But he states there is no intent to proceed with it.

City Hall was just one of five major civic projects completed over a seven-year period ending in 1979. Other buildings included an education centre, a federal building, Sheppard Centre, and Beecroft Manor for seniors. Photo by Lorraine C. Parow/First Light

The study also called for the widening of Yonge from four to seven lanes; large-scale, high-density development along Yonge from Highway 401 to just south of Finch; and low-density construction just east and west of Yonge. This growth would bring in 66,000 workers and 33,000 residents. The study showed foresight as it inferred in a schematic approach that development could include such items as a civic centre and a ring-road concept. "It was a far-reaching and in-depth study that touched on a lot of things that should be in a downtown development," says O'Neill, who joined the city staff in 1970. In fact, many of its recommendations, in modified form, have now come to fruition, except for the study's call to have development proceed farther east and west of Yonge than is currently permitted. This was a "planners' pipedream," says O'Neill, something that couldn't take place, at least in the foreseeable future as viewed from the 1968 perspective. Nevertheless, the Parkin-Jones study, which was far ahead of its time but not practical back then, provided the concept upon which future Yonge Street studies were based.

Eventually, in 1969, North York politicians were persuaded to scale down this plan. What they came up with was the District 11 Plan—Yonge Redevelopment Area. New construction was restricted to six small blocks in the Yonge-Sheppard node, and only 7,000 residents would be allowed (employment figures were not made available). As a result of this plan, five major projects were constructed over a seven-year period to 1979: City Hall, the education centre, the Federal Building, Sheppard Centre, and Beecroft Manor for seniors. And just on the edge of this development, just east of Yonge on Sheppard, was the former CIL Square (now the North York Square).

One of the politicians who had been on the scene since 1969 was then-controller Mel Lastman. Lastman had been a colorful and somewhat outlandish businessman before he turned to politics. As owner of Bad Boy Appliances,

he went as far as selling refrigerators to Eskimos in the Arctic; he sold two-dollar bills for one dollar in Toronto and New York, and repeated the scheme in Rome with lire. He also dressed up as a beggar and asked people on the street for quarters. He rewarded those who gave him 25 cents with a $100 bill. Lastman in turn was rewarded with publicity worth much, much more. And now he gets added exposure on his weekly cable television show, "Straight Talk," which, for 15 years, has allowed North Yorkers to phone in and air their beefs. A showman and shrewd businessman, now politician, he knew the value of a dollar, both development- and tax-wise. It wasn't long (two 2-year terms) before Lastman became mayor.

In the late 1970s, Metro Council (consisting of Lastman and other politicians from North York, Toronto, and four other municipalities that make up the greater Toronto area)

decided on a grand scheme to decentralize downtown Toronto, which was fast becoming overcrowded. Two sub-centres were proposed, one in North York. Large-scale, high-rise development would take place from just south of Sheppard to just north of Finch, bringing in 60,000 jobs and 30,000 residents. Taking up the challenge, North York councillors initiated a review of the Yonge Redevelopment plan. They wanted to enlarge the plan and increase densities to reflect the changing times— shades of the original Parkin-Jones study! Once again, area residents raised concerns about the scope of this new plan; they feared living in the shadows of towering buildings and facing increased traffic through their streets. Lastman and other councillors met with ratepayer groups in the redevelopment area. "I listened to their concerns and a few months later I introduced a revised plan that was acceptable to all of them, without any

Facing page: Mel Lastman, shown here proudly displaying the city slogan in front of the Civic Square, had been a colorful and somewhat outlandish businessman before turning to politics and becoming North York's mayor. Photo by Lorraine C. Parow/ First Light

The Yonge Redevelopment plan has unleashed a recent flurry of construction projects in the downtown core. Photo by Lorraine C. Parow/First Light

Officers C. Schewieg (left) and W. McCormack are on patrol in North York for Metro Toronto Police Division No. 32, one of four divisions serving the city. Photo by John O'Brien

changes in density or height of buildings," Lastman says.

In 1979, council approved this somewhat scaled-down plan, the "Lastman Compromise," or the District 11-48 Yonge Street Centre Plan. It extended the north and south boundaries of redevelopment on Yonge, and allowed for 25 million square feet of new construction. It also called for 24,000 residents and 47,000 workers. All of this formed the foundation for the current downtown.

In 1983, development in the Yonge core took another giant step. Metro Council, with some prodding by Lastman and other North York politicians, decided to build another subway station on Yonge, right on the doorstep of City Hall, and smack in the middle of the redevelopment area. City planners reviewed the 1979 plan, and the council soon approved their recommendations to again extend the Yonge redevelopment area boundaries.

The amount of new construction would be increased to about 36 million square feet, with 66,000 workers and 33,000 residents accounted for. A ring-road system would be installed just east and west of Yonge to provide a buffer for the surrounding community. This revised plan has provided the impetus for the present growth in the Yonge core.

As for the near future, new building applications are expected to be more upscale and up-to-date than in the past. For example when the Sheppard Centre, a complex of retail outlets, offices, and residences, was built in the mid-1970s, it was Canada's first multi-use, self-contained development. Nearly 15 years later, it still looks modern and new. But it needs redesigning and refacing in order to be more accessible and acceptable to today's downtown. It's expected that the new owners of the centre, Olympia & York and Counsel Trust, will begin this refurbishing soon.

In 1988, new construction consisted mainly of condominiums, with four developments erected in the Yonge-Finch area, and two in the Yonge-Sheppard core. This has provided thousands of residents with comfortable and exclusive accommodation, steps from shopping and transportation. Other new construction included three large commercial-office projects—Place Nouveau at Yonge and Finch, the North York Corporate Centre at Yonge and Highway 401, and Coscan's office building at Sheppard just west of Yonge. These buildings are expected to be occupied by 1989.

The second phase of the City Centre Development is in the Civic Square. An 18-storey office tower, with 500,000 square feet of space, is to be built adjacent to the Petro Canada Centre. Phase two of the North American Life Centre at Finch and Yonge will also get under way, with another 21- or 23-storey office building to complement an existing 23-storey structure.

Proposed developments include a high-rise office complex (Gibson Square) on the west side of Yonge across from the City Centre Square. Penta Stolp will build this office tower on top of a glass-enclosed galleria. The galleria will contain an interior rose garden to replace the one that existed outside on the site for years. Pedestrians will be able to see the garden in its new enclosure from Yonge Street, or view it up close in the galleria. They will then be able to continue through the building to the exterior of the west side, into spacious Gibson Park. The park will stretch for a city block along the north side of Park Home Avenue. "This will be the finest urban park in Canada," Stroud says. When the property immediately to the north on Yonge is developed, its street level will also have a vista of historic Gibson House, once the home of pioneer David Gibson.

Other proposed projects include Menkes' combination 23-storey office-condominium-retail complex at Yonge and Empress; Elmwood Development's two condominium towers and

an office building at Yonge and Elmwood; Bramalea's two 23-storey condominium towers just off Yonge and Sheppard on the east side; and Marathon Realty's 23-storey office building at the southwest corner of Yonge and Sheppard, with a 21-storey office structure by Southwest Sheppard Investments just behind Marathon's.

Across the street on the northwest corner of Yonge and Sheppard is a significant development involving the historic Dempsey Brothers Hardware Store and the bus terminal just behind. Canderel and Prudential Assurance

One significant development on the northwest corner of Yonge and Sheppard is the new bus terminal just behind the historic Dempsey Brothers Hardware Store. Photo by Lorraine C. Parow/First Light

New residential projects, like these apartment complexes in the Don Mills area, have provided thousands of residents with comfortable and exclusive accommodation, only steps away from shopping and public transportation. Photo by Glen Jones

Before the end of the century, the Yonge Street core will eventually house some 66,000 workers and 33,000 residents, and will contain about 36 million square feet of developed property. Photo by Lorraine C. Parow/First Light

plan a 23-storey office tower, plus a low-rise office building. The Dempsey store, built in 1860, will be relocated to the rear of the project and will become a luxury restaurant. The original owner of the building was Joseph Shepard, a general merchant and miller. (Sheppard Avenue, although spelled differently, was named after him.) Shepard's store sold various goods, housed a post office, and was a coach depot and regional drop-off point for milk that was carted down to Toronto. The store was sold to Benjamin R. Brown

in 1888, and in 1921 the Dempsey family took it over. The bus terminal, which is a major terminus for bus links along Sheppard, has caused traffic problems as a result of buses attempting to exit to and enter on Sheppard without the benefit of traffic lights. The terminal will now vanish underground. Buses will then enter the improved and more efficient terminal by turning onto Beecroft just to the west where there are lights. This will facilitate better traffic flow on Sheppard and into the intersection at Yonge.

Just east of Yonge on Sheppard, Seneca College, in conjunction with developer Penta-Stolp, plans to build its $100-million Seneca Square complex, including an education centre, a high-rise office tower, and a shopping concourse. It is all part of the college's seven-year plan to merge 22 teaching locations into seven major campuses.

South on Yonge along the fringe of the downtown development is the massive Maclean Hunter site—23 acres assembled and now owned by Loblaws owner Galen Weston. This land parcel

could include high-rise offices, hotels, stores, condominiums, a recreation complex, and cultural facilities, becoming the largest development in North York history. The Yonge-401 area provides for future expansion of the downtown. But in order for major development to take place on the Maclean Hunter property, a comprehensive review of the downtown plan would be mandatory, says Ken Stroud. Issues such as major road improvement and traffic and sewer capacity must be addressed.

In the north end, just south of Finch on the east side, is a second large site—the 16-acre Northtown shopping centre property owned by North American Life. Potential plans call for more than 600,000 square feet of commercial-retail development, with a possible residential component. Originally built in the 1950s, the low-rise suburban-style plaza was a style suited for its time, but over the years it has become obsolete. A new development would reflect today's more modern North York downtown.

And much farther down the road? "We're an awakening giant," Stroud says. "There are all kinds of sites downtown not yet assembled." With this potential, many more applications similar in scope to recent ones are expected. "We haven't reached the peak of development yet." The likelihood of major projects such as offices outside the greater downtown core are remote, however. But there is the possibility of a new east-west transit line bisecting the downtown area and joining North York's core development to other major centres, such as the city of Scarborough's civic centre far to the east, and west possibly to the Spadina Subway line in North York.

As for Lastman, he predicts that, "What you see now [in the downtown area] is nothing compared to what will be there." What can be more exciting? Says the mayor, characteristically, "Well, perhaps one thing will thrill a politician more . . . the additional $25 million in business and realty taxes we will receive every year starting in 1989."

CHAPTER 4

Weaving the Ethnic Tapestry

Representing more than 100 countries and speaking over 80 languages, North York's residents weave a rich tapestry of cultures. This diverse ethnic mix makes the city one of the most cosmopolitan urban centres in the world.

Caravan is just one of the many community-wide events in downtown Toronto, and the festival of arts, culture, food, and history draws thousands of people annually during the summer months. Photo by John O'Brien

by Helga V. Loverseed

North York has a large number of ethnic communities. The city's residents come from over 100 countries, and over 80 different languages are spoken here—more than in downtown Toronto, where 56 are spoken. Its diverse ethnic mix makes North York one of the most cosmopolitan urban centres in the world. British settlers founded the city, but there was a tremendous influx of newcomers after World War II, and according to a 1981 census only 36 percent of North Yorkers today can trace their ancestry to the British Isles.

Nonetheless, the British, or those of British origin, still make up a sizeable portion of the population. From the early nineteenth century to World War II, they were responsible for laying the groundwork of the city that we know today. In the 1950s there was a surge in immigration, adding to the British mix people of many nations—Italians, Jews, West Indians, Chinese, Latvians, Germans, Ukrainians, Japanese, East Asians, Poles, Greeks, and Latin Americans.

Many immigrants came from the poorer areas of war-torn Europe. After the war, opportunities were limited and the future looked bleak. Italians, Greeks, Poles, and Jews came to Canada hoping to better themselves and to provide a promising future for their families. Canada was seen as a land of plenty, and indeed it was.

In the 1960s and 1970s, immigrants who came out of economic necessity were joined by those fleeing political repression. Refugees from Chile, Laos, Vietnam, Kampuchea, Korea, Sri Lanka, Argentina, and Uganda poured into Metro Toronto.

Those who live in this cosmopolitan city find it hard to imagine that, a mere century ago, North York was only large tracts of open land and wilderness. It entered the twentieth century as a rural backwater, but in the last 20 years the community has developed at an astonishing rate—so much so, that those who knew it in the 1960s would

scarcely recognize it today. Physically, economically, and culturally, North York has changed in every way.

North York has become a prime residential area, but in the early 1700s not many people would have wanted to live here. The city then was covered in dense bush. The only folk who inhabited these regions were native Huron Indians. Agricultural nomads, the Indians tilled the land, then moved on as game and fish became exhausted. With the coming of the White man, the Indians became guides and traders of fur.

By the mid-1800s most of the Hurons had retreated northwards. Their numbers declined rapidly, diminished by disease and intermarriage with Europeans, and they were driven further into the bush—victims of circumstance and dishonest treaties drawn up by colonial rulers. Land was needed for settlers, and those who ran British North America (as Canada was called) wanted it at any price.

Today, a small number of the descendants of Canada's "People of the Land" reside in Metro Toronto, of which just an estimated 350 speak their own languages. But they are very active in the community. The Native Awareness Committee, based in Willowdale, educates and informs the public about Canada's aboriginal peoples by providing guest speakers, holding arts and crafts displays, and showing films about the role they have played in the country's history.

The first Europeans to come to Central Canada were French-speaking explorers and voyageurs, hardy backwoodsmen who, like the Indians, lived off the land. The French and their Indian guides were the backbone of the fur trade, and although large companies such as Hudson's Bay and the North West Company were later run by Scots (a huge ethnic group in the 1800s), it was the French and aboriginal peoples who laid the foundations of Canada's wealth.

French-speaking Canadians are found throughout Ontario. Metro Toronto is home to an estimated 100,000, but those include immigrants from countries where French is spoken: Viet-

The Japanese Cultural Centre provides facilities and instruction for judo, karate, and other traditional martial arts. Photo by John O'Brien

nam, Tunisia, Algeria, Morocco, Belgium, and, of course, France itself. The greatest influx of francophones came in the 1970s when Quebecers, fed up with the nationalist policies of the Parti Québécois, moved here to seek greener economic pastures.

One direct result of this francophone "invasion" has been an interest in bilingual education. North Yorkers and Torontonians of all backgrounds and political stripes are enrolling their children in French-speaking schools. According to recent government figures, people who speak both of Canada's official languages get better jobs with higher salaries than those who are unilingual. French immersion classes, which begin in grade 5, are available in eight elementary schools, and two secondary schools have extended French programs.

Francophone North Yorkers can continue their education at college and university level. The Glendon campus of York University, at Bayview and Lawrence avenues, runs a wide range of bilingual programs. The Newnham campus of Seneca College of Applied Arts and Technology also offers bilingual classes.

Other non-English speaking groups are served by the Heritage Language program which is run by North York's

Board of Education. Under this program, foreign language instruction is given to children from Junior Kindergarten level to Grade 8. Every May, 17 language groups from the Woodbine/Vanier Centre Heritage Language program stage "Multifest," a festival with stage presentations, cultural displays and ethnic food.

Though today's North York is made up of people from all corners of the globe, North York's first citizens came mostly from England, Scotland, Ireland, and the U.S. Like the immigrants of today, they were driven from their own countries by political turmoil and economic hardship. The British came because of overcrowding and a repressive class system. The American War of Independence brought republican government to the United States, but many Loyalists wanted to remain faithful to the Crown and were attracted to Upper Canada (as Ontario was called) because it was still under British rule.

Both groups benefitted from the system of land grants introduced by John Graves Simcoe, Upper Canada's first governor-general. Each settler was given 200 acres of land. These plots became orchards, mills, and farms, which only 50 years later formed the foundation of a thriving agriculture industry.

By taming the wilderness, the pioneers turned the northern part of the Township of York (as North York was then called) into prime farmland, and they established the many villages and hamlets which made up this part of Ontario. They also founded North York's first churches. In the nineteenth century, churches served as social centres as well as temples of religion, and were the backbone of a hardworking, God-fearing society.

The Asbury and West United Church was one of the earliest places of worship in the township. The church can trace its origins to 1812, when Henry Mulholland purchased 375 acres of land in what is now the Bathurst and Lawrence area. The first Asbury and West United Church was a simple log building. It was subsequently replaced by a frame, clapboard

The Asbury and West United Church was one of the earliest places of worship in the township. Today, it is one of the 20 United Churches in North York and represents only one of many religious denominations. Photo by Dawn Goss/First Light

Above and facing page: Jews comprise the second-largest ethnic group in North York, and many are active in the programs offered by the Jewish Community Centre, a 700-volunteer body offering a wide variety of social, recreational, theatrical, and cultural activities. Photos by Peter Tang/First Light

structure, built in 1845. Named after Francis Asbury, the first Methodist Bishop (the Methodist churches merged with the United churches in 1923), this building was destroyed by fire in 1898. One year later, a new brick church, built for $2,400, rose on the same site.

This church, too, was replaced in 1951. By this time, the Asbury congregation had merged with that of the West United Church on College Street, which began in 1855 as a Sunday School in a temperance hall at Queen and Spadina. On Sunday, March 30, 1947, the two congregations joined.

Today the Asbury and United Church is one of 20 United Churches in North York, representing only one of many religious denominations. The city has religious institutions of every kind—Greek Orthodox, Lutheran, Mennonite Brethren, Roman Catholic, Jewish, Pentecostal, Baptist—a reflection of its diverse ethnic population.

People from countries other than Great Britain and the United States really started to make themselves felt after World War II. Until then English-speaking settlers dominated the population of York Township, weathering political and economic storms caused by the War of 1812, the Rebellion of

1837, World War I, and the "Dirty Thirties."

Immigration to North York started in a small way after World War I, when urbanites from Toronto seeking a quieter lifestyle came to what was then a rural community. War veterans and Europeans slowly swelled their ranks, particularly after the Depression, but it wasn't until the early 1950s that large-scale immigration got under way.

The largest influx of immigrants to the province came from Italy. One of the first Italian Canadians was Captain Philip de Grassi, who arrived from Jamaica as early as 1831 and settled on land near the Don Valley. But he was unusual. For the most part, they came from Veneto and Fruili in the north, Abruzzi in central Italy, and Sicily and Calabria in the south. Five thousand came in 1950 alone. By 1956 these had been joined by another 13,536.

The Toronto area is home to the largest number of Italians outside the city of Rome. Italians, or those of Italian background, still make up the bulk of North York's ethnic population. The city is home to some 93,000, or 40 percent of Metro's total number of 223,000.

In the 1950s North York expanded rapidly, as people abandoned city living for life in the suburbs. The construction industry boomed, and many of the newcomers found work building roads, bridges, sidewalks, homes, and hospitals.

Though they were willing to work hard, they were often cold and lonely. Life in a hostile climate and alien culture wasn't all roses. Few of the immigrant workers could speak or understand English. To help them overcome their isolation, the church and benevolent clubs and societies stepped in. Soon the Italians formed their own associations and community organizations, such as COSTI (Centro Oganizativo Scuole Techniche Italiane), founded in 1962. COSTI (renamed COSTI-IIAS, Community Organization Serving the Immigrant—Italian Immigrant Society) was originally started to aid Italians in the construction trade.

It now runs educational and social welfare programs for all immigrants, not just Italians.

COSTI's North York office on Lamberton Boulevard offers babysitting services, tutoring for immigrant children, and re-training courses. Staff members speak English, French, Italian, German, Spanish, Russian, Portuguese, Romanian, Hindi, and Punjabi, and they help newcomers through a maze of government bureaucratic procedures—straightening out problems with workmen's compensation, pensions, and other public services.

The raison d'être of the centre is to foster a sense of community among North York's diverse ethnic populations, and COSTI-IIAS involves itself in many local enterprises such as the International Bazaar, the International Christmas, the Arts and Crafts display, the North York Winter Carnival, and the Citizenship Court at North York City Hall.

The Italian Canadian Benevolent Corporation is also actively involved in community affairs. Incorporated in 1971, the corporation is headquartered at Lawrence Avenue West and Dufferin Street in a complex known as the Columbus Centre. The Columbus Centre houses a sports and recreational area, the Joseph D. Carrier Art Gallery, Villa Columbo (a social centre for people over 50), and Caboto Terrace (homes for independent senior citizens). The multi-lingual staff works closely with disadvantaged persons, running blood clinics, counselling those with drug- and alcohol-related problems, and aiding the Italian Canadian Diabetic Association.

Jews comprise the second-largest ethnic group in North York, numbering around 68,000, or 70 percent of Metro Toronto's total Jewish population. Some came to Canada as early as the 1880s, after the notorious pogroms in Russia and Romania. But most ar-

Religion has always played an important part in Jewish life, as have music and the arts. Here, a 13-year-old youth marks the traditional rite of passage into manhood by carrying the Torah during his Bar Mitzvah service. Photo by John O'Brien

rived, like the Italians, in the post-war years.

Those years were busy ones for Ontario's Jewish community. Pooling their resources and manpower, they helped to rescue and resettle the many thousands of Jews who had fled the Nazi regime. The first displaced persons, including over 1,000 orphans, arrived in 1947. By March 1950, 11,064 Jews had come to Canada.

Two North York museums recall the horrors of the Nazi era. The Holocaust Education and Memorial Centre on Bathurst Street, dedicated to the 6 million Jews who were murdered, is a resource centre which traces the story of the Jews' flight to Canada and the creation of the State of Israel. The Lodzer Centre Holocaust Congregation also has a resource centre outlining the hor-

rors of Hitler's Germany. The centre is a synagogue as well, one of 36 located throughout North York.

North York's Jewish community is very active in the arts. The Leah Posluns Theatre, the Koffler Gallery, and the *Canadian Jewish News* are just some of the cultural enterprises with which the community is involved. Some of these groups operate under the aegis of the Jewish Community Centre, a 700-volunteer body, which offers a wide range of social, recreational, theatrical, and cultural programs.

The Jewish Information Service on Bathurst Street coordinates community activities and organizations. Members of the staff here are equally fluent in Hebrew, English, French, and Yiddish. Service clubs such as B'nai Brith also serve the Jewish community,

as does the Toronto Jewish Congress, which has its headquarters in North York. B'nai Brith, like other branches across Canada, helps to raise money for Israel and runs educational programs for children, adults, and seniors.

Various other North York organizations aid Jewish and other immigrants. The Ontario Welcome House on Wilson Avenue is an offshoot of the Ontario Ministry of Citizenship and Culture. Here staff members help immigrants work their way through the wide range of public services available in the community, including schooling, health care, housing, and employment. When necessary, the multi-lingual staff translates into English documents needed for education or employment.

The North York Inter-Agency and Community Council is an alliance of autonomous organizations and individuals who concern themselves with social, educational, health, and community services. The council functions as a combined information exchange, planning and service development body, and public educator. It also works toward improving relationships among North York's many ethnic groups.

A Committee on Community Race and Ethnic Relations was appointed by the City of North York in 1979. At the time, it was the first such committee in Canada. It works with various North York institutions and agencies, encouraging them to develop programs and services that are responsive to the needs of racial and ethnic minorities. The committee was also instrumental in the development of the

Gryfe's Bakery at Baycrest and Bathurst is well known for its bagels. Mr. Gryfe takes pride in the fact that a number of prestigious brokerage firms send delivery services to pick up his fresh bagels daily. Photo by John O'Brien

Reflections of apartment buildings are seen in the pool of the Ontario Science Centre. Photo by Derek Trask/The StockMarket

Multilingual Information Gathering System, which enables doctors to gather medical data from patients who do not speak English.

North York's ethnic communities do a lot to help immigrants through their own cultural networks and community centres. In recent years North York has welcomed a growing number of newcomers from Chile, Argentina, Ecuador, Uruguay, and Colombia. The Latin American Community Centre on Milvan Drive aids Spanish-speaking migrants by running a legal aid clinic and teaching courses in English.

The A.R.S. Social Services Centre is a part of the Armenian Community Centre. It provides numerous services to immigrants and the elderly, including an Armenian language day school, a summer camp, and a seniors' club which runs English classes and social outings.

Like the Jews, Armenians have been victims of ruthless genocidal campaigns and have been cruelly persecuted for their religion, which is believed to be among the oldest forms of Christianity in the world. Every April the centre commemorates the killing of Armenians during World War I, when 1.5 million people perished in their struggle for a homeland. This bears special significance since Armenia, as such, no longer exists. Having been fought over by many nations, today it is divided among three states—Turkey, Iran, and Russia.

Latvia is also a country that has lost its independence. In 1940 it became a part of the U.S.S.R., but North York's Latvians keep their traditions alive at the Latvian Canadian Cultural Centre, which houses a Latvian Library and Resources Centre, a book store, a credit union, and a permanent art ex-

The Armenian Community Centre provides numerous services to immigrants and the elderly, and its activities include an Armenian language day care school, summer camp, and a seniors' club. Photo by Peter Tang/First Light

hibit organized by the Latvian Association of Artisans and Craftsmen. The centre runs cultural programs and provides facilities for a Latvian school ("Valodina"), the Latvian National Youth Association in Canada, and Latvian girl guide and boy scout groups, choirs, and folk dance ensembles.

In recent years a number of affluent, middle-class people of Greek origin have moved into North York. Most of Metro Toronto's 80,000 Greeks live downtown in the Danforth Avenue area, but as they move up the economic scale they tend to look for homes elsewhere. Greek immigration to Ontario peaked between 1966 and 1970. It is estimated that during those years, one tenth of Greece's population left. World War II, a devastating civil war, and a military government had upset the economy, bringing poverty to many families who could scarcely afford to put food on the table.

The Greek Orthodox Church (there are two in North York) helped these immigrants to settle in their new homeland. The priests wrote letters (many early migrants were illiterate) and interpreted Canadian regulations. The church continues to play an important role in the lives of Greek North

Yorkers. Three churches—St. Demetrius, St. George, and the Annunciation of the Virgin Mary—were amalgamated to form Greek Community Metropolitan Toronto Inc. Situated in Don Mills, it administers several seniors' programs and a school for the teaching of Greek, and organizes various festivities for the community.

The Japanese Cultural Centre, also in Don Mills, was conceived in the 1950s to meet the social and recreational needs of the Japanese Canadian community. Dedicated to the "Issei," hardy Japanese pioneers who came to Canada at the turn of the century to build roads and work in lumber mills, it opened in 1963 after many years of fund-raising by the Japanese community.

The centre's mandate is to "develop a comprehensive program of guided leisure time"; to "make the community aware of the unique qualities of Japanese culture"; and to cooperate with and further whenever possible "charitable causes which promote the welfare of the entire community." The centre, which offers a wide range of cultural and educational activities, is one of North York's most beautiful buildings. An elegant, harmonious

North York's Latvian Community keeps its traditions alive at the Latvian Canadian Cultural Centre, which houses a library and resources centre, a bookstore, a credit union, and a permanent art collection. Photo by Peter Tang/First Light

Facing page: St. Demetrius Greek Orthodox Church—amalgamated with St. George and Annunciation of the Virgin Mary churches—form the Greek Community Metropolitan Toronto Inc. Located in Don Mills, it runs a school for the teaching of Greek, seniors' programs, and organizes various festivities for the community. Photo by Peter Tang/First Light

Left and below: The Japanese Cultural Centre in Don Mills meets the social and recreational needs of the Japanese Canadian Community, and is dedicated to the "Issei," the hardy Japanese pioneers who came to North America at the turn of the century to establish an Asian community here. Photos by Peter Tang/First Light

structure surrounded by a traditional rock garden, it was designed by Japanese-Canadian architect Raymond Moriyama, who also built the Ontario Science Centre.

Talented Japanese Canadians are found in every profession, especially in the fields of law, dentistry, medicine, and teaching. Unfortunately, they have faced their share of prejudice. During World War II, the Canadian government sent many Japanese and their families to internment camps. After the war ended, church groups and the YMCA helped the evacuees to find homes and employment. Toronto was the focal point of resettlement because many Japanese Canadians were attracted by job opportunities available in business and industry there.

Immigration from Japan virtually ground to a halt until 1967, when a new immigration policy was formulated abolishing discrimination on racial grounds. In the period between 1957 and 1971, 1,965 Japanese arrived in Ontario. The majority settled in Metro Toronto.

North York is home to several other groups of Asian and Pacific origin—including Koreans, Laotians, Kampucheans, and Filipinos. In recent years, there has been a tremendous influx of Chinese. Like the Japanese, the Chinese came to Canada originally to work in lumber camps and to help build the railways at the turn of the century, but in the past decade large numbers have moved to North York, attracted by good working conditions and the city's bustling business environment.

Some of these "new" Chinese have come from the British colony of Hong Kong in anticipation of its reverting to the People's Republic of China. Others have moved to North York from Toronto's Chinatown. Centred around Spadina Avenue and Dundas Street West, Chinatown is where Chinese-speaking immigrants often locate first, before they become more educated and fluent in English. Second-generation Chinese have moved out of the downtown area into surrounding communities, one of which is North York. The Chinese presence is most visible around Victoria Park Avenue, where restaurants and retail stores celebrate the cultural heritage of this group.

Another relatively new immigrant population is that of Indo-Pakistani origin. More than 16,000 North Yorkers, making up the city's seventh-largest ethnic group, the Indo-Pakistanis come from Bengal, Gujarat, Punjab, Sri Lanka, Bangladesh, Pakistan, and Uganda. They speak different languages, have different traditions, and adhere to at least five different religions, including Hinduism, Sikhism, Christianity, Buddhism, and Islam.

A substantial number of East Indians came as refugees in the early 1970s after dictator Idi Amin overthrew President Obote in Uganda. Amin, who exterminated thousands of his own people in his quest for power, threw the East Indians out of Uganda. These Asians were well-educated, often wealthy, entrepreneurs. Their success was resented by locals and Amin played on racial fears.

At the same time, many East Indians, facing a racial backlash, left Kenya and Tanzania, where they also belonged to the entrepreneurial and professional classes. East Africa's loss has been North York's gain. Out of five typical East Indian immigrants, one is a teacher, one is a doctor, one is an engineer, and the remaining two are in business.

North York's Black community is as varied as that of the East Asians. Its people comprise fifth- and sixth-generation Canadians, including descendants of Loyalist slaves; Blacks from Atlantic Canada who have moved to Ontario to find work; Africans; Americans; British; and most recently people from the West Indies. Immigrants have come from many islands—Antigua, Barbados, Dominica, Grenada, Montserrat, St. Lucia, St. Vincent, St. Kitts, and Trinidad and Tobago. Some 80 percent of the 150,000 Blacks in Metro Toronto come from Jamaica.

Jamaican Canadians are located throughout Metro, but a large number live in North York, especially around

The North York Jewish Community Centre provides facilities and programs geared to physical as well as cultural needs. Photo by Peter Tang/First Light

Ukrainian dancers are famous for their high kicks and gymnastic techniques. This performance was at Gala at the Inn On the Park. Photo by John O'Brien

the Jane-Finch area. They have added energy and spice to both the cultural and sports scenes. Metro Toronto is home to many jazz, reggae, and steel band musicians. (The summer Caribana Festival is one of Toronto's most lively and colorful celebrations.) Sprinter Ben Johnson recently became the world's fastest man, beating American Carl Lewis. Johnson became an international celebrity when he ran 100 metres in a mind-boggling 9.83 seconds.

Despite their achievements, North York's Blacks have sometimes faced racial prejudice. Barbadian-born Donald Moore, a revered community leader who has done much to help Black North Yorkers integrate into their new homeland, recalls that when he first came to Canada in 1912, he was unable to find work as a tailor because of his race. At that time, Blacks were able to find only two types of employment—as laborers or railway porters. Now 96, retired, and living on Drewery Avenue, Moore comments: "The foremen told me they would be glad to hire someone of my calibre, but they said the other workers would refuse to work beside me."

Determined to do something about improving the lot of his people, Moore got involved in community work. With the help of church, labor, and political groups, he formed the

That same year he received the Jerome Award (named in honor of Canada's ace sprinter Harry Jerome), in recognition of his fight against racism.

The battle against racial prejudice is by no means over, but the situation for Ontario's Blacks is much improved. In 1962 the provincial government passed a Human Rights Code that prohibits discrimination on grounds of race, color, nationality, ancestry, or place of origin. Today there are numerous government and city agencies to which people can turn for help.

Dr. Dan Hill, a distinguished, American-born Black, is now Ontario's ombudsman—a job which involves handling complaints about various government departments, agencies, or employees. Hill sums up the situation this way:

This is the great thing about Ontario. You've got agencies and people and the press who will fight for you . . . We've built, thank goodness, in Canada, a system of government agencies and institutions that support multi-racialism and multi-culturalism and that are against racism and discrimination.

Whatever problems we may see in the Canadian social structure are always balanced off by the other fine things about it, and the great people and the opportunities that abound in this country.

Negro Citizenship Association. In 1954 Moore led a delegation to Ottawa that helped sway the government into easing immigration restrictions which, at that time, were blatantly racist. The Ontario government had passed a Racial Discrimination Act in 1944, but there was still prejudice at the federal level.

Moore has been highly honored for his substantial contribution to society. In 1982 the City of Toronto gave Moore its Award of Merit, in recognition of his unpaid role as liaison person between the federal immigration department and the Black community. Two years later, the province of Ontario awarded him the Bicentennial Medal.

Hill describes himself as an "ardent North Yorker" and has, among other achievements, been director of the Ontario Human Rights Commission, a writer, a lecturer, president of the Ontario Black History Association, and a professor at the University of Toronto, where he served as special advisor to the Toronto committee on race relations. He is also, incidentally, the father of singer Dan Hill.

But perhaps the last word should go to Mayor Mel Lastman, a high-profile member of the Jewish community, who comments, " . . . there's no question the ethnic quality of North York makes this municipality such a great place to work and live."

CHAPTER 5

Investing in Opportunity

North York is a city that invests in its future, offering an exciting business environment and excellent educational and health care facilities.

As part of a two-tower structure, the Xerox Canada building encompasses more than one million square feet of space. Photo by Lorraine C. Parow/First Light

by Wendy Priesnitz

The polished aluminum and cement shopping plaza is a cluster of service businesses and a restaurant, typical of any city corner . . . except that these shops proclaim their names in Chinese letters and the parking lot is full of BMWs and Cadillacs. And big, red neon letters spell out the words "Hongkong Bank." This is North York.

A few miles and worlds away, in the gentrified Avenue Road neighborhood, grocers and florists set out their greenery in neat sidewalk displays. Here one finds antique and art galleries, a bicycle shop, food, clothing for the haute couture two-year-old; brick sidewalks, trees and flowers in pots; bistros, sidewalk cafés, and at least two restaurants in every block. This is North York.

Bathurst Street, with its jumble of storefront strip plazas, is yet another world. Cars climb curbs to park by the Bagel Factory or Springer's Deli which advertises "strictly kosher meats." Across the street is Daiters Deli, famous for its cream cheese and lox. Down the way, Negev Importing's window is draped with a string of Israeli flags. On the corner, in front of the Blue and White Super Market, veggies and plants perch on upturned red plastic milk cases. This is North York.

Just around the corner, and across from Bagel World, the Tin Sing restaurant serves up a Cantonese and Szechwan buffet next door to a tiny West Indian take-out. Keep travelling and the eateries become La Traviata and Lorenzo's Pizza. Turn north now, along streets peppered with Jamaican pattie shops, past squat, anonymous-looking factories housing a hodgepodge of furniture manufacturers, printers, machine shops, woodworking shops. This is North York.

Then suddenly, 23 storeys of silver metal and reflective blue glass soar into the sky, narrowing to a dynamic flared roof by means of a centre-column waterfall of sheer glass. A marble and

North York currently is home to at least 17,000 business operations. Photo by Lorraine C. Parow/First Light

Although North York is home to many large operations such as IBM, more than 70 percent of the city's business establishments employ fewer than 10 people. Photo by The StockMarket

The new City Centre is shown under construction, with the completed Petro Canada tower and the Novotel Hotel in the background; both existing structures were designed by Canadian architect Raymond Moriyama. Photo by John O'Brien

Facing page: This view looks south on Yonge Street toward York Mills Valley and the city of Toronto from beyond the Procter & Gamble tower. Photo by John O'Brien

granite entrance leads to a half-million square feet of corporate offices, stores, a health club, restaurants, and theatres. This, too, is North York.

Diversity and excitement are two of the hallmarks of this enigmatic city. Woven into its texture are many contradictions and contrasts. North York is just as much home to Joe's Painting as it is to IBM Canada, with more than 70 percent of the city's business establishments employing fewer than 10 people. The historic is elbowed aside by the modern as a redevelopment boom takes hold and suburbia gives

way to big city. A manufacturing-based economy metamorphoses into a service-based one. But the contradictions are bound together into a dynamic whole by a pervasive spirit of entrepreneurship.

Just a few decades ago North York was just another suburb of Toronto, but the suburban model of the sixties does not fit anymore. The image of sleepy, tree-lined streets punctuated by the occasional convenience store or shopping mall has been replaced by that of a dynamic, exciting city of the eighties. North York's business community is, like the city itself, in transition. But a consciousness of its entrepreneurial past remains; it is a stable business community, in touch with its roots while developing new leaves on its flourishing tree.

This, also, is North York: The door to the rough-hewn log building opens to reveal the blackness that is a village blacksmith shop. The forge, bellows, anvil, tools, and fire sit waiting to fashion shoes for the horses and oxen, repair implements for the farmer, make new forks for the housewife, or replace iron tires on the wooden wheels of a carriage. This is a nineteenth-century artisan's building at Black Creek Pioneer Village, one of Canada's foremost museums of living history, located on the old Stong farm

property at Steeles Avenue and Jane Street.

As the humble pioneer blacksmith shop symbolizes, commerce has played a major role in North York's development since 1796 when Governor Simcoe opened Yonge Street as a trading route between the southern metropolitan settlement of York and areas to the north. By the early nineteenth century, a network of complementary village sub-centres had begun to emerge at crossroads along the roadway. These commercial hubs are still thriving neighborhoods today, even as a bold and brassy new $3-million, big-city-style downtown emerges along Yonge Street where none existed before.

Amid the traffic and urban sprawl sits a poignant reminder of North York's past. Historic Zion School-house SS No. 12 sits incongruously on Finch Avenue between the glass towers of Don Mills Road and Leslie Street. Built in 1869 by the citizens of L'Amaroux, this one-room schoolhouse is the last of its kind in North York, and an important link with the rural roots of this community.

One early and significant North York settlement was the Village of York Mills that grew up in the valley at what is now the intersection of York Mills Road and Yonge Street. In 1870 it had a population of one hundred people. But its history goes back further

The Zion School served the people of L'Amaroux for the better part of a century, and, after school hours, it became a community centre used for meetings, dances, and concerts. It was closed in 1955, but continues to function today as a living museum. Photo by Lorraine C. Parow/First Light

than that. By the 1820s early residents had constructed an 18-by-20-foot schoolhouse of 18-inch unhewn logs on the hill east of Yonge Street. It had a fireplace at one end whose chimney often caught fire during cold weather, and two outhouses behind the building.

In those days, teachers were often ex-soldiers or retired businessmen whose main qualification was the ability to keep order while pupils memorized or recited their lessons. But the educational climate greatly improved later in the century, under the guidance of Egerton Ryerson, a Methodist minister and constant visitor to North York. Ryerson was provincial Superintendent of Education from 1844 to 1876, and is credited with developing the Ontario public school system as it exists today.

A second York Mills school, called SS No. 3, was constructed of red brick on the northwest corner of Yonge and John Streets in 1947. And a third, two stories high with a bell tower, replaced it in the 1890s. The school housed 37 students in 1908.

Why did the village's early settlers choose to live a difficult six miles from the town of York? Standing at the bustling intersection today, with its stark white and glass office towers reflecting the still-remaining green areas, that is not a difficult question to answer. The pioneers likely realized that this point, where the main highway north, the West Don River, and what was an east-west concession road met, would be a natural site for industry.

And it was. A thriving little town grew up in the valley which was to become known as Hogg's Hollow. Even that nickname traces its origin to commerce, having been first used in connection with a housing development that was opened in 1856 by John and William Hogg. They had bought the property with their inheritance from their father, James, the valley's most successful miller.

Milling was one of North York's earliest and most common industries, aside from agriculture. As early as the 1700s, plentiful waterpower had led to the establishment of gristmills, distilleries, and woolen mills.

Evidence of early mills still remains within view of the seventh fairway of the Don Valley Golf Club, just northwest of the Yonge and York Mills intersection. Thomas Arnold, an early settler, saw the potential for water power on the site and constructed a dam by anchoring heavy logs into the clay bank and cutting a sluice into the corner to form a mill race for his sawmill. In the late 1830s new owner Cornelius van Nostrand, finding his mills paralyzed by spring floods, came up with a solution that typifies the foresight that has been characteristic of North York's business community. He converted the mills to steam in what was one of the earliest applications of steam power to industry in Canada.

Water had another commercial application at this intersection. The Gooderham property, which fronted on Yonge Street, had a spring that was tapped and bottled by a company called Mineral Springs Limited from 1906 to 1925. This water was used by O'Keefe Beverages in the early 1930s after a fire destroyed its main Toronto facility. O'Keefe erected a windmill and maintained the grounds until the property was sold for apartments in the 1950s. But the brewing company, now named Carling O'Keefe, still has its offices in the area.

York Mills is also home to such Canadian giants as London Life, the Canadian Federation of Independent Business, and Sunoco. The new Yonge Corporate Centre is a 735,000-square-foot joint venture of the Cadillac Fairview Corporation and London Life Insurance Company overlooking the golf course. On the northeast corner of the

York Mills Centre, built by the York-Trillium Development Group Ltd., boasts 540,000 square feet of offices, retail space, a six-storey public atrium, and a subway/bus terminus. Photo by Lorraine C. Parow/First Light

The Willowdale area of the 1980s is hardly the same as in 1865, when the Canada Gazetteer and Business Directory listed most Willowdale residents as having the occupation of farmer. Photo by Dawn Goss/First Light

intersection, the York-Trillium Development Group Ltd. has built the spectacular York Mills Centre, 540,000 square feet of offices, retail space, a six-storey public atrium, and a subway/bus terminus.

But long before granite towers and architects, the pattern of early commercial development was emerging along Yonge Street. In fact, since 1844, when the roadway underwent the revolutionary process of macadamization (small broken stones combined with a binder of tar) all the way north to Richmond Hill, the move toward development has been strong. And when the Northern Railway started up in 1853, the farming areas north of York were opened up even further to development.

North up Yonge from York Mills was the village of Willowdale. The

Canada Gazetteer and Business Directory of 1864-65 lists 26 Willowdale residents with occupations other than farming, out of a total population of 200. According to the list, the business community of the day included a tanner, currier, coppersmith, saddle and harness maker, carpenter, insurance agent, blacksmith, hotel proprietor, general merchant, flour and gristmill proprietor, sawmill proprietor, provincial land surveyor, and a carriage maker.

There was a teacher, too, who presided over the Willowdale School, SS No. 4, built at the corner of Yonge and Ellerslie Streets. Teaching in those days was a thankless and under-rewarded occupation. By the late 1800s the profession had improved greatly, but not sufficiently to hold the interest of lively

students who wanted most to be out working on their families' farms.

Educational opportunities in North York are now among the best in the country. A recognized leader, the North York Board of Education provides a balance between excellent academic and technological programs and values education for over 60,000 elementary and high school students and 55,000 adults.

Commerce, too, has evolved. From those few early hand-to-mouth manufacturing enterprises, the city is now home to at least 17,000 business operations. And as in the 1800s, increased and improved transportation routes continue to facilitate business growth. The city is located near Pearson International Airport and is serviced by major east/west (Highway

401) and north/south transportation corridors (Don Valley Parkway and Highway 404 combination, Highway 400 and the Allen Expressway). The subway runs from downtown Toronto to Finch Avenue along Yonge Street and to Yorkdale Shopping Centre in the west end. Plans are under way to build an east/west subway line along Sheppard Avenue.

In spite of good transportation and the positive mind-set of those entrepreneurial, spirited pioneers of commerce, the development of North York's business community has not been without its problems. One of the largest was the Great Depression, which hit North Yorkers hard. Toronto firms paying Toronto taxes fired their suburban workers first to save on city relief payments, creating an unemployment rate

in North York of 40 percent. Conver-
sely, many Toronto residents who did
lose their jobs, and consequently their
houses, moved north because land was
cheap and often available for squatting.
At the same time, North York had few
industries and, therefore, a shaky tax
base.

But with a growing local market
due to a swelling population, competitive tax rates, and an abundance of
commercial space, businesses bounced
back, and again found it hard to ignore
the lure of the great north. De Havilland Aircraft of Canada was one of
those companies, having opened an aircraft manufacturing plant north of
Sheppard Avenue, between Dufferin
and Keele Streets, in 1928 when land
was still cheap. After World War II
was declared, the federal government
arranged for the closing of Sheppard
Avenue south of the plant and the leasing of the land to De Havilland so that
it could expand to accommodate the
war effort. In May of 1953, the Royal
Canadian Air Force opened a supply depot on the site, and De Havilland
moved into a new building. Although
the De Havilland plant remains, and
there is still an active airport on the
site, the huge tract of prime land is a

valuable candidate for development in
the future.

After the Depression, a mini-land-
boom occurred, a hint of what was to
come for the municipality. Hundreds
of lots held by land speculators caught
by the Depression were now sold off,
and some of the parties involved became major players in the development
boom. Housing tracts sprang up
quickly, often as isolated pockets with
few shopping or community facilities.

During this post-World War II
population explosion, improvements
were made to the school system to help
it cope with the fast-growing number
of school-aged children moving into
the community. Back in 1928, the Newtonbrook, Willowdale, and York Mills
schools had merged into an administrative unit called the First Township
School Area. This unit was expanded
in 1950, many one- and two-room rural schools were closed, and a school
board administration building was
opened.

In 1953, under the Municipality
of Metropolitan Toronto Act, the present Board of Education was put in
place. There were over 700 teachers
and 23,000 students in 2 secondary
schools and 45 elementary schools. It

soon became apparent that the new trustees faced an unparalleled expansion of school buildings and facilities to meet the needs of Canada's fastest-growing municipality. The budget that had been a little over $500,000 in 1945 expanded to nearly $6.5 million in 1955.

In 1954 the Don Mills Development Company began building the first planned community in Canada. It was a revolutionary concept. The community was carefully planned to integrate industry, housing, churches, parks, community facilities, schools, and an 80-acre town centre which included a 44-acre shopping centre. The natural landscape was preserved wherever possible during construction. The plan was to be completed in 1960 at an estimated cost of $200 million, but business at the shopping centre was so good that it expanded a few years later.

The development of the Don Mills industrial parks was strictly regulated, with controls on outside storage, noise, signs, size of parking lots, and architecture. Among the first major industrial companies to locate there were Barber-Greene Canada Limited and Philco. But others, although they complained about the stringent controls, soon moved there too. Ironically, years later when a new industrial subdivision was being planned north of the original Don Mills community, some of the same industrialists who had complained about the restrictions were now so converted that they petitioned North York Council to impose the restrictions on their new neighbours.

These controls, coupled with proximity to the Don Valley Parkway, ensure that Don Mills remains a popular

and prosperous business area. New developments, such as the six low-rise buildings that make up the Wilket Creek Business Park at Eglinton and Leslie, are still being constructed. IBM has one of its main research facilities in the area, and its corporate neighbors include Imperial Oil, People's Jewellers, Rothman's, and Wrigley Canada Inc.

Each section of the city is colored by the type of commerce located there. Small manufacturing businesses, traditionally an important component of the North York business mosaic, are no exception. North York has long been the industrial heartland of Metropolitan Toronto, with manufacturing concentrated in 18 industrial parks located in three relatively narrow north/south corridors. In the west, four large indus-

IBM's main research facility is located in the Don Mills area. Photo by Glen Jones

trial areas run along both sides of Highway 400, south from the northern city limits at Steeles Avenue to Highway 401. Another large concentration of industrial zoning is located south from Steeles Avenue, between Keele and Dufferin streets, all the way to the city's southern boundary. Eight smaller parks are scattered along the Canadian National Railway line between Leslie Street and the Don Valley Parkway, south from Highway 401.

High-tech, metal fabrication, furniture manufacturing, and printing and publishing businesses are industrial leaders in the city. Early business development was centered around the manufacturing sector, with the number of firms mushrooming from just 6 in 1922 to 1,200 by 1966. And the growth continues. Industrial building

permits issued in 1987 were worth more than $60 million, compared with just under $20 million four years earlier.

Although small companies predominate, large manufacturers are also finding life attractive in the city. North York is home to companies like Dow Chemical, C-I-L Inc., Union Carbide and Cyanamid Canada, as well as high-tech giants like Burroughs, Unisys Canada, Epson Canada Limited, Sony, Advanced Fiberoptic Technologies Corp., Intercon, and Northern Telecom.

Motorola Canada Limited, a high-tech company, is a North York pioneer of sorts. Long recognized as a world leader in the electronics industry, it moved its corporate headquarters and one of its major high-tech development and manufacturing centres to an expan-

Don Mills is a popular and prosperous business area; corporations and businesses like Imperial Oil, IBM, and Wrigley Canada Inc. have located here. Photo by Glen Jones

Office workers from companies located in the area, like Union Carbide (dark building in background), can relax at lunchtime or after work at the many fine cafes and restaurants in the downtown area. Photo by Dawn Goss

Facing page, top: Motorola Canada Limited, long recognized as a world leader in the electronics industry, moved its corporate headquarters and one of its major high-tech development and manufacturing centres to a large site at Steeles and Victoria Park in 1967. Photo by Dawn Goss/First Light

Facing page, bottom: North York is home to many chemical and pharmaceutical producers. This is the Ortho Pharmaceuticals Building. Photo by Dawn Goss/First Light

sive site at Steeles and Victoria Park in 1967. At that time, Victoria Park cut through miles of farmland, and the company had to run its own bus service to get employees to and from work.

Spar Aerospace Limited is another innovative technological firm prospering in North York. The 17-year-old company, housed in a new 70,000-square-foot plant in the Ormont Drive Industrial Area, is famous for the Canadarm, a component of the United States' space station program. Research-and-development is also under way for a Mobile Servicing Centre for the space project.

Many large corporations are also located in Flemingdon Park, a 100-acre prestige industrial estate first developed in the early 1960s. The development was also designed to include multiple-rental housing, a golf course, shopping centre, school, swimming pool, and tennis courts. The park is home to Blue Cross, Canada Wire and Cable, Bata International, and a host of smaller companies.

Health care products and services constitute another large component of the North York mosaic. Pharmaceutical multinationals Ortho Pharmaceuticals and Connaught Laboratories are both headquartered in the area. And the city is home to no less than 15 hospitals and major health care facilities, a number of them holding special places of distinction within the local and national health care scenes.

Metro Toronto's first suburban hospital, Humber Memorial, is still going strong in North York. Established in 1950 by a group of 57 community organizations, this well-equipped facility has 352 beds and offers full inpatient services. Humber's special community services include an out-patient alcohol treatment unit and a diabetes educational program.

Canada's most frequently used hospital, Sunnybrook Medical Centre, is located on 100 acres of parkland on Bayview Avenue. Originally designed as a veterans' hospital and built at a cost of over $20 million in 1948, the 1,190-bed facility is now affiliated with the University of Toronto and serves the entire community with 620 acute care beds. But it still retains its commitment to the elderly and has declared their care, and the diseases of aging, as one of its major programs.

In addition, it has major programs in spinal cord injury, oncology, mental health, rehabilitation medicine, and car-diovascular disease. The Aids for Living Centre provides patients with prosthetic and orthotic devices; the Toronto Bayview Regional Cancer Centre serves thousands of cancer outpatients each year; the W.P. Scott Geriatric Day Hospital serves the needs of the elderly population living independently in the community; and numerous psychiatry and family practice clinics are available for a variety of needs. Sunnybrook also houses Canada's first regional trauma unit for the treatment of multiple-injury patients.

As a leader in the provision of quality health care in Canada, Sunnybrook

The Baycrest Centre for Geriatric Care was founded at the turn of the century as a Jewish home for the aged, and now consists of five main facilities providing social, recreational, emotional, and medical services. Photo by Peter Tang/First Light

Facing page, top: Sunnybrook Medical Centre serves the entire community, but still retains its commitment to the elderly, toward which its major programs are geared. Photo by Lorraine C. Parow/First Light

Facing page, bottom: Lyndhurst Hospital is one facility of many in the North York area providing high-quality health care. Photo by Peter Tang/First Light

depends on the expertise of its staff. The hospital currently employs more than 3,500 people, including a medical-dental staff of close to 300. Physicians' outpatient offices are organized through the Sunnybrook Hospital University of Toronto clinics. The hospital provides an attractive milieu for world-class researchers, furthering knowledge in many areas such as spinal cord injury, emergency medicine, and cancer.

North York is well served by a number of community-oriented hospitals. North York General houses a major obstetrical centre with a full-scale genetic counselling program, and operates the Seniors' Health Centre, a multi-level care and nursing home facility. NYGH has made the corner of Leslie Street and Sheppard Avenue a focal point for the provision of health care to the community. The first Mental Health Clinic in North York was opened there in 1965 on the site of the present School of Nursing.

In the west, York-Finch General Hospital and Northwestern Health Centre are both medium-sized acute-care community hospitals providing a full range of health care services. Of similar size is Branson Hospital, sponsored by the Seventh-Day Adventist Church. In addition to being a community acute-care facility, Branson has an active health promotion centre with programs for smoking cessation, weight control, fitness, nutrition, and stress management.

Rehabilitation, long-term, and specialty care are provided at a variety of facilities, including Childrens' Hospital, St. Bernard's Convalescent Hospital, St. John's Rehabilitation Hospital, and the Hugh MacMillan Medical Centre.

A continuum of health care for the elderly is provided by a model complex on Bathurst Street that includes health care, a home for the aged for debilitated patients, and a hospital. Baycrest Centre for Geriatric Care, established in the early 1900s as the Jewish Home for the Aged, now comprises five main facilities which all work together to provide a combination of social, recreational, emotional, and medical services.

North York General Hospital houses a major obstetrical centre with a full-scale genetic counselling program and also operates a Seniors' Health Centre and a nursing home facility. Photo by Peter Tang/First Light

York-Finch General Hospital and Northwestern Health Centre are both medium-sized acute-care community hospitals providing a full range of health care services. Photo by Peter Tang/First Light

Branson Hospital is sponsored by the Seventh-Day Adventist Church, and has an active health promotion centre with programs for smoking cessation, weight control, fitness, nutrition, and stress management. Photo by Peter Tang/First Light

The Canadian National Institute for the Blind provides rehabilitative and support services to the visually impaired. Photos by Lorraine C. Parow/First Light

tion skills. Signing classes are offered on a regular basis to the general public.

The Canadian National Institute for the Blind is the only private charitable organization in Canada providing rehabilitative and support services to the visually impaired. The CNIB national headquarters, provincial office, training facilities, and a residence for the visually impaired are all located in two buildings on a 12-acre site.

Just across the street from the CNIB is a facility which is unique to Canada. The Canadian Memorial Chiropractic College is the country's only school that provides professional education including practical training and clinical experience leading to qualifications as a Doctor of Chiropractic. The college is a privately run institution with a four-year program for 600 students who have completed a minimum of two years of basic university study. It also houses an outpatient clinic providing treatment to the general public.

Services for the deaf and blind are also provided at two facilities located within a few minutes walk of each other on Bayview Avenue. The Bob Rumball Centre for the Deaf is a multi-purpose complex which provides a unique combination of residential and outreach services for the hearing impaired. Programs include health care, education, recreation, vocational rehabilitation, and training in communica-

Being the sole training facility for the chiropractic profession in Canada, the college has an active research division. In addition to an impressive list of medically oriented projects, the college is actively sponsoring investiga-

tions into such topics as a descriptive analysis of sports injuries clinics, and issues of career and family relating to women chiropractors. College president Dr. Ian Coulter is also principal researcher of a study investigating chiropractic versus medical treatment of low back pain.

The preventive aspect of health care is addressed by the North York Public Health Department, which provides a variety of health protection services, including immunization and dental treatment programs for school children, birth control clinics, and services for seniors and new mothers. Department staff is also responsible for health inspection in restaurants, food stores, and public swimming pools.

Despite the size of the city's health care industry, manufacturing continues to play a significant role in North York's economy. However, there is also a shift from blue collar to white as corporate headquarters and professional and service businesses snap up

the proliferating high-quality office space. The most active office development centre outside the downtown area is strategically positioned at the crossroads of Highway 401 and the Highway 404/Don Valley Parkway combination. The Consumers Road Office Park houses a variety of both new high-rise and older, smaller office buildings. Consumer's Gas, Inducon, Burroughs, Honeywell, and Control Data are all located here. In the 1970s, Manufacturers Life established the standard in suburban office design with its Lansing Square development. Phase Three of the project, an eight-story, 150,000-square-foot glass, stone, and marble building continues the tradition. Also making a major impact on the skyline in this area are Marathon's Atria North and Oxford Development's Parkway Place.

Further north, adjacent to Highway 404 at Finch, is the Cosmopolitan Corporate Centre, an ambitious, mixed-use development. Encompassing 850,000 square feet of space are four buildings clad in reflective blue glass and linked by an enclosed pedestrian promenade. Included in the development are a 225-room hotel, a two-level, 30,000-square-foot retail atrium, and a $4-million Bally Matrix fitness centre.

The retail sector is also developing quickly in North York. In 1987, $20 billion, or 14 percent, of Canada's retail sales were located within its trading area.

One of the major retail products is food. Food merchandising has changed dramatically since the days when everyone grew their own. Some of the earliest retailing took place at the York Outdoor Market. Twenty-eight producers banded together to open the market in June of 1926 at the city limits on Yonge Street. It was moved in 1931 to the old streetcar barns near York Mills Road, where it remained until 1952. With the trend to supermarkets and shopping centres, it degenerated into a flea market and was no longer used by the farmers. So it was sold for $250,000, and the proceeds were used to build the first part of the North York Municipal Building. A few stalwart farmers moved the market to Yonge and Finch for a year or so, after which it was relocated yet again, this time further north on Yonge into the town of Thornhill.

It was around this time that North York hopped onto the shopping centre bandwagon in a big way. In fact, an article in the *Ontario Hydro News* in May of 1971 noted that North York had witnessed more shopping centre openings than any other place in Canada.

The first one-stop shopping centre in the Toronto suburbs opened at Lawrence and Bathurst in 1953 and is still in business today. The Lawrence Plaza opened with a Loblaws food store, 2 restaurants, 2 banks, 31 retail stores, and free parking for 2,000 cars in its floodlit lot. In the summer of 1955, Henry Morgan and Co., a Montreal retailer later taken over by the Hudson's Bay Company, opened the first suburban department store there.

A few years later the Bayview Village Centre opened on the northeast corner of Bayview and Sheppard

Avenues. And in 1960 a reporter, describing the opening of the U-shaped Newtonbrook Plaza at the corner of Cummer Avenue and Yonge, raved about "the latest in counter-top automatic vegetable sprinklers to keep all vegetables at the peak of freshness" in the plaza's Steinberg's grocery store.

One-inch headlines blared out the start of construction in June 1961 of what was to be called Sayvette City, at the southwest corner of Yonge and Steeles, where Towne and Countrye Square is located today. The 140,000-square-foot Sayvette Department Store was located in a 37-acre complex that newspapers called "Metro's largest complex of department stores and shops." By 1964 the papers announced a new shopping centre for the same site, with 50 new stores and a new name: Towne and Countrye Square.

A broader concept of the shopping centre made outdoor malls obsolete in 1964, when the spectacularly upscale Yorkdale Shopping Centre opened adjacent to Highway 401 between Dufferin and Bathurst streets. The T. Eaton Company's real estate department had purchased the tract of land in the early 1950s, planning to build a major suburban store there. In 1960 Eaton joined with fellow retail giant Simpson's and New York developer William Zeckendorf, who was responsible for Montreal's Place Ville Marie. Walt Disney included the resulting mall in his Bell Telephone Expo Film of Canada. The mall has in recent years been dubbed "The New Yorkdale," after a modernization project expanded it to more than 1.4 million square feet and 230 stores.

Fairview Mall, opened in 1970 at Don Mills Road and Sheppard Avenue, was the Toronto area's first two-level regional enclosed shopping mall. A promotional brochure excitedly described a new type of escalator which would provide for "easy movement between levels . . . on gently-inclined 'moving walks.'" The $20-million project was developed by the Fairview Corporation of Canada Limited when it was the pri-

The Yorkdale Shopping Centre, opened in 1964, has recently been dubbed "The New Yorkdale" after a modernization project expanded it to more than 1.4 million square feet and 230 stores. Photo by Dawn Goss/First Light

Fairview Mall was the Toronto area's first two-level regional enclosed shopping mall. Photo by Dawn Goss/First Light

The Highland Farms food terminal is just one of the grocery "superstores" that have met great success in the North York area. Photo by Dawn Goss/First Light

Steele's West Market is an indoor market with a multicultural bazaar theme. Photo by Dawn Goss/First Light

vate real estate wing of the Bronfman family, and before it merged with the Cadillac Development Corporation in 1974 to become Cadillac Fairview. It has recently undergone a spectacular $90-million renovation which has more than doubled its size.

The 1980s have seen a new thrust in retailing in North York that is just as revolutionary as the shopping centre was in its time: the superstore. In 1986 the city welcomed IKEA Canada, with its largest furniture warehouse in North America. This superstore includes more than 260,000 square feet

of furniture and housewares, and a restaurant. The grocery business has also had great success with the superstore idea, with Highland Farms food terminal, Knob Hill Farms in the west end, and Steeles West Market—an indoor market with a multicultural bazaar theme.

Hospitality and tourism are also growth industries in North York. The city has 10 premier hotels, with more than 300 meeting rooms. The Inn on the Park is a flagship for the Four Seasons chain. Located across from a multi-acre parkland at Eglinton and Leslie, it

North York's newest hotel is the Novotel, a 260-room corporate-style facility with a European flavor. Photo by Lorraine C. Parow/First Light

The Prince Hotel is North York's largest, with more than 400 rooms and 16 meeting halls. Photo by Lorraine C. Parow/First Light

The Space Science program at York University contributes to more than half of all space science research at Canadian universities. Photo by John O'Brien

is a destination and convention facility with 21 meeting rooms. The city's newest hotel is the Novotel, a 260-room, corporate-style facility with a European accent. Its pinkish tower with green-tinged windows stands out among the glass and granite of the new Yonge Street downtown. The city's largest hotel is The Prince, with over 400 rooms and 16 meeting rooms. Other hotels include Holiday Inn Yorkdale, Ramada Inn, Relax Plaza, Skyline Triumph, Radisson Hotel Don Valley, and the Yorkdale Inn.

The communications industry has a strong foothold in North York, as well. Two major companies, Southam Communications and MacLean Hunter, produce more than 500 trade and consumer magazines from their plants in the city. The community itself is served by more than 30 neighborhood and ethnocultural weekly newspapers, as well as the four Toronto dailies. In addition, the Global Television Network has its facilities in Don Mills.

An examination of the elements of the city's business base reveals two other players. York University and Seneca College, both post-secondary educational facilities, contribute to the business community with their small business development, training, and research facilities. They also bolster the local economy by employing large numbers of people.

The fact that York University is North York's largest employer would be enough to give it a prominent place in the mosaic. But more importantly, it has an international reputation for excellence in business administration, environmental studies, and a full range of science, fine arts, and education programs. Its space science program contributes to more than half of all space science research at Canadian universities. Approximately 41,000 students from around the world study there on a full- and part-time basis in more than 200 degree programs.

Founded in 1959 on the University of Toronto campus at Bayview and Lawrence avenues, York grew so fast that it moved to a 600-acre campus between Jane and Keele streets, south of

Steeles Avenue, in 1965. Its motto, *"tentanda via"* (The way must be tried), defines the spirit embodied in the school's dynamism and excellence.

York University students are seldom at a loss for ways to occupy their time. There are more than 50 clubs and 32 varsity sports teams. In fact, the school boasts major sports facilities designed to international standards, including the National Tennis Centre and the Metropolitan Toronto Track and Field Centre.

Seneca College is a major community educational resource for the people of North York. It was founded in 1967, with over 800 full-time and 1,000 part-time students in a converted factory at Sheppard Avenue and Yonge Street, which it outgrew in less than a year. It now has around 10,000 full-time and 80,000 part-time students at 18 campuses. Its facilities include the 1,100-seat Minkler Auditorium, which offers professional facilities for theatrical performances, concerts, and other cultural events. Along with the Sports Centre, it is used throughout the year by many community organizations.

An ambitious seven-year plan is under way to consolidate the college's many teaching locations. Plans for Seneca Square, a new $100-million complex on the site of the original college, include a four-storey education centre, office tower, and shopping concourse. Seneca's business-oriented facilities include a new communications campus, its Centre for Entrepreneurship, a Business and Industrial Training Division, a Centre for Precision Skills, and a variety of other skills development courses.

Other post-secondary educational institutions include the Institute for Aerospace Studies, the Canadian Forces College, the Ontario Bible College, Canadian Centre for Advanced Film Studies, and private trainers like Control Data Institute and the Devry Institute of Technology. In addition, the Community Industrial Training Committee provides specialized career skill training programs with the co-operation of Seneca College, the North

York Board of Education, organized labor, local and provincial governments, and private sector employers.

The ethnic character that makes North York's business community such a lively one is also a vital characteristic of its educational community. Schools are rich in cultural and linguistic resources: students from more than 125 countries and speaking 75 different languages make up at least one-third of the public school population. The North York Board of Education offers one of Ontario's most comprehensive programs of heritage language instruction, in partnership with community and parents groups. Over

York University was founded in 1959 on the University of Toronto campus at Bayview and Lawrence avenues, and grew so fast that it moved to a 600-acre campus between Jane and Keele streets in 1965. Photo by Lorraine C. Parow/First Light

Seneca College began in 1967 with more than 800 full-time and 1,000 part-time students in a converted factory. It now has 10,000 full-time and 80,000 part-time students at 18 campuses. Photo by Lorraine C. Parow/First Light

10,000 students from non-English-speaking countries are enrolled in English as a Second Language courses. And a parallel set of services, called Standard English as a Second Dialect, helps students from English-speaking Caribbean countries adjust to the life and language of North America.

French language instruction receives first-class treatment in North York. Immersion is provided from senior Kindergarten to the end of secondary school for those students who display a superior level of proficiency in oral and written French. And one school, Ecole Etienne Brûlé, targets itself solely to those whose mother tongue is French.

French is also an important component of the program provided by the public school board's sister system. The Metropolitan Separate School Board educates more than 33,000 young people in the City of North York in 53 Catholic elementary schools and 11 secondary schools. There are three schools that provide a French-language education for francophone children, in addition to regular, extended, and immersion programs in the regular separate schools.

Based on Catholic principles, this board's academic and extra-curricular programs are designed to help children develop to their full potential—spiritually, physically, and emotionally. The Separate School supporters of North York elect six of the 24 board trustees. The board also has a *Conseil de l'enseignment de la langue francais* whose three members are elected by francophone Catholic ratepayers.

The degree of educational choice in the city is vast. Parents can also enroll their children at one of 16 Jewish-sponsored day schools. The Board of Jewish Education sets general guidelines and standards for these private schools, but each school has its own distinct philosophy and hires its own teachers. Curriculum includes courses required by the Ontario Ministry of Education, as well as instruction in the Bible, Hebrew, Jewish traditions, and the history of Israel and the Jewish people.

There are numerous other independent schools from which to choose. Located in the beautiful and historic F.P. Wood home and estate, Crescent School is a non-denominational private boys' school for grades 4 through 13. A private girls' school, Havergal College, has a strong academic program plus a broad range of extracurricular activities including music and sports. The Toronto French School provides an enriched bilingual program with very high standards, particularly in math, science, and languages.

The lure of private schools often involves specialized, alternative, or enriched programs with low pupil-to-teacher ratios. In North York, the public school board, true to its slogan, "Champions in Education," has been a pioneer in offering such programs. In the 1970s, faced with protecting its numbers as enrollments began to decline alarmingly, the Board of Education introduced a strong program of public relations and program specialization.

The Alternative and Independent Study Program is one such specialized school. AISP, as it has come to be called, caters to the self-motivated, responsible, and independent student who seeks a less structured approach to education. It features small classes with individualized instruction and informal, personal contact with teachers.

Claude Watson School for the Arts delivers the Board of Education's enriched artistic educational program. By means of an extended school day and a modified academic program, students who have successfully completed an audition process are able to develop their talent and appreciation in the visual or performing arts.

A similar program is offered for talented female athletes. The Seneca-North York Sports Program for Women's Athletics responds to the challenge of matching an academic timetable to a training program that allows athletes to compete at the international level. World-class, medal-winning teenage gymnasts Mary Fuzesi and Monica Covacci are both students at the school.

These are just some of the high-calibre services that North York is able to offer as it emerges as an exciting and vibrant city with a prospering economy. Although the city's population is remaining relatively stable, employment levels are among the highest in Metropolitan Toronto, due in large measure to commercial development in the Yonge Street corridor and the revitalization of the Don Mills area.

The city's administration has actively worked to create a climate that encourages commercial and industrial growth. Mayor Mel Lastman has a personal background as an aggressive retailer and is committed to helping local businesses flourish. The city created a Department of Economic Development in 1985, and has an industrial development specialist on staff. The department provides the encouragement and information required to attract new companies and measures the city's pattern of economic development and growth.

Also supporting the business community are numerous business organizations. Foremost among these is the North York Business Association, founded in 1980 to represent the interests of the growing economic community and to promote communication and interaction among businesses and between the business and educational sectors. The association co-sponsors,

with York University, an "Entrepreneur of the Year Award"; supports high school co-op education programs; hosts dinners, network trade shows, and seminars; and lobbies government about a variety of issues that affect the local economic community. The association, soon to be renamed the North York Chamber of Commerce under the auspices of the Metro Toronto Board of Trade, is a young, aggressive, and dynamic association firmly committed to growth, progress, and community service—just like North York itself.

Walk the golden mile-and-a-half of Yonge Street from just south of Highway 401 to Finch Avenue and you can see, hear, and touch the evidence of the city's dynamism and strength. Since 1984, construction cranes, gleaming corporate towers, and office workers pouring into new buildings by the thousands have been the order of the day. This type of development is a major force in today's North York business picture, as available office space is becoming scarce and expensive in downtown Toronto. Companies who locate in North York can find first-class accommodation at about 35 percent of what they would have to pay downtown. Consequently, a number of major corporations have located their offices along this portion of Yonge Street. The aluminum-clad Procter &

The Canadian Government Building is on Yonge Street. Photo by Glen Jones

The aluminum-clad Procter & Gamble building encompasses 370,000 square feet of office space. Photo by Lorraine C. Parow/First Light

Gamble building, recently finished by Menkes Developments, encompasses 370,000 square feet of office space. North American Life Insurance Company, after operating its Canadian headquarters in downtown Toronto for over a hundred years, recently joined the trend and moved to North York. Its two-tower project, developed in partnership with Xerox Canada, encompasses over one million square feet of space.

Other downtown projects include the Camrost Group's distinctive 23-storey Madison Centre north of Sheppard; Inland Properties' 300,000-square-foot Yonge Norton Centre; the 29-storey Olympia and York office tower; and the Avro Group's 1.4 million-square-foot complex attached to the Civic Centre. The largest development in the area when completed, the Avro Group development will house Petro Canada's regional headquarters. The jewel is the City Centre, which emerged in 1987 from a muddy excavation site to encompass more than two million square feet of gleaming office, shopping, and leisure space.

But perhaps more than anything, Dempsey's hardware store, a familiar sight to all who travel past the Yonge and Sheppard intersection, typifies the city's relentless push for growth and renewal. In the mid-1800s this area was a little hamlet called Lansing. In 1860

Joseph Shepard built a large red brick general store there. Benjamin Robert Brown bought it in 1888 and turned it into a thriving hardware business. In 1921 the store was bought by two brothers, George and William, who named it Dempsey Brothers Limited. It also housed the post office and the offices of the local weekly newspaper, *The Enterprise*. The business became a landmark in the community, was passed down to George's two sons, and prospered until the inevitable redevelopment squeezed it out.

The Canderel Ltd. development group, along with the Prudential, purchased the property early in 1988, and plans to incorporate the building into a $160-million office tower development plan. The North York Historical Board has approved a plan to move the old building half a block west along Sheppard, where it will be restored and see new life, probably as a restaurant.

A similar plan is already in place further south along Yonge, near where the enterprising residents of the village of York Mills first built their mills and blacksmith shops. At the Yonge Corporate Centre at Yonge and York Mills Road, history collides with the future in an unsettlingly comfortable way. Polished granite and glass towers reflect two 130-year-old whitewashed workers' cottages with green shutters, which have been restored, linked, and expanded to accommodate a first-class French restaurant.

This juxtaposition of old and new seems, to the passerby, to bode well for a positive future of continued business and industrial health in North York. The city's challenge for the future lies in protecting this balance between growth and tradition, and retaining the multi-cultural exuberance that is such an important part of its business mosaic.

Facing page, top and bottom: Madison Centre is just one of the many new developments springing up along Yonge Street. Photo by Lorraine C. Parow/ First Light

Highway 401 is one of the busy transportation arteries feeding into the North York area. Photo by John O'Brien

CHAPTER 6

Creating a Cultural Showcase

With concerts, festivals, theatres, art galleries, historic sites, and fine libraries and museums, North York sets the stage for a lively cultural scene.

Black Creek Pioneer Village is a "living history" museum run by the Metropolitan Toronto and Region Conservation Authority. Photo by Lorraine C. Parow/First Light

The Centre for Advanced Film Studies in North York was the brainchild of Norman Jewison, producer of the Oscar-winning Moonstruck. The centre ranks with the best film schools in Hollywood and Europe. Photo by John O'Brien

by Helga V. Loverseed

North York is within easy reach of the many arts and cultural attractions found in Toronto—among them, the O'Keefe Centre, the CN Tower, the Royal Ontario Museum, and the bustling St. Lawrence market. But it also has a lively cultural scene of its own. The city stages festivals, concerts, and arts and crafts workshops, and has many theatres, cinemas, art galleries, historic sites, museums, and libraries.

North York's libraries are among the most modern in Canada. They have a wide range of books, magazines, and research material, and they also lend films, records, videos, "talking books," and digital discs. Several branches have facilities for plays and concerts. The Fairview branch, for example, has its own stage, used by local theatre groups and entertainers.

There are 19 branches throughout the city. Most were built after World War II, and are a far cry from the skeleton library run out of one of the rooms of the Memorial Community Hall in the 1940s. The Community Hall was used for social and cultural gatherings of various service clubs, with only one room set aside for the lending of books.

Later the library was located in the basement of Willowdale United Church. Librarians were volunteers be-

longing to the Queen Mary McKee Home and School Association. In 1954, to keep up with public demand, a portable building was placed at the junction of Yonge Street and Park Home Avenue. Bookmobiles, introduced that same year, served readers who did not live close to the building. A permanent library was erected in 1959.

The newest branch is the North York Central Library, which opened on May 28, 1987. It's situated in the North York City Centre, next to City Hall. Designed by celebrated architect Raymond Moriyama (who also built the innovative Ontario Science Centre and the Japanese Cultural Centre), the North York Central Library is a futuristic glass-and-concrete structure—a jewel in the crown of North York's new "Downtown, Uptown."

This literary and cultural showpiece is large (it sprawls over 160,000 square feet) and its six storeys are stacked with books. The library houses a mind-boggling 250,000 volumes (and has the capacity for an additional 150,000), hundreds of which are written in the many tongues spoken in Metro Toronto. Books and periodicals in 28 of those languages can be found in the Languages, Literature and Fine Arts Department on the second floor.

North York, with its large ethnic community, celebrates its heritage in its own unique way. Every June, North Yorkers of every background and race take part in Caravan, a colorful festival of arts, culture, food, and history. Started some 20 years ago as a modest community event in downtown Toronto, Caravan has blossomed into a Metro-wide festival which draws thousands of people annually. It's now one of Metro Toronto's prime summer attractions.

Events are staged at "pavilions" —theatres, church halls, and community centres—throughout Metro Toronto. The pavilions are named after cities, countries, or geographical areas, and visitors are issued "passports," which are stamped as they move from place to place.

There are over 40 pavilions, several of which are in North York. "Skopje," at Overlea Boulevard, highlights the culture of the Macedonians. Visitors, met by hosts in national costumes, are treated to folk dances and typical Macedonian food—stuffed peppers, shishkabob, beans with sausages, and the like.

At "Thessaloniki" on Thorncliffe Park Drive, a Greek orchestra plays loud, lively Greek songs and dances; while at "Tokyo," the Japanese pavilion on Wynford Drive, all is harmony and elegance. Dancers in kimonos demonstrate graceful, classical dancing, and there are demonstrations of flower-arranging, origami, calligraphy, and brush painting.

North York is also the scene of a popular winter festival—the Winter Carnival, held on the second weekend in February. More than 75 North York cultural and community groups get involved in this three-day event, which is staged at Black Creek Pioneer Village, the ideal setting for such traditional winter activities as ice sculpting, pancake breakfasts, and romantic sleigh rides through the snow.

Such activities go back to the days of the pioneers. North Yorkers have always enjoyed social get-togethers. In the nineteenth century, when the city was a rural backwater, barn-raising bees were all the rage.

By the turn of the century, bees had given way to other kinds of cultural gatherings such as Sunday school picnics, church socials, and plowing matches. Festivals were popular then, too. In 1918, at the height of World War I, a Flax Festival was organized on the farm of Billy Wallace in Willowdale. (Another Flax Festival, commemorating this one, was staged in August 1983.) The festival celebrated the growing of flax, which was turned into linen—a much needed commodity in the manufacturing of biplane wings. It was a grand affair. The skirling sound of the 48th Highlanders sailed through the air as farmers mowed down the crops.

In 1913, Joseph Kilgour's 380-acre Sunnybrook Farm (now Sunnybrook Medical Centre) was chosen as the site for the first Provincial Plowing Match. Held on a different farm every year, the match attracted farmers from south of the border. The final plowing match in North York took place in 1934 on Maryvale Farm, north of Lawrence Avenue on the west side of Victoria Park. (The farm was owned by businessman Frank O'Connor, who founded Laura Secord Candy Shops and the United States-based Fanny Farmer Candy Shops. O'Connor later became a senator.)

North York has numerous reminders of those early days. The city has

over 70 architecturally or historically significant buildings. Some are private homes. Others have been turned into museums administered by the North York Historical Board.

The 17-person board, appointed by the City of North York Council, is responsible for managing the historic sites. It acts as the Local Architectural Conservation Advisory Committee (L.A.C.A.C.), advising on the designation of historically and architecturally important properties, as outlined by the Ontario Heritage Act. The board also educates North Yorkers about their heritage, by organizing walking tours and historic, cultural events.

The David Gibson House (5172 Yonge Street), North York's finest example of the Neo-Classical "Georgian Survival" style, comes under its jurisdiction. An elegant, well-proportioned red and yellow brick structure, it boasts a handsome doorway with a semi-elliptical fan transom and sidelights—a popular addition to the homes of gentlemen of the mid-1800s.

Built in 1851, the house belonged to surveyor, rebel, and public official David Gibson. Today it's manned by costumed guides who give interpretive talks on North York's early history.

The historic David Gibson House, built in 1851, is managed by costumed guides who lecture on North York's early history. Photo by Lorraine C. Parow/ First Light

Twenty-three-year-old Ofra Harnoy is one of the world's leading cellists. She debuted at Carnegie Hall at age 17. Photo by John O'Brien

The home is also used for displays of arts and crafts.

Another famous house is the Tudor Revival home at 3590 Bayview Avenue, which once belonged to writer Mazo De La Roche. Roche was best known for her Jalna books, which portrayed life in nineteenth-century Ontario. While living in her North York home from 1939 to 1945, she wrote nine novels, including *Whiteoak Chronicles, The Building of Jalna,* and *Finch's Fortune.*

Historic illustrator C.W. Jeffreys lived in the Ontario Gothic farmhouse at 4111 Yonge Street. Built in the 1830s by Rowland Burr, who was involved in the upgrading of Yonge Street, the house served for awhile as a manse for the former York Mills Pres-

byterian Church. After Jeffreys bought it in 1922, it became something of an artists' colony. He and his wife Clara were popular hosts, and members of the famed Group of Seven frequently met in their parlor.

Jeffreys himself was a well-known artist. After working for the *New York Herald* and the *Toronto Globe,* he started illustrating scenes from Canada's history. A stickler for accuracy, he once paid $100 for a Dutch book on firearms so that he could correctly depict the muskets of Champlain and his men. Today his works grace public buildings, books, galleries, and magazines. Jeffreys died at York Mills in 1951, and in 1972 Imperial Oil donated its collection of his historical drawings and paintings—the largest ever assembled—to the Public Archives of Canada.

Talented and well-known artists continue to make North York their home. The Cavoukian family of Melrose Avenue has produced two renowned portrait photographers and Raffi, a popular children's entertainer. Artin Cavoukian, who uses the professional name of Cavouk, has photographed dozens of artistic superstars and heads of state—among them, Queen Elizabeth and Prince Philip, Lord and Lady Mountbatten, former Ontario premier William Davis, singer Anne Murray, violinist Yehudi Menuhin, and pianist Vladimir Ashkenazy.

Known for making his subjects appear natural and relaxed, Cavouk is a master of what he calls "painting by camera." His son Onnig, who began working at his father's studio in 1963, is also a renowned portrait photographer. Their work has been displayed all over the world, including the U.S.S.R.

Singer Dan Hill is another famous North Yorker. Although he now lives in downtown Toronto, he was born and raised in Don Mills and spent his early years singing in Shier's coffeehouse in Willowdale, a favorite hangout for "folkies" in the seventies. Hill, who is a talented songwriter as well as singer, has won five Juno awards, and his songs have been recorded by superstars such as George Benson. His own number, "Sometimes When We Touch," has sold 3 million copies around the world.

North Yorker Ofra Harnoy is a classical cellist of international renown. Only 23 years old, Harnoy has performed in countries as far afield as England, Japan, China, Italy, and Israel. She has played with leading orchestras such as the Cincinnati Symphony, under the leadership of Erik Kunzel. The youngest winner in the 31-year-old history of the New York Concert Artists Guild competition, she debuted at Carnegie Hall when she was only 17 years old.

North York, as well as nurturing the careers of such world-renowned artists, has played host to many. Eddie Fisher, Joel Grey, Shelley Berman, and Vincent Price are some of the stars who have played the Leah Posluns Theatre. Over 10 years old, the theatre produces five full-scale plays every year, ranging from comedy to drama. The Tony Award-winning musical *Applause* closed last year's busy season.

Attached to the theatre is the Leah Posluns Theatre School—one of the largest drama schools in Metro Toronto. Courses are taught in creative drama, acting, script writing, musical theatre, scene study, and the role of the director. They are aimed at all levels of experience, from amateurs to working professionals.

Drama courses are also taught at one of North York's "alternative" schools—the Claude Watson School for the Performing Arts. Here students combine an academic education with training in dance, music, drama, and the visual arts. North York also has a summer music school for children and adults, held every August at A.Y. Jackson Senior Secondary School.

North York's educational establishments are very much part of its cultural scene. The Glendon Gallery, for example, is on the Glendon Campus of York University. The city's first public art gallery, the Glendon houses a small but comprehensive selection of historical, modern, and contemporary Canadian and foreign applied and decorative arts.

One of North York's largest and most popular theatres is the Minkler Auditorium at the Newnham Campus of the Seneca College of Applied Arts and Technology. Built in the shape of an amphitheatre, the hall has a seating capacity of 1,116 and is equipped to handle everything from big band concerts to films and plays. One of the highlights of the year is "Kids' Kapers," a series of seven children's shows presented on Sunday afternoons. A second facility, the 250-seat Studio Theatre, is also located here. An intimate "theatre-in-the-round," it is ideally suited to specialized cultural events.

The Minkler Auditorium is the home base of the North York Symphony. Considered to be among the best in Canada, the 90-member orches-

The North York Puppet Centre is an unusual museum featuring more than 500 marionettes from Canada and other countries. The staff presents a variety of shows and stories for its young audience. Photos by Lorraine C. Parow/First Light

Facing page: Numerous cultural events, such as the fall pioneer festival and North York's Winter Festival, are held at Black Creek Pioneer Village, and the site is used as an interpretive centre for schoolchildren. Photo by Lorraine C. Parow/First Light

tra runs a five-concert subscription series featuring works by classical masters such as Beethoven, Liszt, and Tchaikovsky. On Sunday afternoons there are programs highlighting music by Strauss, Richard Rodgers, Cole Porter, Bizet, and other nineteenth- and twentieth-century composers.

An offshoot of the Symphony Association is the Sinfonia of North York, which performs a four-concert Young People's Series. Children who subscribe get a unique chance to involve themselves in music. They can sit with the 37-member orchestra while it is playing. Another group under the auspices of the North York Symphony Association—the North York Concert Orchestra—brings music to the community by playing in public places like

shopping malls and senior citizens' homes.

A relative newcomer on the cultural scene is the National Chamber Orchestra of Canada, an ensemble of internationally renowned professional musicians. Based at the Cringan Hall Auditorium at Earl Haig Secondary School, it offers a varied musical program—matinee concerts and music in parks and libraries. As well as supporting young, creative talent, the ensemble has a particular interest in researching and presenting lesser-known Canadian works.

A particular favorite with North York's children is the Puppet Centre, an unusual museum with over 500 marionettes from across Canada and from 35 different countries. A joint project

Above and facing page: Black Creek Pioneer Village is a "living history" museum, where costumed "pioneers" go about their daily tasks. Photos by Lorraine C. Parow/First Light

of the Ontario Arts Council, the Ministry of Citizenship, and the Metropolitan Toronto and North York Boards of Education, the Puppet Centre is educational as well as entertaining.

Every Saturday from September to June, the staff, in the style of traditional "Punch & Judy" shows, presents a variety of stories, from "Aesop's Fables" to "The Princess and the Pea." Kids have fun, and at the same time they learn about puppetry, an ancient craft dating back to Egypt and classical Greece.

Summer brings a host of outdoor entertainments. The Skylight Theatre, performing at an open-air amphitheatre in Earl Bales Park, stages ambitious large-scale productions for over 3,000 people. Past successes include the Dora Award-winning musical, *The Count of Monte Cristo*. In August, Skylight's Young Company presents a se-

ries of drama workshops throughout North York and a variety of dance, music, and multicultural events.

North York's large ethnic communities have their own cultural centres where they perform plays, concerts, and traditional song and dance. The Latvian Canadian Cultural Centre (which becomes the Latvian Pavilion during Caravan) hosts folk dancing, choral, and theatre groups. The Japanese Canadian Cultural Centre (also a Caravan pavilion) organizes spring and fall art exhibits, and each spring runs the Haru Matsuri (Spring Festival).

The Armenian Community Centre keeps alive the traditions and culture of Armenia by perfoming historic plays. The centre is also the home of the renowned Hamazkain choir.

The Joseph D. Carrier Art Gallery, situated in the Columbus Centre built by the Italian community, features exhibitions by local, national, and international artists.

The Koffler Gallery is a branch of the Jewish Community Centre of Toronto. As well as showing exhibits of decorative art and design, it offers educational and interpretive programs, panel discussions, and a film series open to all North Yorkers. At the Koffler Gallery School of Visual Art, would-be artists can take a variety of courses in pottery, life drawing, painting, watercolor, drawing, design, cartooning, and clay, wax, and stone sculpting.

Coordinating all these artistic and cultural activities is the North York Arts Council, a non-profit umbrella organization for literary, performing, and visual artists, their friends, and patrons. With a membership of over 500 individuals and 80 groups, the NYAC acts as an advocate for the city's cultural community, striving for better funding and facilities while raising the profile of local artists.

To that end the NYAC has published an anthology of prose and poetry written by members, and it organizes two annual exhibitions—the juried Eye on Art and the non-juried Open Show. It also runs a gallery, a studio/ workshop, and a Film/Video festival, held every fall. Throughout the year, member artists and writers have the opportunity of giving and attending workshops. They publish their works in a monthly newsletter and give poetry readings, which are open to the public.

North York's history is highlighted at the Black Creek Pioneer Village, a unique "living history" museum where costumed "pioneers" go about their daily tasks. Run by the Metropolitan Toronto and Region Conservation Authority, the museum is used as an interpretive centre for schoolchildren, but numerous cultural events are held here as well. During the summer the Theatre Passe Muraille performs *1837—The Farmer's Revolt* by renowned playwright Rick Salutin, an

Black Creek Pioneer Village is a major tourist attraction, with more than a quarter of a million visitors from all over Canada and the U.S. visiting every year. Photo by Barry Dursley/First Light

enactment of the events which led to the Rebellion of 1837.

Seasonal celebrations such as a fall pioneer festival, nineteenth-century Christmas festivities, and North York's Winter Festival are also held here. At the Visitor Centre, with its gallery, gift shop, audio-visual theatre, and dining room, visitors can attend lectures and buy history books outlining life in "Upper Canada" (as Ontario was once known).

Black Creek Pioneer Village is a major tourist attraction; over a quarter of a million visitors from all over Canada and the United States come here every year. It's remarkably authentic. The site is surrounded by high-rise apartment blocks and the campus of York University, but it looks and feels as if it belongs to another era.

The museum recalls the small rural settlements that once made up the northern part of York Township (which later became the Township of North York, then the City of North York). The village lies on what was originally the farm of Daniel Stong, a Pennsylvania German who came to the Jane and Steeles area in 1816. In 1874 Jacob Stong was appointed Justice of the Peace, and after the establishment of the Canadian National Exhibition five years later, he was appointed a director and judge.

The tiny log cabin which was Daniel's first home and the two-storey building which replaced it still stand. Over 20 other buildings have been added, including a water-driven gristmill; a one-room schoolhouse; a blacksmith's barn; a weavers' shop; a carriage works; and a Mennonite meeting house.

The buildings were gathered from around the City of North York (and other parts of Ontario), transported to Black Creek Pioneer Village, then re-erected on the site. They look as if they are part of a real pioneer community. Ladies clad in long frocks and poke bonnets smile and wave at visitors, their feet clattering on the wooden sidewalks. The giant wheel of Roblin's Mills swishes and thumps as it turns in the foaming water, and in the surrounding fields, horses whinny a welcome.

The exhibits at the Ontario Science Centre are very much the hands-on variety, and the facility mixes education with entertainment. Photo by Dawn Goss/First Light

Animals were very much part of nineteenth-century life, and there are plenty here. Sheep graze in meadows bordered by rough-hewn pioneer fences. Oxen, their massive, horned heads moving slowly from side to side, nuzzle visitors' cameras, hoping no doubt for a tasty snack. To North Yorkers who lived in the city prior to World War II, before it became the thriving metropolis of today, these scenes bring back fond memories.

The Ontario Science Centre, at Don Mills Road and Eglinton Avenue, is a quite different kind of museum. Black Creek Pioneer Village is relaxed and slow, permeated with the atmosphere of an era when time was measured by the pace of a horse. The Science Centre, all hustle and bustle, represents the world of tomorrow.

The centre was the Province of Ontario's official commemorative project for the Centennial of Canada's Confederation, held in 1967. It was conceived

originally as a museum of science and technology but, rather than build just another repository for artifacts, the Ontario Government, together with the Centre's Board of Trustees, decided to change the emphasis of the museum to make it an interpretive centre where visitors could interact with the technological displays.

Housed in 12 halls, the exhibits run the gamut of scientific and technological discovery—from mining to space exploration to solar heating. Would-be inventors have a field day, pushing buttons, flicking levers, turning cranks, and chatting to computers. This is very much a "hands-on" place, a learning center that mixes education with entertainment.

A continuous program of workshops and scientific demonstrations supplements the more than 800 exhibits. The laser show is a big favorite, especially with North York's schoolchildren, who come here frequently on field trips. Under the tutelage of white-coated "scientists" (in real life, the centre's student guides), children learn how laser beams work. The guides keep the audience enthralled as they fill the room with smoke, pop balloons, and produce crackling flames—all in the interest of science.

Throughout the year the centre stages special exhibitions and festivals. At the Ontario Film Theatre there are jazz concerts and movies from around the world. The films, which include foreign avant-garde movies not shown in regular cinemas, are presented by the moviemakers themselves, who discuss their work with the audience.

The Science Centre is also used as a backdrop for making movies. In recent years, Hollywood film companies have flocked to Metro Toronto, attracted by favorable tax breaks, a favorable dollar, and well-trained crews. Jerry Lewis, Mary Tyler Moore, and Sophia Loren have all been on location here.

North York also has recently become the home of the Centre of Advanced Film Studies, housed in the mansion once owned by E.P. Taylor. The brainchild of Norman Jewison, producer of the Oscar-winning *Moonstruck* starring Cher and partly filmed in North York, the school ranks with similar prestigious establishments south of the border. Its opening means that young filmmakers can now study their craft under conditions formerly found only in Europe and Hollywood.

Film crews frequently use the Science Centre as an "airport" because its concrete concourse looks rather like a terminal building. One of North York's most modern and unusual buildings, the centre sits on the edge of a ravine that is part of Ernest Thompson Seton Park, the 180-acre Don River conservation area. A dramatic 200-foot concrete bridge spans the ravine, linking the main entrance with the Tower Building. Banks of escalators join this core with the Valley Building, 90 feet below, beside the West Don River.

As visitors descend on the escalators, they are serenaded by birdsong, piped through speakers in the roof. A solid wall of glass runs along the right-hand side. Outside are dozens of trees. Entering the exhibit area one is plunged into semi-darkness. This is a subterranean world of black walls, illuminated by glowing neon—a theatrical effect which sets the mood for the dazzling exhibits on display.

The centre's designer is Japanese-Canadian Raymond Moriyama, a gifted architect who has created some of Metro Toronto's most outstanding landmarks, including the Metro Reference Library on Yonge Street and the Scarborough Civic Centre. Always ahead of his time, Moriyama designed his "temple of technology," as he described the Science Centre, when he was only 30 years old. Still changing the face of North York, Moriyama helped to design the new Mel Lastman Square, centre of North York's booming downtown. The $250-million square will have cafés, shops, a reflecting pool, and an amphitheatre.

In so many ways, the richness of life in North York is increasingly remarkable. In festivals and galleries, in song and on canvas, in print and in the poetry of concrete and steel—a proud young metropolis is unveiling wonders of its own.

The Ontario Science Centre was built as the official commemorative project for the Centennial of Canada's Confederation in 1967. Photo by Lorraine C. Parow/First Light

CHAPTER 7

Keeping Fit

Sports and recreational activities abound in fitness-conscious North York. Olympic champions and senior citizens alike train in the city's hundreds of parks and sports facilities.

During the summer months, many of North York's recreational areas, like Serena Gundy Park, become centres of equestrian activity. Photo by Derek Trask/The StockMarket

by Karen Shopsowitz

A typical day in North York is often comfortably crammed with a schedule of sports and other recreational activities, no matter what the season. This is, after all, The City With Heart, and to that end the personal fitness and health of each of its residents seems to be of continual concern. The more than 290 parks in the City of North York alone are testimony to this. The fact that there are numerous arenas, community centres, fitness clubs, and other facilities eliminates any doubt as to one of this city's main priorities.

Just about any activity is represented: from bocce ball, lawn bowling, and mini-golf to more mainstream pastimes such as hockey, skiing (both downhill and cross country), soccer, and golf at public and private courses. Impressive statistics abound, such as these from the city's Parks and Recreation Department: at this writing, there are 16 indoor swimming pools, 19

An active interest in sports seems inherent in many North York residents. Here, a thousand balloons are released at the lighting of the Olympic Flame at the 1987 Ontario Games for the Physically Disabled. Photo by John O'Brien

The North York area is crammed with opportunities for recreational and fitness activities. Here, Olympic torch bearer Diana S. Beevor-Potts makes her way past the new eastern headquarters of Petro Canada, the official sponsor of the Cross Canada run. Photo by John O'Brien

outdoor pools, 25 community centres, 19 arenas, 10 outdoor artificial ice rinks, one fitness centre, one ski centre, one stadium, 219 tennis courts, 182 playgrounds, 95 bocce courts, 82 baseball and softball diamonds, one fitness trail, 30 soccer and football fields, seven horseshoe pitches, four lawn bowling greens, and three cricket pitches. As well, there are leagues and organizations for every age group and sport imaginable. Local offerings include, for example, an extensive North York Hockey League for young, developing players; a North York Minor Football Association for boys 8 to 18; a North York Soccer League for boys and girls; the North York Senior Walkers; numerous softball and baseball leagues; a women-only football league; and strong high school sports programs. One quickly gets the point. Variety—as well as accessibility—is enjoyed by North York residents who want to keep fit.

Many of the facilities and organizations have histories that reflect the desires of a growing community. Consider, for example, the work of the North York Tennis Association, which operates 24 community clubs in parks scattered across the city. The association is operated by George Fowler and Alex Cooper, two gentlemen who have

been involved with the NYTA since its inception 20 years ago. The NYTA's official season kicks off in early May, although some courts open their gates earlier, depending on the weather. In a move to attract more and more players to its ranks, the NYTA recently introduced in-school programs, in which older teens tell youngsters about the benefits of tennis, and a city-wide tournament held for the first time in early June 1987.

The tournament is one of the more visible programs offered by the NYTA. But both Cooper and Fowler are quick to point out the importance of the ever-growing house leagues, as well as an indoor program made possible by "bubbles" fitted over a handful of NYTA courts. Best of all, membership in the NYTA family of clubs is accessible to just about any North York resident. Membership costs are kept unbelievably low, with adults paying between $40 and $50 for the season, and junior players between $15 and $20. A priority for the NYTA is attracting beginners as well as more experienced players, and hence clinics are run through July and August as well as in the winter.

The Willowdale Lawn Bowling Club has an even longer history, dating back 26 years. It's the largest lawn

North York's parks and scenic areas provide a variety of recreational opportunities for all age groups. Photo by Greg Locke/First Light

bowling club in Canada. (It's worth noting here that throughout any discussion of sports and recreation in North York, the words "largest" and "best" are bound to come up; this is very rarely a matter of publicists' puffing.) Last year the club consisted of 400 members, ranging in age from early twenties to late eighties. The club came about after a former policeman, W. Gordon Fraser, approached the city's councillors with a petition signed by over 340 people.

The city complied with the club's requests in 1962, and the Willowdale Lawn Bowling Club officially opened in a small building behind a library in the heart of the city. In 1976 the club moved a few steps away to its present location, which it rents from the city. Last year, North York treated the lawn bowlers to a $50,000 additional structure to house lockers and other equipment.

Over the years the club has produced its share of champions, and it even hosted an international women's tournament in 1981, attracting players from over 15 countries. In the summer of 1988 the Willowdale club hosted three Ontario tournaments.

Once a week Ruth Holesh, a native of South Africa and now a North York resident, leads a group of blind and near-blind bowlers to the three well-manicured Willowdale club greens.

Holesh's own interest in involving the blind in the sport stems from an accident she had in 1959, when she was knocked down by a truck and lost her sight for three weeks. Even after she regained her sight, she was told she might never play lawn bowling again.

But lawn bowling was—and continues to be—her favorite sport, so she searched her own hometown for a club where she could continue to play. When Holesh moved to North York in 1978, she found a recreational league in nearby Mississauga. Because Holesh was interested in competing as well as enjoying the game, she organized her own league in North York.

While the league has been affiliated with the Canadian Blind Sports Association since its inception, the 1988 season saw Holesh's league affiliated with the Ontario Lawn Bowls Association, a move to which Holesh has always aimed. She also hopes to continue to lead her players to tournaments around the world. Most recently she sent a blind bowler to a tournament in Great Britain. In 1985 Holesh led a team of blind bowlers to Australia for a world tournament, bringing home three gold medals and one silver medal.

Winning medals seems to go hand in hand with amateur sports in North York. The city has produced its share of Olympic-class athletes, including skaters, gymnasts, swimmers, and

Above and facing page: North York has produced its share of world-class athletes, and track and field events are popular at athletic facilities around the area. This is a high school track meet at the Metro Toronto Track and Field Centre at York University. Photos by Lorraine C. Parow/First Light

runners. Ben Johnson, the "world's fastest man," and gymnastics medalist Curtis Hibbert are among the Olympians who have honed their skills at local facilities.

The North York Aquatic Club admits that its goal is to be the best swim club in Canada, and as such it aims to produce a strong roster of champions. In 1984 NYAC contributed Alison Dozzo, Bernhard Volz, and Sandy Goss to Canada's Olympic squad. In 1986 NYAC also had the distinction of being Ontario's biggest swim club, with 270 members. NYAC has won the Ontario Team Championships in 1983, 1985, and 1986.

Right from its lowest-level programs NYAC is geared to producing champions, and it takes its role seriously as a training ground for future elite swimmers. The club has three full-time and several part-time coaches, and operates out of nine local pools—at high schools, the city's beautiful Douglas Snow Aquatic Centre, and Glendon College. NYAC is one of the few Canadian swim clubs to be affiliated with a university—in this case, the University of Toronto. The affiliation means that swimmers can start with NYAC as youngsters, swim through their high school years, and continue through university until they retire from competition.

Several of the top swimmers at NYAC are also students at the Athletic Program for Gifted Athletes offered at Earl Haig, a local high school. The "elite athlete" program allows top athletes an opportunity to participate competitively in their sport while earning a high school diploma. It was the first such program to be offered in Canada. Students take advantage of more accessible classroom hours; and classes deal with not only the usual high school subjects, but also topics such as sports psychology, and others aimed at preparing the athlete for life after athletic competition.

York Mills Valley Park affords an excellent opportunity for a pleasant afternoon stroll. Photo by John O'Brien

The school is also affiliated with Sport Seneca, which offers athletic programs to young gymnasts—both rhythmic and traditional—as well as skaters and trampolinists. As one would expect, several national champions have come out of the Sport Seneca program. Top coaches, top athletes, and top facilities make this marriage of academics and athletics a success. Seneca College also offers degree programs in physical education and coaching, for older, college-age students, also at its North York campus. The school's trampoline program consistently produces provincial and national champions.

Top athletes—and some students at Earl Haig—also train with the Upper Canada-North York skating club, which sent ice dancers Melanie Cole and Michael Farrington to the Calgary Winter Olympics. Head coach Roy Bradshaw, who competed on the world team for his native Britain, notes that the club boasts one of the most elite groups of dancers in Canada. Several of the club's teams have skated both nationally and internationally. To keep his squad in top form, Bradshaw relies on resource people, including members of the National Ballet Company, Toronto's Studio Dance Theatre, and Prince Edward Island's Charlottetown Festival. Bradshaw's reliance is understandable; after all, he says, the Russian skaters use the Bolshoi Ballet as their advisors.

International competition is, of course, nothing new to North York's athletic contingent. Across the city and at its northern borders sits York University, home of the Metro Track and Field Centre as well as a training ground for the country's national gymnastics squads. York's gymnasts have fared consistently well, under the tutelage of longtime coach Tom Zivic, as well as Bob Carisse and Naosaki Masaaki. In 1987 Curtis Hibbert, a then 21-year-old member of the York and national squads, placed second at the world championships. His team took a strong overall ranking of 14 at the championships. Tamara Bompa, York's women's gymnastics coach and an international judge, also took a top honor in 1988, when she was recognized with a national award for her officiating duties.

Other York University athletic teams are just as renowned. In 1988 the Yeomen hockey squad claimed the national title. The university also fielded several Ontario championship teams—in men's and women's gymnastics, synchronized swimming, women's track and field, women's volleyball, and men's ice hockey. York's women's track and field team also won the national title. In individual events, the university produced 18 Ontario champions, 41 Ontario All-Stars, 12 National Champions, and 21 Canadian All-Stars. Across campus at the Metro Track and Field Centre, nationally and provincially ranked athletes—as well as veterans of the Olympics, the Commonwealth Games, and other prestigious competitions—meet to train in a variety of disciplines. Several local

events, such as the annual York-Finch Hospital Wonder Run, also use the centre as a starting point for 10-kilometre races and related events. The Metro Track and Field Centre is also the home of the Bobby Orr Sports Medicine Clinic, a facility founded by Dr. Charles Bull, known for his work with Canada's world hockey squads and with other international-class athletes in a variety of sports.

There are other sports medicine clinics located in North York as well, with equally impressive personnel manning their facilities. One of the first clinics to be created in the entire Metro Toronto area is at North York General Hospital. Established in 1975 by Dr. Morris Bent, it is headed by Dr. Robert Brock, who has been the Canadian Figure Skating Association's team doctor

North York resident and teacher Audra Noble is living testimony to the importance that locals attach to personal fitness and health. Photo by Derek Trask/ The StockMarket

since 1985. Brock was part of the 1984 Olympic medical team, and was Canada's Chief Medical Officer at the 1988 Winter Olympics. His clinical staff includes a roster of physiotherapists, an orthopaedic surgeon, volunteers, interns, and general practitioners specializing in sports medicine. The clinic also has referral privileges to specialists who include an ophthalmologist and a plastic surgeon. While many of the patients who visit the clinic are world-class athletes, recreational sports buffs are also welcome, and make up the bulk of the hospital's patient list.

In 1987 the Jewish Community Centre transformed an empty classroom located near its front entrance into the North York Health and Sports Injury Clinic. The clinic is outfitted with top-of-the-line equipment such as a whirlpool, an ice machine, and a range of high-tech gadgetry—bicycles, treadmills, a Cybex machine used for muscle strengthening, and another machine which uses ultra-sound and

sound waves. The staff includes doctors, physiotherapists, nutrition counsellors, sports medicine specialists, and several other professionals. Drs. Bull and Clarfield of the Bobby Orr Clinic at York University also back the Jewish Community Centre's clinic.

Ideally located, the clinic augments a first-class facility geared to athletes of all ages and ability. The JCC offers a stroke recovery program, for example, as well as a number of seniors' programs. This is a community facility in the truest sense of the word—membership here is open to everybody. Sports facilities are excellent: separate health clubs for men and women, two indoor running tracks, a gym, indoor and outdoor swimming pools, outdoor tennis courts, a Nautilus room, indoor squash and racquetball courts, an outdoor running track, and other attractions. Programs include sports leagues in floor hockey and basketball, exercise classes, and social activities for all ages.

North York offers leagues and organizations for every age group and sport imaginable, and has an extensive hockey league for young, developing players. Photo by The StockMarket

Located a few miles east of the Jewish Community Centre is the North York "Y," another fitness and recreation centre that is a mainstay of the city. Built in 1980, the "new" North York YMCA boasts first-class facilities, such as a 25-metre temperature-controlled swimming pool, a variable-depth training pool, racquetball, handball and squash courts, indoor and outdoor running tracks, individual exercise areas, a full-size gymnasium, whirlpools, steam rooms and saunas, changing rooms, a pro shop, and a snack bar. Like the Jewish Community Centre, it hosts a packed schedule of social events, seminars, and classes for participants of all ages and interests.

The third major community recreation facility in North York is the Columbus Centre, nestled in one of the city's large Italian areas. Again pro-

grams are open to all members of the community, and the facilities are top-notch. The stress here is on health and fitness, and cultural and community interests. The centre is home to the first-rate Joseph Carrier Art Gallery, a resident theatre and music performing company, a variety of programs for children and teenagers, as well as seminars and memberships geared to both individuals and corporations. As well, the centre houses a first-class dining room, Ristorante Boccaccio, and has full catering and party facilities.

The City of North York itself operates a fitness club—the Cummer Park Fitness Centre, which it refers to as its "best-kept secret." This facility has the usual and expected amenities, at lower membership rates than most. It also offers special month-by-month memberships at certain times of the

Built in 1980, the new North York YMCA boasts a 25-metre swimming pool, raquetball, handball, and squash courts, indoor and outdoor running tracks, a full-size gymnasium, steam rooms, and saunas. Photo by Glen Jones

year, a medical membership (for track use only), summer tennis memberships, and special prices for students and seniors.

Of course the city is also responsible for a full roster of sports and recreation activities, centred around its numerous arenas, swimming pools, parks, and other facilities. One of the highlights in North York's recreational program is the new Douglas Snow Aquatic Centre. The centre is named after the city's Commissioner of the North York Parks and Recreation Department from 1957 to 1984, who is now retired but still living in North York. Located adjacent to City Hall, the centre is a leisure pool complex that accommodates competitive swimmers from the North York Aquatic Club and pleasure dippers of all ages. Programs are open to residents and non-residents, and lessons are available for tots, youngsters, teens, and adults. The pool is open at various hours for leisure swimming, at which time participants can take advantage of such special attractions as a slide, a "Tarzan rope," a water jet, and a climbing net. Also on deck are a sauna and whirlpool and, steps away, a therapeutic whirlpool for people who need to do specific exercises prescribed by a physician.

Along with all the arenas, pools, and other facilities, there are some 25 community or recreation centres located in North York, each offering its own schedule of programs and activities geared to neighborhood residents. Swimming programs are also offered at local high schools in the city.

The city publishes several calendars through the year, listing contacts for each of the various leagues and sports organizations in the area. There are organized leagues for archery, ball hockey, baseball, cricket, fastball, figure skating, football, soccer, softball, swimming, track and field, water polo, volleyball, skiing, hockey, and more. Also offered are a co-ed recreational softball league for adults, and a summer hockey school for children.

The headquarters for almost every amateur sport in Ontario are located in North York. The Ontario Sports Cen-

The Douglas Snow Aquatic Centre is adjacent to City Hall and offers a pool complex that accommodates both competitive swimmers and pleasure dippers. Photo by Lorraine C. Parow/First Light

DON'T LOSE YOUR COOL
COME IN
FOR A RELAXING WHIRLPOOL

Douglas Snow Aquatic Centre

Mayor
Mel Lastman

Commissioner
Gordon Hutchinson

The Douglas Snow Aquatic Center is named after the city's Commissioner of the North York Parks and Recreation Department from 1957 to 1984, who is now retired but still living in North York. Photo by Lorraine C. Parow/ First Light

tre Inc. hands out information and acts as administrator for such bodies as the Ontario Track and Field Association, the Ontario Cycling Association, the Ontario Water Ski Association, the Ontario Sailing Association—in total, over 75 associations and federations.

During the warmer months, one of the nicer and more popular parks in the area is Earl Bales, with its walking trails and rolling hills. In summer the park is the home of Skylight Theatre, an outdoor performing arts company that specializes in Shakespearean productions, and throughout the year the Earl Bales Senior Centre is in full operation.

In the winter, the Earl Bales Park is transformed into a skier's dreamscape. As soon as the snow falls, the park becomes the North York Ski Centre, which offers, quite literally, skiing in the city. There are three intermediate slopes and one beginner's slope, two T-bars, and one rope tow as well as several kilometres of cross-country trails that lead skiers through 161 acres of parkland. A chalet and snack bar warm skiers between runs,

and rental of all equipment for both downhill and cross-country skiing is available, as are lessons taught by the centre's ski staff. Every winter Ski Telemark, a local organization, runs its program of clinics and races. Telemark skiing combines elements of cross-country and downhill skiing; the word "telemark" refers to a turn used in this type of skiing.

Even in a mild season, if it's wintertime, then snow is guaranteed at the North York Ski Centre, at least for downhill enthusiasts. As long as the temperature stays low enough, the ski centre can cover over 4.5 acres of skiable terrain with the man-made snow. Downhill runs are also lit for night skiing. During the Christmas holidays, special ski camps are offered to both children and adults, and every year the centre puts on its own ski celebrations. Throughout the season skiers get ongoing weather and ski condition reports from the centre's information phone line.

Once the snow melts, the park is again geared to the needs of warm-

Earl Bales is one of the last original North Yorkers, after whom the city named a recreation and ski centre. Photo by John O'Brien

-weather athletes. Up the street from the Earl Bales Park sits the Esther Shiner Stadium, a fairly new facility that has already been used for special events such as the 1987 Ontario Games for the Physically Disabled. The Duke and Duchess of Windsor visited that year's edition of the games while on a trip to Toronto. The stadium seats 2,000 spectators, and its lighted sports field can be used for soccer, football, and field hockey. Also available are a six-lane, 400-metre running track with a synthetic surface; sprint and hurdle runways; long jump, triple jump, high jump, and pole vault areas; and an electronic scoreboard, a broadcasting booth, and a snack bar.

The Civic Stadium is home to York University's Yeomen football squad, as well as home field of the North York Rockets, the city's two-year-old professional sports squad and entry in the recently rejuvenated Canadian Soccer League. Along with a regular schedule of home and away games, the Rockets run a soccer school, featuring the club's head coach Grezgorz Lato

Right and facing page: The 1987 Ontario Games for the Physically Disabled were held at the North York Civic Stadium, a new facility that has been used for special events such as this. Photos by John O'Brien

Sarah Ferguson, the Duchess of York, greets the crowd at the Ontario Games for the Disabled. Photo by John O'Brien

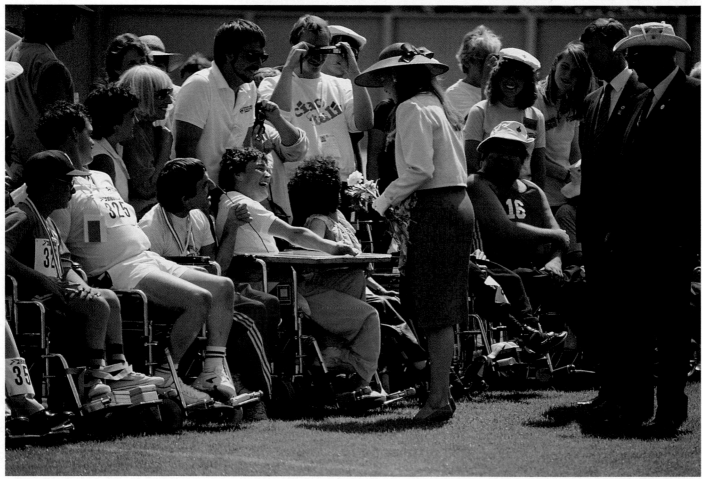

and the team's players. The Rockets offer young summer-league players a goal for which to strive.

While the Rockets attract a lot of local support, other annual sporting events are just as well regarded. For example, every year the city's seniors get together for a sports and fitness tournament that lasts two weeks and involves a variety of active pastimes, such as tennis; shuffleboard; table tennis; bocce; horseshoes; lawn, carpet, and five-pin bowling; darts; badminton; walking; swimming; and golf. With several seniors' community and activity centres located in the city, there is never a shortage of players for any tournament. Winners compete in the provincial "Actifest," which was held in 1988 in Brampton, Ontario.

North York was the first city in the area to initiate a "seniors' games." Since its inception, other local municipalities have followed by creating their own tournaments specially for older athletes.

Along with the Senior Games and the North York Senior Walkers group, which meets once a week for Sunday morning walks and once a month for seminars with health and fitness experts, there is also a seniors bowling league, run out of the Newtonbrook Bowlerama located near the city's downtown area. The Golden Age Bowling League, which dates back at least 25 years, gives older bowlers a chance to play the game and socialize with other seniors.

In addition to Earl Bales, there are several other park areas in the city. Notable are Sunnybrook Park and the adjacent Edwards Gardens and Civic Garden Centre. Edwards Gardens, with its beautiful network of trails, is a favorite for wedding parties and photo buffs, as well as walkers and runners. Nestled in the heart of the adjacent Sunnybrook Park are the Central Don Stables, a city riding academy that specializes in all equestrian disciplines. (It also boards the Toronto police force's horses.) During the summer, the soccer and playing fields of Sunnybrook are transformed into first-class equestrian fields and the site of the annual "Classic" tournament. This world-level event attracts at least 500 horses and an estimated 60,000 spectators, and includes classes for dressage, jumper and hunter riders. The family crowd pleasers include a celebrity novelty race, a dog show, and an antique carriage exhibition.

In 1984 the Classic acted as a team trial for that summer's Olympic squad. Prize money for the 1986 Classic World Cup was $60,000. With the continued success of the event, national sponsors have contributed their support to add to the event's coffers. The City of North York has a longtime

Central Don Stables, in the heart of Sunnybrook Park, is a city riding academy that specializes in all equestrian disciplines. Photo by Jack Holman

history of equestrian excellence, having produced its share of Olympic champions, such as national team member Terry Leibel. For years E.P. Taylor bred racehorses on his estate in North York, located a few miles north of Sunnybrook Park. Nowadays filmmaker Norman Jewison and his associates have taken over the estate, making the beautiful home the site of the newly established Canadian Centre for Advanced Film Studies.

The Classic is a huge undertaking; organizers note that it takes ten days to put up needed tents and get the fields in shape for the event, and three days to pack up and move out of the park with nary a trace. Just days after the Classic, the park's regulars are back on the fields playing cricket or soccer.

The annual Run for Research, Sunnybrook Hospital's 10 km run, also winds its way through part of Sunnybrook Park, as do several other annual running events. There is no shortage of events for runners throughout the city—annual editions of the Speedy Baycrest Fun Run and the York-Finch Wonder Run are on the North York schedule.

Sunnybrook is representative of the wide range of sporting events available in North York, and of the city's adaptability. One week the park is the site of a friendly cricket match; the next week it's filled with horse trailers, and spectators anxious to catch a glimpse of equestrian excellence. Then, a week

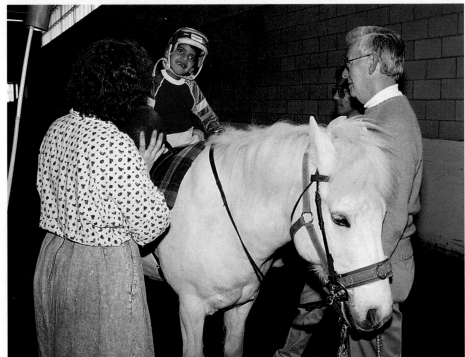

later, trails are busy with cyclists, walkers, and joggers. In the winter one can expect to see cross-country skiers, and more-intrepid joggers along the footpaths. A luge toboggan club even used one of the park's steep hills as a training route one winter.

Thanks to good planning and an understanding of local interests, recreational facilities are plentiful in North York. Be they amateurs or professionals, weekend recreation buffs or internationally ranked pros, youngsters or senior citizens—The City With Heart is also "the city of good sports."

The North York area has a tradition of equestrian excellence. These people are given a chance to saddle up during a program put on by the Community Association for Riding for the Disabled. Photo by Peter Tang/First Light

EPILOGUE

by Helga Loverseed

If one thing could be said to encapsulate the feeling of North York, it would be the city's new "Downtown, Uptown"—a vibrant urban core of condominiums, public buildings, parks, and gleaming office towers. Forged out of the North York portion of Yonge Street (the strip that runs from Sheppard Avenue in the south to Finch Avenue in the north), it has been created in a scant five years by the government, entrepreneurs, developers, and construction companies. They have invested almost $2 billion (with another $2 billion on its way over the next seven years), and in the process changed the face of the city.

"Downtown, Uptown" is only two miles long, but it has become the heart and soul of the city. Office buildings and civic structures have sprung up like mushrooms. The Xerox building, the North American Life Centre, the Petro Canada Complex, the Madison Centre, Novotel, the Central Library, the North York Community Hall, and the Douglas Snow Aquatic Centre are just some of the structures that have altered the Yonge Street of old, and new buildings are rising daily to join the ever-changing skyline.

Procter & Gamble have just moved to an ultra-modern corporate head office here. Roy Kendall, the conglomerate's president, speaks for many businesspeople when he says, "We decided to move to downtown North York because it made good business sense. Some of Canada's major companies and developers are investing millions of dollars in creating a downtown that is attractive for both business and residents. We are delighted to be part of it."

Anchoring the numerous developments is the Mel Lastman Civic Square. Flanked by a futuristic City Hall, the square is named after North York's business-minded mayor, who, along with his councillors, citizens' groups, and local business organizations, has done much to put the "new" North York on the map.

There are, of course, many modern cities in Ontario. After World War II, when Canada's population increased—a result of prosperity, the "baby boom," and immigration— new communities were founded all over the country. Regionalization was introduced in the 1970s to streamline local government and decentralize major urban centres such as Toronto and Hamilton. Cities such as Mississauga, Etobicoke, and Scarborough, now part of Metropolitan Toronto, were created to cope with the Toronto and Hamilton overspill. Regionalization ended their role as "bedroom communities," and places like North York became separate entities.

What makes North York unique is how quickly it has developed its own identity. Despite having on its doorstep Toronto, an urban centre over three times its size, North York has found a personality of its own. It's an exciting, diverse, and entrepreneurial city and it evolved from rugged wilderness in a mere century and a half—an achievement which would no doubt astonish its early settlers.

In the 1800s North York was a collection of villages and hamlets scattered throughout York Township. Travelling from one to the other along muddy, potholed roads could take hours. Toronto (or York as it was then called), 20 miles to the south, was a good day's journey away. Today the buses and subway trains of the TTC (Toronto Transit Commission) whisk commuters between North York and Toronto in less than half an hour—cause for astonishment indeed.

By the turn of the century, improved roads, electricity, telephones, automobiles, and a radial railway brought the communities of York Township into increasing contact with Toronto and the rest of the outside world. But at that point they were still independent entities. The City of North York, which later engulfed them, lay far in the future.

Interestingly enough, one village—Lansing—became more of a central focal point than the others, probably because of its location. Lansing was situated at the corner of Sheppard Avenue and Yonge Street. Then, as now, this was a major intersection.

In the 1860s the corner of Yonge and Sheppard became the centre for transportation and business. Settlers, salesmen, and farmers from all over York Township gathered in the brick building on the northwest side—the Dempsey Brothers store—where they caught up with the news and discussed business and politics. In the new "Downtown, Uptown" North Yorkers continue that tradition. The face of the city may have changed, but the Yonge Street strip is still the centre of the action.

As Brian W. Dunn, Vice President of McLeod Young Weir Investment Services puts it, "It was natural for our company to expand right along with downtown North York. This area is fast becoming a major new focus for business and investment within Metropolitan Toronto. No other city centre in Canada has such strength and vibrancy in its core."

While the Yonge/Sheppard corridor had attracted entrepreneurs for over a century, it was a long time before it took on the characteristics of today. The "Downtown, Uptown" concept isn't new; plans were on the drawing board a decade ago. But after North York became a city in 1979, many of the ideas for a city centre were rejected, or at least modified. Feasible projects were finally approved, and in the last five years the dream of "Downtown, Uptown" has finally become a reality.

Clearly "Downtown, Uptown" didn't just happen. For a long time, the hamlets and villages of York Township just chugged along at a steady but slow pace. Little development took place in the 1920s and '30s. World War I and the Depression hampered any large scale projects. But in the late 1930s, urban workers started casting their sights northward. Fed up with overcrowded conditions and expensive housing in Toronto and Hamilton, they started moving to York Township.

Like the Great War before it, World War II slowed down development, but after the conflict was over North York simply took off. The war had left Canada a wealthy and highly industrialized nation and dozens of foreign companies moved in to get a slice of the action. The country's economy boomed.

The healthy balance sheet fuelled a population explosion (at one point North York had the highest birth rate in the country) and created a demand for labor and expertise. The rural character and small-town ambience of this little 1940s community, where everybody knew everyone else, was destined to change in a big way.

In the 1950s, immigrants from the far corners of the world poured into Canada seeking greener economic pastures. Not all of them ended up in large cities. Many of them were drawn to up-and-coming communities like North York where housing was reasonably priced and readily available, and where they felt there would be less competition and more opportunity.

Newcomers from Italy, Greece, Israel, Great Britain, Hong Kong, Poland, the U.S.S.R., India, and the Caribbean flocked here to find jobs, start businesses, and seek higher education for themselves and for their children. The population soared. During World War II North York was home to 27,000 people. By 1950 that figure had climbed to 150,000. Today North York has a population over 560,000; 95 percent, it is estimated, arrived after 1951.

These "new" North Yorkers have helped make the community what it is today. North York is not only one of the five largest cities in Canada, it is one of the most cosmopolitan centres in the world. The city's residents trace their roots to over 100 nations, and more than 80 languages are spoken here—cultural differences which lend variety and spice to North York's lifestyle, and

which are actively nurtured through numerous educational programs and community activities.

Governing such a fast-paced city has not been without its headaches. Local government is challenging at the best of times, but North York's mayor, Mel Lastman, and his council have had to be more flexible than most. They've frequently had to change policies or modify legislation at very short notice, merely to keep abreast of the latest changes.

But then, the goals of the mayor and his council are not merely to keep North York rolling along. Their aims are high: they want to make the city the envy of other communities around North America. As Mayor Lastman puts it: "North York's new downtown will be the envy of all. We are not content with simply building the newest and best office centre in Canada. We want to create the newest and best downtown, which is more than just a place to do business."

The dream of "Downtown, Uptown" has certainly become a reality.

As soon as the snow falls, many of North York's parks and rural areas become ideal winter recreation spots. Photo by Harry L. Cantlun/The StockMarket

An entrepreneurial spirit, innovative ideas, and a propensity for hard work have contributed to its success. Things can only get better. Before the turn of the century, the Yonge Street core will house some 66,000 workers and 33,000 residents.

Despite North York's obvious prosperity, its story has in some ways just begun. The City With Heart, created only 10 years ago, is clearly a city that works. One of the greatest challenges for the future will be to keep it that way.

Meanwhile, other communities witnessing the success story that has unfolded north of Toronto will no doubt take their cue from what happens here. Standing at the threshold of the 21st century, North York is not just a model for the present: it is a prototype for a bright and abundant future.

PART 2

Enterprising North York

CHAPTER 8

Manufacturing

Producing goods for individuals and industry, manufacturing firms provide employment for many North York area residents.

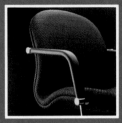

THE UPJOHN COMPANY OF CANADA

The Upjohn Company of Canada ranks among the largest of Canada's research-based pharmaceutical companies. When corporate headquarters was first established in 1935, however, it operated only as a sales office from a small rented facility on Adelaide Street in downtown Toronto.

The story of Upjohn is one of growth and expansion. A number of factors have contributed to its success. The basic factor was summed up in a statement made by the immediate past president, Stuart S. Alexander: "Upjohn Canada's leadership role in the Canadian pharmaceutical industry is based on our commitment to serve the needs of Canadians to the best of our ability."

Upjohn Canada's parent company, The Upjohn Company, is located in Kalamazoo, Michigan. It, too, started from modest beginnings. Founded in 1886, Upjohn has grown from a small U.S. partnership with a single product to an effective international organization with subsidiaries in more than 35 countries and marketing outlets in

The high-speed labelling of vials.

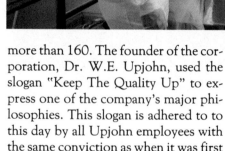

more than 160. The founder of the corporation, Dr. W.E. Upjohn, used the slogan "Keep The Quality Up" to express one of the company's major philosophies. This slogan is adhered to to this day by all Upjohn employees with the same conviction as when it was first formulated.

From the start the firm's major business interest and emphasis has been human health care—beginning with pharmaceutical products, but now including home health care services as well.

The addition of raw materials to the high shear mixer is part of the process in the production of Motrin®.

Today The Upjohn Company also has worldwide agricultural operations committed to the search for new products for animals and plant production. This business includes an extensive line of veterinary pharmaceutical products, feed additives, animal health products, and agronomic and vegetable seeds.

Subsidiaries of these two interests have also been established in Canada. Upjohn HealthCare Services has its head office in Don Mills, sharing quarters with The Upjohn Company of Canada at 861 York Mills Road, and TUCO Products Inc., the agriculture/veterinary subsidiary, operates from Orangeville, Ontario. Both subsidiaries serve all of Canada. Upjohn HealthCare Services provides home nursing and paramedical care to Canadians from branch offices located in all provinces.

In 1954 The Upjohn Company of Canada moved its headquarters, which at that time consisted of office and distribution facilities, to 865 York Mills Road in the Don Mills area of North York, one of the most desirable corporate neighborhoods in the country. This move resulted from the company's entry into the manufacturing and packaging aspect of the pharmaceutical industry. This was The Upjohn Company's first such facility estab-

Tablet compressing takes place at the rate of 4,000 tablets per minute.

lished outside the United States. To accommodate this, further expansion was undertaken at the Don Mills site in 1958. Very soon after that, distribution centres were established in Montreal, Winnipeg, and Vancouver.

The Upjohn Company of Canada has always sought to recruit the very best personnel. Graduate pharmacists from the University of Toronto made up the corporation's first sales force. The firm still employs only university graduates to fill its sales force positions, and includes among its contingent of experts persons holding a variety of university degrees and postgraduate degrees—M.Sc., Ph.D, Pharm.D., and M.D. Upjohn's employees constitute its greatest asset, and all "Upjohners" are proud of the company they work for and are very loyal to its principles. All these hardworking individuals enjoy a unique camaraderie and are on a first-name basis with everyone else in the company.

When Upjohn Canada moved to Don Mills more than 25 years ago, it was a move away from the confines of the city to an area where there was room for growth. Members of the staff who were there at the time tell of looking across the road to where the Prince Hotel is now located and seeing a farmer busily at work in his fields. All this has changed, as has Upjohn. The story of Upjohn is one of constant growth, development, and expansion.

In 1985 Upjohn acquired the building across Upjohn Road at 861 York Mills—the one it shares with Upjohn HealthCare Services. Located there is the Toronto Distribution Centre, Upjohn's order desk, and the credit department. This acquisition enabled Upjohn to expand within 865 and create more office space. The year 1988 saw the completion of a two-storey extension at the south end of the 865 York Mills building, which now houses modern laboratories for quality assurance and research.

Upjohn currently employs more than 450 people across Canada. In excess of 300 employees work in the North York facility, which now encompasses 185,000 square feet.

From the beginning Upjohn Canada has worked closely with all members of the health care community to provide the best in pharmaceutical products and services. Today it is a fully integrated pharmaceutical firm involved in the research, manufacture, distribution, and marketing of a wide range of pharmaceutical products, both prescription and over-the-counter. Who among you has not sought relief with that well-known product Kaopectate®.

Upjohn has established some very significant partnerships in the fight against diseases. Its medical department

Visual inspection of sterile products.

co-ordinates and plans many clinical studies with Canadian physicians to ensure that appropriate products are thoroughly researched and tested in Canada prior to marketing. For example, Upjohn recently sponsored the Cross National Collaborative Study in which clinical researchers in Montreal and Toronto, and at 16 additional centres in 14 other countries, investigated the role of Xanax® in the treatment of panic attacks. This is the largest clinical-therapeutic study of a disease ever undertaken by any pharmaceutical company at a given time.

In addition to clinical studies, Upjohn conducts epidemiological studies to continue the investigation and research on drugs that are being marketed. One significant such study was the Evaluation of Medications for Insomnia in Canada, which involved collecting and analyzing data from thousands of Canadians to determine the effects of benzodiazepine hypnotics in the treatment of sleep disorders.

One of Upjohn's most exciting partnerships resulted in the formation of The Victoria/Upjohn Clinical Research Unit, initially a three-year, million-dollar venture, between the

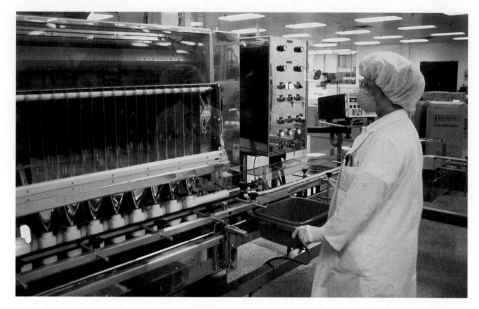

At a rate of 200 bottles per minute, tablets are packaged at the Upjohn Company of Canada.

company and the renowned Victoria Hospital in London, Ontario. This innovative collaboration is designed to expand the scientific interchange among Upjohn, Canadian researchers, and physicians, as well as to open new avenues of research. The unit has conducted several studies on new and existing drugs, concentrating on the areas of renal disease, lupus, respiratory dysfunction, hypertension, cancer, heart disease, depression, and post-operative

care. Recently a multiyear extension of this collaborative venture was signed to facilitate further expansion of the research efforts.

Upjohn has a major commitment to assisting physicians in becoming more fully informed on new disease concepts. A highly trained field force of 80 sales representatives and 20 medical sciences liaison representatives are employed to ensure that physicians, pharmacists, and professors of medicine, dentistry, and pharmacy are provided with the latest medical education and research results. Upjohn's Visiting Professors Program, in which experts in various health-related fields are sponsored in their visits to hospitals and universities, also helps maintain a high level of awareness of the latest medical concepts and findings among Canadian physicians and pharmacists.

One of Upjohn's strong points is specialization in its sales approach. Upjohn's general sales force communicates product information to physicians and pharmacists in cities and towns throughout Canada. As several Upjohn products are specialized products used only by hospital physicians, a separate hospital sales force provides product information to major teaching hospitals associated with schools of medicine. In addition, as many of its most innovative products are used to treat diseases of the central nervous system, further specialization is practised

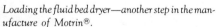

Loading the fluid bed dryer—another step in the manufacture of Motrin®.

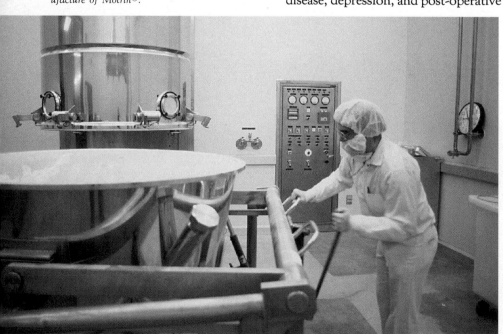

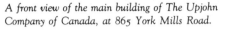

by a small sales force, known as medical specialist representatives, which calls on psychiatrists in major Canadian centres to keep them aware of the pharmaceutical progress in their area of expertise. All Upjohn's sales representatives possess a thorough knowledge of disease concepts and treatments; this knowledge is continuously updated through private study and participation in sales conferences.

Scholarships, grants, prizes, and charitable donations are other ways by which Upjohn helps promote medical knowledge and its application. Winners of Upjohn awards are selected from the student bodies by professors of pharmacy in nine faculties of pharmacy and by professors of medicine in

A robot makes a sample preparation in the quality-control laboratory.

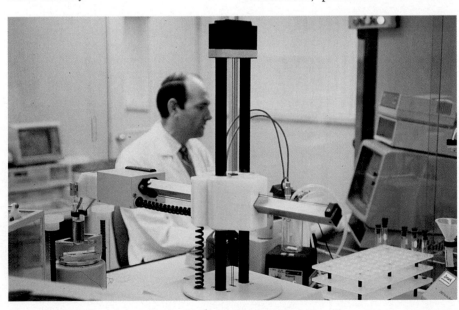

15 faculties of medicine in Canada. Chosen by the Canadian Society of Hospital Pharmacists, five hospital pharmacy residents are recipients of an Upjohn prize for excellence. In collaboration with the College of Family Physicians of Canada and Federation des Médicins Omnipraticiens du Québec (the association of general practitioners in Quebec), postgraduate study awards are given to practising physicians. As well, the Upjohn Award in Pharmacology is presented each year to a distinguished Canadian pharmacologist selected for the award by the Pharmacological Society of Canada. Upjohn supports the Dr. W.E. Upjohn Lecturer at the Canadian Medical Association's annual conference.

Charitable donation efforts at Upjohn focus primarily in three basic areas: health care institutions and foundations, provincial and national

A front view of the main building of The Upjohn Company of Canada, at 865 York Mills Road.

health and welfare associations, and community/public service and civic causes.

Upjohn manufactures a mix of fine products designed to treat a wide range of diseases. They include Ansaid® and Motrin®, potent anti-inflammatory and analgesic agents that have helped reduce the suffering of many arthritis patients; Halcion®, an effective medication for insomnia; Xanax®, an anxiolytic used for treating anxiety sufferers; Loniten®, an antihypertensive medication for the treatment of severe high blood pressure; Prostin® VR, a prostaglandin product used to keep blue babies alive until they can have their heart defects surgically corrected; Trobicin®, a potent antibiotic used to treat penicillin-resistant gonorrhea; and Cytosar®, an anti-cancer agent that has produced remissions in a substantial number of leukemia patients.

One of Upjohn's latest and most exciting products, and certainly a departure from its usual product line, is Rogaine®, the first prescription drug approved in Canada for the treatment of male-pattern baldness.

The Upjohn Company of Canada looks back with a sense of pride and accomplishment on its contribution to the health of Canadians during its first 50 years. All its employees are dedicated to continue to provide the very best in quality of product and service for the future well-being of the Canadian population in the years to come.

CROWN FOOD SERVICE EQUIPMENT LIMITED

In many ways the success of Crown Food Services Equipment can be credited to the strong family commitment of the Stritzl family. Owner and president Joe Stritzl plays an active role in most of the company's operations. Maria, Joe's wife, looks after sales, scheduling, production, and marketing, while their daughter Kim is the purchasing assistant. But, with 38 employees, annual sales exceeding $3.5 million, and an international market, Crown Food Service Equipment, a designer and manufacturer of commercial cooking equipment, has certainly moved beyond the ordinary.

Joe Stritzl, who began sheet metal training in Austria, came to Canada in 1953. Two years later he started working for a restaurant equipment company and refined his skill in the sheet metal trade. Twenty-five years later, after working up to plant manager, Stritzl left to form his own company in 1981, initially as a partner but now as a full owner. Justifiably proud of his company's growth, Stritzl points out that the industry's biggest trade show called Crown a "miracle" because in a short period of time it was able to offer a complete line of fully approved equipment.

Crown's products are high-quality, stainless-steel cooking appliances, often custom made, for high-volume and specialty restaurants. Steamers, boilers, kettles, skillets, and compart-

The high-quality stainless-steel commercial cooking equipment manufactured by Crown Food Service Equipment Limited is not only visible in the kitchens of popular restaurants in the Toronto area but is exported throughout the United States, Europe, New Zealand, and the Orient. Much of the equipment is custom designed to meet the specific requirements of a client. Shown here are the SX-II model steam convection oven (left) and an oyster bar (above), which is in use in many fish restaurants.

ment cookers are Crown specialties. With many innovative features, they are particularly easy to use and adapt easily to special purposes.

Crown products are hard at work at such well-known Toronto restaurants as The Fish House (in North York), Whaler's Wharf, Pier 4, and Sammy's Pasta Pasta. As well, Crown products have found a hungry international market. Eighty percent of sales go to the United States, and Stritzl also has customers in Europe, New Zealand, and the Orient. "I'm the only person I know who's exporting to Japan," he says.

Crown's 30,000-square-foot premises on Oakdale Road in the Downsview area of North York is a model of efficiency and sensible marketing. A new showroom attractively displays the extensive product line, allowing cus-

tomers to fully appreciate the quality and features of each item in a friendly, family atmosphere.

The success of Crown and the quality of its products are not only a reflection of the hard-working and proud Stritzl family, but also of the commitment and dedication of Crown's employees, who, as Stritzl points out, are the best in the business. "I came here with five dollars in my pocket," says Stritzl. "And Canada has been the greatest country in the world."

Maria Stritzl, who oversees sales, scheduling, production, and marketing, also adds a personal touch to products in the company brochures.

CANADA CUP INC.

"We were three young guys, and the last thing we knew about was failure," recalls Tom Thomas of the days in 1964 when he, Jack Hanson, and Hugh Brown plunged into business. But what they did know, through their experience in the plastic industry, was the enormous impact this new unique product would have in the marketplace. That knowledge, plus a lot of hard work, resulted in the formation and success to this day of Canada Cup Inc., Canada's largest manufacturer of disposable cups, containers, plates, cutlery, and other items for the consumer and food-service industry.

The entrepreneurs started off making just one cup, using high-speed, thinwell, injection moulding—a revolutionary new technique. In 1966 the company took over a small competitor, increasing its size to the point where it had to relocate from Scarborough to a larger facility in North York. In 1971 the firm was acquired by Dart Industries Inc., headquartered in Los Angeles, kicking off a period of even more spectacular growth. In 1972 Canada Cup merged with Polychemical Ltd., another Dart company with plants in Edmonton and Mississauga. The following year Polycup Ltd. in Montreal was acquired. In 1974 a fourth foam cup plant was set up in Vancouver, and two years later a new plant was built in Montreal. From 1971 to 1981 Canada Cup grew tenfold.

In 1981 Dart Industries and Kraft Inc. merged and formed Dart & Kraft, a $10-billion company that decided to sell off its smaller holdings, including Canada Cup. A group of four investors led by Tom Thomas bought the firm back in 1983.

At that time GoTech Inc. was incorporated to sell Canada Cup technology abroad. In 1985 Canada Cup acquired Dixie Canada Inc. of Brampton, maker of disposable paper cups, giving the firm its seventh plant and a presence in both the plastic and paper disposable markets. The following year the owner of Canada Cup agreed to sell the company to the James River Corporation of Richmond, Virginia.

Canada Cup remains very autonomous, maintaining its own research and engineering departments. Recently the company developed, together with Husky Injection Molding Systems of Bolton, Ontario, yet another major manufacturing technique—injection blow moulding—for clear, widemouth containers uses less clear plastic to make the same size glass or cup and reduces raw material usage by up to 60 percent.

Another important development of Canada Cup was its creation in 1980 of its Collectibles Division. Using six-color process printing and its own in-house art department, the Collectibles Division produces heavier, more durable cups that can be printed with high-quality graphics. Emblazoned with everything from Max Headroom to Ronald McDonald, they are now being shipped as far as the United States, Singapore, Europe, and the Caribbean.

Today Canada Cup employs 740 people, including 272 at its three North York plants in the Yorkdale area. The product line has grown to 150 items, using injection and injection blow moulding, thermoforming, foam moulding, and paper technology.

"Our company's success is the result of many loyal and dedicated employees and customers working together," says Thomas. Customers include McDonald's, Coca-Cola, Burger King, Kentucky Fried Chicken, Harvey's, Swiss Chalet, and St. Hubert's to name a few. In 1987 the firm produced an astounding 4.5 billion units and had sales of $79.2 million.

Tom Thomas, president and chief executive officer of Canada Cup Inc., arrived in Canada 33 years ago from Holland and has resided in North York for the past 25 years. "The North York area is an excellent location in which to do business," he says. "I've seen it grow from a large village to a really thriving, bustling metropolis."

A small sampling of the Canada Cup product line.

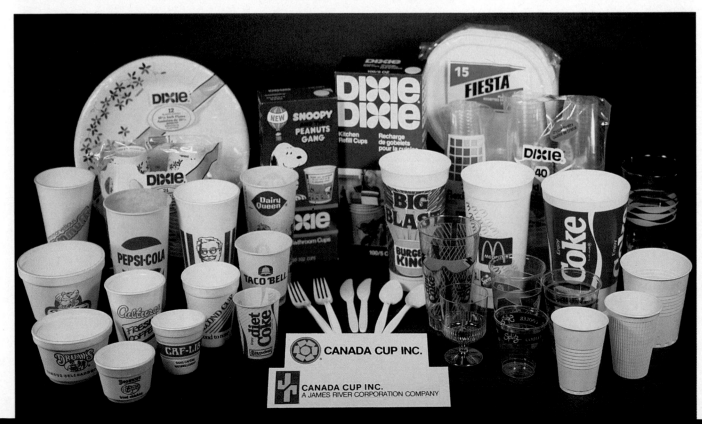

FIBERGLAS CANADA INC.

Fiberglas Canada Inc. faces and meets the challenge that has been shared by almost all Canadians since the foundation of the country—that of energy conservation and efficiency in one of the most forbidding climates in the world. The company realizes that Canadians require more energy per capita than any other nation, and thus need the very best insulation products available. Founded on the principles of conservation and efficiency, Fiberglas Canada has converted a tremendous investment in research and development into a range of products that extends far beyond insulation.

Fiberglas Canada is a relative newcomer to North York, having, in October 1986, moved its Canadian headquarters north from Toronto and into a glittering new glass-encased building on Yonge Street, which offers more efficient space and a centralized location for its employees. The modern structure belies, however, a tradition of serv-

ing Canadians for nearly 50 years.

The company was incorporated in 1939 by the late Colonel W.E. Phillips, whose interest in glass technology began with his family's glass and mirror business, and led to the founding of Duplate Canada Limited, maker of safety and thermal glass. The colonel then envisioned a productive future for glass fibres being made by a process developed by Owens-Corning Fiberglas Corporation in the United States. He subsequently struck a licensing deal with them and formed Fiberglas Canada, which was (and still is) jointly shared by Duplate Canada Limited (now PPG Canada Inc.) and Owens-Corning Fiberglas Corporation of Toledo, Ohio.

Colonel Phillips was obviously correct in his foresight about the myriad applicability of glass fibre technology because since 1939 the firm has undergone rapid expansion and diversification. Significant points in the company's development include the

opening of its first insulation plant in Sarnia (1948), the opening of a textile plant in Guelph (1951), the institution of an insulation plant in Edmonton that marked the arrival in Canada of a manufacturing process combining the latest European and American technology (1960), the creation of a research and development facility (1967), the opening of a chemical plant for the manufacture of polyester resins in Guelph (1974), the start of production at the insulation plant in Scarborough (1978), the initiation of production at the insulation plant in Mission, British Columbia (1980), the purchase of assets of Victomix Inc. of Victoriaville, Quebec, which gave the company the latest technology to produce modified bituminous membranes for hot asphalt or torch applications in roofing instal-

Fiberglas Canada Inc. manufactures a complete line of commercial and industrial insulation products including Fiberglas Base Cap Roof Insulation.

lation (1984), and the opening of a new $11-million Technical Centre in Sarnia (1985).

Today Fiberglas Canada ranks 203rd among Canadian companies, with annual sales of $400 million and 2,500 employees. The corporation is the country's leading manufacturer of glass fibre products and an acknowledged world industry leader in research and development. It ranks 35th in the nation in research expenditures, putting 2.3 percent of gross sales into this component of its operation compared to a Canadian company average of only one percent. More than 100 scientists, engineers, and technicians are employed by the firm.

The organization is now divided into two main groups: Insulation and Textiles, and Reinforcements and

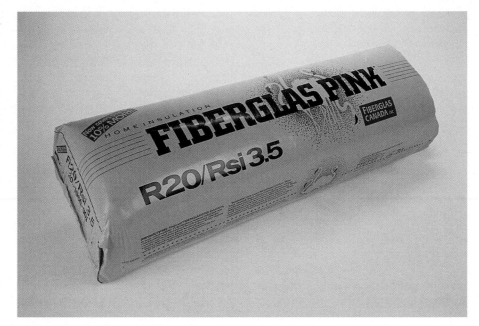

Fiberglas Pink, Canada's leading brand of home insulation.

Fiberglas Canada Inc. is Canada's only manufacturer of textile and reinforcement glass.

Chemicals (TRC). Insulation group products are used in residential, commercial, and industrial construction, and include its best-known product, FIBERGLAS PINK home insulation. Other house-building products include GLASCLAD insulating sheathing and BASECLAD basement wall insulation. Commercial and industrial products include roof and wall, tank, pipe, boiler, duct, and equipment insulation, as well as insulations for automobiles, mobile homes, home appliances, ships, aircraft, railway cars, and cold-storage facilities.

The TRC group produces glass fibre materials and thermosetting polyester resins, sold primarily to the glass fibre reinforced plastics industry, which in turn uses Fiberglas Canada products to make everything from boat hulls to processing equipment for the pulp and paper industry. Glass fibre materials are also sold to weavers who make fabrics for the manufacture of filter bags, radial and belted tires, insect screening, non-combustible materials, and electrical insulation.

The company is also moving into other energy-saving fields, recently developing its Habitair Energy Centre system that provides heat recovery, ventilation, hot water, and background cooling for houses.

Led by president and chief executive officer F. W. Henkelman, the head office employs nearly 200 people, whose functions include marketing, industrial relations, finance, treasury, purchasing, computer operations, traffic, and support for plant and branch operations.

Fiberglas Canada is also keenly interested in employee health and safety. A computerized health-monitoring system was introduced in 1979 that stores medical data on all employees involved in manufacturing and notifies the health nurse at every plant when an employee's medical examination is due. As well, an Industrial Hygiene Group monitors all plants on a regular basis and evaluates environmental conditions by measuring and testing chemicals, physical agents, and noise levels.

Despite the firm's diverse concerns, it remains focused on the key imperatives of conservation and efficiency. Fiberglas Canada Inc. has strongly supported the federal government's super-efficient housing initiative, which aims to reduce home heating costs by 80 percent—a goal that parallels the company's goals of supplying the best and most affordable insulation products possible for the residential market and continuing its role as a major supplier to the nation's construction and manufacturing industries.

PETRO-CANADA

Since its creation by an act of Parliament in 1975, Petro-Canada has been a symbol of pride for Canadians. In one of the most energy-dependent countries on earth the need for a Canadian-owned oil and gas corporation with a national marketing capacity, an aggressive exploration policy, and a genuine dedication to the future of Canada was imperative in this crucial, challenging, and often volatile industry.

Considered too costly and financially risky by some, Petro-Canada had defied the skeptics and grown into the important Canadian-oriented energy corporation its founder envisioned. In assets, sales, exploration, and product development, it is a dominant force in the industry.

Petro-Canada is prominent in the minds of Canadians, giving proof that Canadians can compete with the rest of the world and confidence that the largest Canadian-owned petroleum company in the land is active, today and for tomorrow.

Petro-Canada began operation in early 1976 after the federal government transferred its existing energy interests to the Crown corporation, including a 45-percent share of Panarctic Oils Ltd. and a 15-percent interest in Syncrude Canada Ltd. Later that year Petro-Canada bought control of Atlantic Richfield Canada (ARCAN), a subsidiary of Atlantic Richfield of the United States, for $342 million. In 1979 Petro-Canada concluded the $1.5-billion acquisition of Pacific Petroleums Ltd. from Phillips Petroleum Company of the United States. The acquisitions continued into the 1980s as Petro-Canada bought Belgian-owned Petrofina Canada Inc. for $1.6 billion in 1980, British-controlled BP Refining and Marketing Canada Limited for $416 million in 1983, and the downstream portions of Gulf Canada Ltd. in Ontario and the Edmonton refinery in 1986 for a total of $900 million.

The acquisitions and growth of Petro-Canada since 1975 have made it a major Canadian corporation with more than $8 billion in assets, $5 billion in annual revenue, and 7,000 employees. It ranks 11th on the *Financial Post's* list of the 500 largest Canadian companies.

The corporation has proven its ability to find and develop oil and natural gas on land, underwater, and in the Arctic; in the heavy oil deposits of Western Canada; and, more recently, off the shores of Eastern Canada, at Hibernia and Terra Nova off Newfoundland and the Venture gas field off Nova Scotia. With refineries in Quebec, Ontario, Alberta, and British Columbia, Petro-Canada has the capacity to process 65,000 cubic metres of crude oil per

Pumpjacks at Bellshill, Alberta.

A well is tested by flaring in the Terra Nova discovery area on Canada's East Coast.

day—about 21 percent of the total Canadian capacity. These refineries are also capable of a range of special processes, including the production of petrochemical feedstocks, high-quality lubricating oils, and synthetic crude oil.

To most Canadians Petro-Canada produces gasoline. Indeed, the company is the largest single gasoline retailer in Canada with more than 3,800 retail outlets providing some 44 million litres of refined products to 650,000 Canadians each day. The retail network is also an efficient one, selling 20 percent of the nation's gasoline with only 18 percent of its retail outlets. In its effort to create a nationwide, integrated network, Petro-Canada encourages its dealers to operate as independent business people with strong ties to their

The Trafalgar Refinery in Oakville.

communities. Few Petro-Canada stations are owned and operated directly by Petro-Canada.

Wholesale and industrial sales are a growing Petro-Canada concern as well, with those markets now served through some 40 distribution terminals and 500 bulk plants, also mostly run by independent dealers. Other markets the company serves include those for home heating oil, agricultural petrochemicals, and specialized lubricants.

Petro-Canada is putting more emphasis than ever on developing high-quality products. In 1986 it was the first to introduce a new gasoline that improves engine efficiency and performance. As well, scientists at Petro-Canada's Sheridan Park research facility in Mississauga recently won international acclaim for developing and testing its Premium Turbo Testing motor oil, now officially approved for all Mercedes-Benz gasoline and diesel car engines.

To move its products to distributors and customers, Petro-Canada uses road, rail, ships, and pipelines. The company owns outright or in part 12 crude oil, natural gas liquids, and refined product pipelines, operating nine of these itself with a combined capacity of more than 100,000 cubic metres a day.

As Canada's national oil company Petro-Canada pays extra attention to operating in ways that benefit Canadians. Not only does the firm employ 7,000 Canadians directly, but it generates thousands of jobs indirectly by seeking Canadian suppliers for everything from drilling rigs to office furniture. Dealers and agents are encouraged to become involved in their local communities, with such projects as women's car care clinics, children's bicycle safety, and youth sports. Retail promotions are aimed at supporting worthwhile Canadian initiatives, such as the restoration of the Bluenose II and the building of hostels for visiting parents at children's hospitals. Donation programs are balanced among all regions, focusing on arts and cultural events, education, and community organizations such as United Way/Centraide. One of Petro-Canada's most exciting recent initiatives was its sponsorship of the 1988 Olympic Torch Relay; the Olympic flame was carried from St. John's to Victoria, British Columbia, and back to Calgary for the opening of the 1988 Olympic Winter Games in Alberta.

Petro-Canada has a special relationship with North York after recently making the city the location of its Ontario regional headquarters. Seeking to bring together employees dispersed throughout four buildings in the To-

ronto area, Petro-Canada looked long and hard for a facility with just the right combination of location and amenities. The choice was the stunning new North York City Centre office tower on Yonge Street just north of Sheppard Avenue, adjacent to the new North York Civic Square and in the heart of downtown North York.

Petro-Canada occupies 12 of the 23 storeys of this architectural marvel, which boasts its own bell tower. Employees enjoy easy access to Highway 401, the Yonge subway line, and the proposed Sheppard subway line. There is also a nearby reflecting pool, skating rink, library, amphitheatre, and wedding pavilion, as well as plenty of high-quality shops and restaurants. As one company official put it, the new location is "the centre of attention."

Petro-Canada is the largest gasoline retailer in Canada with more than 3,800 retail outlets. Most are owned and operated by independent business people with strong ties to the local community.

MOTOROLA CANADA LTD.

Motorola's Canadian head office on Steeles Avenue East in North York.

It says much about the philosophy of Motorola Canada Ltd. that it moved its main operation into the Steeles Avenue/Highway 404 area of North York 20 years ago, a time when there were more cows than people and nearby Victoria Park Avenue was still a gravel path. Never a company to rely on old ideas, Motorola was one of the first major companies to recognize the strategic advantages of northeast North York, such as easy access to major transportation routes such as Highway 401 and the potential for major residential development on all sides. The fact that many other large corporations soon followed is not surprising, but merely typical of how Motorola continually seeks new ways to achieve the highest levels of excellence and efficiency.

Motorola Canada is a subsidiary of U.S.-based Motorola Inc., a world leader in the manufacture of electronic equipment. Motorola products first arrived in Canada in 1944 with the sale of 200 mobile radio sets. By 1957 demand in Canada for Motorola products was so strong that the Canadian Motorola Electronics Company was formed, and by 1959 the production of several lines of two-way radios was in full swing. As growth continued more space was needed, and in 1966 the company acquired 50 acres in North York. A year later 500 people were working in the new 100,000-square-foot facility at 3125 Steeles Avenue East. In 1974 another 60,000 square feet were added, and in 1985 a new 55,000-square-foot facility was built to house its semiconductor operation, corporate affairs, and expansion for communication ac-

tivities. Today the North York facility employs 1,500 people, led by president Marcel Bernard.

Motorola is best known for its communications equipment, which it manufactures as both high-volume standardized products and customized, highly sophisticated systems. In addition, the company has expanded its operations in Canada to include semiconductors, automotive and industrial electronics equipment, data communications, and information processing equipment.

To produce, market, and distribute

these products, the parent corporation has divided its operations into six separate entities—Communications Sector, Automotive and Industrial Electronics Group, Information Systems Group, Government Electronics Group, Semiconductor Products Sector, and General Systems Group. Together these Motorola entities employ more than 2,600 Canadians across Canada. The largest is still the Communications Sector, which has 56 sales and service offices across Canada. The North York facility houses most of the Communications Operation as well as all corporate departments, such as finance and payroll.

Most people do not realize that much of the communications equipment they see used by the police or fire departments is built by Motorola right here in North York. Motorola is the largest designer and manufacturer of ra-

The Motorola MC88100 RISC (Reduced Instruction Set Computing) microprocessor will drive high-performance computing environments ranging from supercomputing and telecommunications to fault tolerant business and workstation computing. The MC88100 RISC microprocessor contains more than 160,000 transistors in five parallel execution units providing 14-17 MIPS performance.

dio communications equipment and systems in Canada; it works with such large and demanding organizations as the OPP, RCMP, CN, and CP Rail. Much of this high-technology equipment is also exported abroad, to the United States, the Orient, Australia, and the Middle East. In fact, Motorola equipment is so world-renowned that Japanese mountain climbers in the Himalayas specifically requested the MCX 100 radio, for which the North York facility has earned an exclusive worldwide product mandate. As well, Motorola was chosen as the official supplier of communications equipment to the 1988 Olympic Winter Games in Calgary.

The Communications Sector also oversees the new Motorola Canada Cel-

The Motorola MCX 1000 mobile radio is a powerful communications tool, which is both easy to use and imbued with the most advanced technology available.

lular Division, which markets cellular telephones, and Motorola Dascan Limited, which designs and manufactures Supervisory Control and Data Acquisition (SCADA) systems for remote control and monitoring of unattended locations in electrical utility, petroleum, and gas networks.

The intricacies of high-technology electronics may escape most of us, but even a layman can appreciate the efficiency and dedication to quality evident at the North York plant. Production is uncommonly clean and well organized. Much of the assembly is done through surface mount technology in which robotic arms put tiny parts into place with amazing speed and precision. Vice-president Lloyd Kubis points out that Motorola was the first to install such technology, used by most electronics manufacturers today, when it did so four years ago.

Other state-of-the-art equipment includes a vibration table that gives products a real-life ride similar to what they would experience on a motorcycle. There is also an environment chamber in which products are frozen and thawed at temperatures ranging from minus 30 to 60 degrees Celsius as they come off the production line.

Computers also play an important role in Motorola production, such as testing radios on all frequencies during manufacture. In addition, Motorola produces a computer-controlled rail-

The Motorola 8500 XL convertible cellular telephone features a 120-number memory, electronic lock, theft alarm, and 32-digit number entry and review.

way system that helps eliminate human error and thus dangerous accidents along train tracks.

As a large corporation Motorola not only sees itself as a supplier of electronics equipment, but also as a bearer of social responsibility. The company has a long history of community involvement, supporting such charitable organizations as the Easter Seals Society and providing technical assistance for special events such as the visits of Pope John Paul II and Queen Elizabeth II, as well as the Ontario Games for the Physically Disabled held in North York.

As a wholly Canadian-managed company with much autonomy, Motorola Canada Ltd. is committed to the future of Canada in an increasingly high-technology world, training and teaching Canadians in some of the most sophisticated engineering environments that exist anywhere. This commitment is reflective of the firm's belief that technological innovation can create a better world. It is a philosophy that led to the first commercially marketed car radio in 1930 and to the marketing of the first portable cellular telephone in 1984. And it is certainly a philosophy that bodes well for tomorrow.

INDUCON

The advantages of locating a business in North York may seem obvious today: Taxes are less prohibitive than in the downtown core, land costs are more reasonable, and the location is convenient for employees—most of whom live in the suburbs nearby—and for moving products along the major transportation routes that traverse the city. There was a time when those advantages were only clear to those willing to look beyond old habits and see a better vision for the future. The Inducon group of companies had that kind of vision.

Inducon began nearly 30 years ago when a young engineer named Andrew Zsolt, a refugee from war-torn Hungary who had to claim he was a farmer to gain entrance into Canada, managed to convince some friends to lend him $21,000 to purchase four lots on Banbury Road in North York. He built 20 houses and sold 19 of them, living to this day in the other. He didn't make much money, but he proved to himself and others that he could turn a dream into reality. Zsolt then turned to industrial design, working 16 hours a day preparing proposals while drawing no salary from his infant company. His labor bore fruit when his first order came in, from B&E Furniture, for a small 10,000-square-foot plant in North York. The clients liked it.

Inducon has repeated that process, on various scales, hundreds of times since then, and the company has grown

Examples of the Inducon office concept are Motorola Information Systems Limited in Brampton (above), Johnson Controls in Markham (below), Cosmopolitan Inn Office Complex (Phase 1), Willowdale (opposite bottom), and West Metro Corporate Centre (Phase 1), Etobicoke (opposite top).

into one of the area's most innovative and respected builders. Today Inducon is divided into two semi-autonomous entities: Inducon Development Corporation, which is wholly owned by Zsolt's family trust, Yorkland Develop-

ments; and Inducon Design/Build, which is jointly owned by Yorkland and Desbil Management Inc., an employee-owned company with its founders William Buck, Kalman Czegledy, and Robert MacKay. Together these two entities own Inducon Design Build Associates, which in turn has consulting, construction, project management, and air conditioning divisions.

What may appear to be a confusing structure is actually an effectively integrated group of companies providing a full range of real estate development services. They employ 525 people (200 at Inducon Development Corporation and 325 at Inducon Design Build), and revenues in 1986 topped $180 million.

Innovation has been the real key to Inducon's success. It was the first to develop the industrial mall concept, putting small incubator units into a mid-size multiple unit complex so that small or new businesses can lease a few thousand square feet and still benefit from an elegant entranceway and reception area, ample parking, and shipping services at the back. The first such mall was at York Mills and Lesmill in North York, consisting of units of 1,900

square feet. This type of business accommodation has grown to be a major type of facility of its kind in North America.

Another innovation was the refinement of the "turn-key" contracting process, in which the customer is provided with a single-source supply of land, building, and fixtures for a predetermined cost or fixed-lease rate.

Perhaps the company's most important innovation has simply been its belief in suburban office space. More than once Inducon has built in what many thought would always be a desolate field, only to have a vibrant community spring up around it. Today Inducon buildings ring Toronto from Oshawa to Oakville and are particularly prevalent in North York.

An excellent example of the Inducon suburban office concept is the Cosmopolitan Corporate Centre at Highway 404 and McNicoll Avenue, featuring four office buildings housing 850,000 square feet of rentable space, a 225-room hotel, and a $4-million fitness centre. Other recent projects of a similar mold are the Oakville Corporate Centre (8.5 acres, 300,000 square feet) in Oakville, the Airport Centre III (10 storeys, 160,000 square feet) near Pearson International Airport, Yorkland Court (12 storeys, 190,000 square feet) at Highway 401 and the Don Valley Parkway in North York, the Westmetro Corporate Centre (four

towers of 155,000 square feet each) in Etobicoke, and the Ambler Centre (45,000 square feet) at Highway 401 and Dixie Road in Mississauga.

Typical Inducon design/build projects include the Motorola Semiconductor Products facility in the Willowdale area of North York; the Alfa Laval distribution centre in Scarborough; the American Motors plant in Guelph; Ford Electronics Manufacturing in Markham; Johnson Controls Ltd. in Markham; Honeywell's head office in North York; shopping centres in Brampton, Tillsonburg, Milton, Keswick, and other centres in Ontario; Ya-

maha's head office; the downtown Toronto Mercedes-Benz service centre; the Airport Hilton; and Inglis head office in Mississauga.

Certainly the most ambitious Inducon project is Lagoon City, a huge European-style resort on Lake Simcoe that has been Zsolt's labor of love for 25 years. Carved out of 1,400 acres of swamp at the northeast end of the lake, Lagoon City will include a 300-slip marina; a $17-million, 165-room hotel; a 9,000-square-foot shopping complex; tennis courts; 5,000 feet of sandy shoreline; the most protected harbor on the lake; and easy access to the Trent and Severn canal systems. Residential units (500 by the end of 1987 and 160 more in 1988) come in single-family homes, condominiums, time-share units, and luxury time-share apartments.

Lagoon City is Ontario's first licensed time-share resort and the province's first urban resort townsite. Located just 120 kilometres north of Toronto, Lagoon City offers year-round recreation—swimming and boating in the summer, and ice fishing and cross-country skiing in the winter. It is expected that there will be 6,500 permanent residents and part-time guests within five years; the final goal is 20,000. Lagoon City represents a $50-million commitment by Inducon to again create something visionary.

REFF INCORPORATED

Since its beginnings in 1964 Reff Incorporated has developed a corporate philosophy and work ethic based on quality, value, and service that has propelled it into the very front ranks of office furniture manufacturing in Canada.

The founders—Robert, Eric, and Frank Zoebelein and Fred Drechsel—first developed modular furniture for residential, educational, and institutional applications. Their thoughtful design and innovative use of technology and materials was highly acclaimed and soon resulted in major contract awards. awards. As well, a succession of unique product introductions quickly established Reff as an industry leader, garnering the company several awards and catching the eyes of some prominent architects and designers.

Impressed by what they saw, these experts encouraged Reff to enter the office furniture market. After its first forays into this new business proved successful, the firm, in 1978, committed all of its resources to the design and manufacture of office systems.

Another major turning point for Reff came in June 1983 at Neocon (the office furniture industry's premier exposition), when it introduced its revolutionary System 6, which would become Reff's flagship furniture system and a standard for much of the competition.

System 6 reflected a natural progression and refinement of Reff's initial commitment to modular engineering, classic design, and quality. Summoning up nearly 20 years of experience and focusing closely on the needs of modern business, Reff had produced a furniture system that guaranteed interchangeability without the loss of modular compatibility.

Reff System 6 provides a flexible furniture system that may be used as freestanding casegoods (below) or in panel-hung systems applications (right).

The clean lines of System 6 are the natural result of Reff's design and engineering logic. The heart of the system is a unique set of connecting devices that ensures strength and ease of assembly and reassembly. Hardware is easily accessible but hidden from view. In addition, the inclusion of all connecting hardware with modular elements allows for easy specification and installation. And of course, the system is designed to adapt to technological needs such as electrical cabling and computer wiring.

Architecturally inspired, System 6 was created to allow for necessary office evolution. Change is viewed at Reff as a response to legitimate needs and not as a dictate of fashion. For example, when solid color laminate finishes were introduced in 1984, both new and existing System 6 users benefited from

the expanded product offering. With a classic design and truly systematic concept, System 6 satisfies virtually all the operational requirements of the contemporary office while providing classic, ever appropriate styling.

Reff has grown into one of Canada's largest office furniture manufacturers, headquartered at 1000 Arrow Road in North York and with show-

Reff introduced a complete line of ergonomic seating in February 1987.

rooms in Atlanta, Calgary, Chicago, Dallas, Houston, Los Angeles, Minneapolis, New York, Philadelphia, Toronto, and Washington, D.C. The company is completely Canadian-owned and -managed.

In November 1986 Reff offered shares in the firm to the public for the first time. With the resulting influx of investment capital, the company, in March 1987, purchased Office Specialty of Toronto, which included a metal furniture production facility that gave Reff a new material dimension. This acquisition has expanded Reff's production space to more than 900,000 square feet. Reff today employs almost 800 people in its plants and showroom facilities.

With satisfied customers such as North American Life, Bank of Nova Scotia, Xerox, Procter & Gamble, Novatel, and the Canadian Imperial Bank of Commerce, and an ongoing program of product development and innovation, Reff Incorporated has a future of continued growth and accomplishment. Its philosophy and the dedication of its people are evident in everything the company does. Today, as it has for more than two decades, the Reff name continues to be synonymous with excellence.

The corporate offices of Reff Incorporated, North York.

ROYAL PLASTICS LIMITED

If anyone out there still believes Canadians are too conservative and provincial to leap to the forefront of technological innovation and international commerce, they should finally be convinced otherwise by the existence of Vic De Zen, a former laborer who has parlayed monumental ambition and revolutionary production techniques into the Royal group of companies, a vinyl building supply empire unrivalled in North America and perhaps the world.

De Zen, a 43-year-old Italian-Canadian, first met with frustration in this country when his lack of English kept him out of the tool and die trade he was trained for. He finally found a job making dies for a vinyl extrusion company, and in 1967 returned to Europe for a year to study the latest developments in that new industry. When he returned De Zen, together with partners Domenic D'Amico, Lorenzo Demeneghi, and Fortunato Bordin started their first company, Royal Plastics Limited, in 1970 in a single 300-square-metre unit with one extrusion machine, supplying vinyl window profiles to window system manufacturers. The company expanded rapidly, outgrowing several units in its original location until it was decided to build a new plant at 4945 Steeles Avenue West

One of the many industrial and commercial buildings developed by the Royal Group.

Royal Group president Vic De Zen.

in North York.

In 1976 De Zen, with the assistance of a $250,000 research grant from the federal government, patented and licensed a new process in extrusion tooling technology that proved enormously efficient and inexpensive to produce. At the same time the use of vinyl (technically known as polyvinylchloride or PVC) generally was gaining popularity as a building material for the 1980s. As a result, Royal Plastics has expanded into many new areas, such as the automotive, swimming pool, appliance, furniture, and even advertising industries.

To facilitate such tremendous growth without creating an unwieldy corporate monster, De Zen has implemented a policy of creating separate companies within the Royal family; they are managed and partially owned by employees who show exceptional skill and ambition in a given area. This method has had the dual advantages of instilling motivation in employees by giving them a vested interest in productivity and quality, and of preventing top workers from taking their skills to the competition.

The many companies that have sprung from Royal Plastics create almost a microcosm of the plastics indus-

try, with each integrated into the overall goals of the group. For instance, there are land development, construction, electrical contracting, plumbing, and even landscaping firms to build the group's own offices and factories. There are also a number of tool-and-die and machine manufacturing companies to make equipment for the group, as well as for outside sales. There is even a restaurant to serve the group's new industrial complex. In total, De Zen has created more than 70 companies that employ 3,000 people and generate sales of $600 million per year.

But despite the firm's apparent diversification, plastic extrusion, particularly of vinyl, remains the core of the enterprise. The virtues of using vinyl for window frames have been known to Europeans for more than 30 years, but it was not until the energy crisis of the mid-1970s that North Americans discovered its excellent thermal properties and durability. As well, vinyl is made from plentiful natural gas and chlorine, and thus less subject to oil price fluctuation than is its chief competitor, alumi-

num. With De Zen's patented vacuum-sizing tool-and-die technology, the benefit of low cost has been added to the equation, making vinyl the dominant material in the window industry, creating new uses for vinyl extrusion, and, in a historic reversal, forcing Europeans to come to Canada for the latest plastics technology.

Today Royal has 15 plants doing custom extruding—in Toronto, Winnipeg, Montreal, Pittsburgh, Fort Lauderdale, and England. The corporation has a firm grip on the American market, even selling 75 percent of its Toronto-made products in the United States. In all the company has 300 extruders, almost twice as many as its nearest North American competitor. Rivals are not likely to come close in the near future either, since Royal constantly strives for product improvement through an extensive research and development department.

Royal's astounding growth over the past 17 years has gone almost unnoticed by the general public, and even by the business community. The company actively shuns publicity and advertising, preferring to concern itself only with its relationship with the individual customer. In fact, sales manager David

Miles of plastic pipe awaiting shipment to all corners of North America at the ultramodern Royal pipe plant (above).

Some of the more than 300 vinyl-extrusion machines that position Royal Plastics as North America's largest custom-vinyl extruder (below).

Woolf recalls with a smile how the firm was forced to produce its first brochure in 1982 for a trade show.

No expense is spared, however, for interested customers. Clients are routinely flown in aboard Royal's company plane to view the facilities. As well, Royal concentrates hard on providing design assistance, such as explaining what manufacturing changes would be necessary to convert from aluminum to plastic materials.

The atmosphere at Royal is very much a reflection of Vic De Zen himself. There are no corporate types, and everyone refers to the president as "Vic." This informality does not translate into lethargy, however. Watching De Zen, with sleeves rolled up, making the smallest adjustments to a machine, inspires fellow workers to reach for the same high levels of product quality and service dependability. "Vic sets a fast pace," says Woolf. "He works long hours and won't let anything go out the door if it's not right. No matter how large a company is, the owner's tone is going to rub off."

The dizzying expansion of the Royal empire is showing no signs of let-

Customers from across North America attend meetings at Royal Group headquarters via a Westwind jet operated by the Royal Flight Division.

ting up. The company is currently putting the finishing touches on a 24-acre industrial/commercial complex at Steeles Avenue and Pine Valley Drive, just north of the North York plant in the town of Vaughan, on a street appropriately named Vinyl Court. The 600,000-square-foot complex contains several of Royal's offshoot companies, a major office building that houses Royal's accounting and legal departments, a bank, and the firm's Italian restaurant.

Royal's location in the western part of North York has also proved to be an important ingredient in the company's success. "There's an excellent work force here," says Woolf. "There's especially a lot of new immigrants, and in many cases we've given them their first chance, and they've done well."

There is one particular Royal legend that perhaps best sums up the man and his business. When the company first started, it was asked by North York's Fairview Mall to repair the vinyl railing around the upper deck of the mall. It was Friday afternoon, the railing was needed Monday morning, and the contractor had been turned down by all the larger established firms. "Impossible," Vic reportedly told the contractor, who then countered with the magic words, "So you're just like all the rest. You just can't do it." De Zen's single extruding machine worked right through the weekend, and the job was ready on time.

As a Royal tanker unloads PVC compound from storage silos, shipments to the United States are loaded onto Royal Freight Lines' Roadex Transport.

CANADA DRY BOTTLING COMPANY LTD.

Canada Dry has a story that closely parallels the history of the country itself. Born in the late 1800s through a mixture of ingenuity and hard work, the company has grown with the nation, changing with the tastes and technology of the times but never altering its goal of achieving the highest product quality. And, like all the best Canadian-born institutions, Canada Dry, maker of Canada Dry Ginger Ale and a host of other soft drink brands, has a reputation that extends worldwide.

The first Canada Dry plant was opened in Toronto in 1890 by John J. McLaughlin, a young entrepreneurial chemist. His first product was called carbonated plain water, a forerunner to today's soda water, which he supplied to drugstores for sale from their soda fountains. But despite its initial success, J.J. McLaughlin knew there were still two ingredients missing from his operation—a way to make the carbonated beverage portable so that it could be enjoyed outside the drugstore, and new, more appealing flavors.

After much experimentation McLaughlin was able to develop techniques for mass bottling, an important first step toward modern production and automation. Then, using recipes

Delivering Canada Dry in the late 1800s.

The original Canada Dry label, which dates back to 1903.

from Great Britain that required exotic spices, he developed and marketed McLaughlin Belfast Style Ginger Ale, a product much darker and sweeter than today's ginger ale. In 1904, after a trip to Europe where he was impressed with the dryness and sparkling appearance of French champagnes, he introduced Pale Dry Ginger Ale. As this search for an improved flavor continued, the company was growing considerably, opening bottling plants in Winnipeg, Manitoba, and Edmonton. In 1907 McLaughlin perfected his product, called Canada Dry Ginger Ale, the "Champagne of ginger ales." It became the most successful soft drink ever created in Canada and the favorite of millions around the world.

Today Canada Dry products reach consumers in 87 countries on six continents. Under the auspices of Canada Dry Limited, its products are bottled and canned by a network of more than 500 franchises worldwide, each carefully scrutinized and obligated to maintain the company's high quality standards. Canada Dry is one of the largest soft drink companies in the world, and its champagne is the biggest-selling ginger ale there is. Canada Dry makes a

host of other flavor brands, including club soda, tonic water, and "C" Plus Orange.

Production of Canada Dry products is absolutely exacting. The water used is purified through a process so effective that it has been taken by astronauts into space and requested as the table water for Royal tours. Using only the best ingredients, Canada Dry imports flavor components from such far-flung places as Nigeria, Madagascar, Sri Lanka, Bulgaria, Indonesia, and Jamaica.

The largest Canada Dry franchise operation is Canada Dry Bottling Company Ltd., located at 2 Champagne Drive in North York, where it has been making Canada Dry products for more than 20 years. This 175,000-square-foot facility produces an astounding 100,000 cases (at 24 units per case) an astounding 7.5 million units per day, distributing them with a fleet exceeding 200 trucks. Led by Tom Collins, director of Canadian operations, Canada Dry Bottling has a work force of 350 people, all of whom help contribute to annual sales topping $120 million.

PRINCIPAL HEATING COMPANY

The secret behind the success of Principal Heating Company is rather straightforward, according to president and owner N.E. Baird. "Quality and price," he credits. "We perform the work quickly, efficiently, and at a lower cost." Although his words may sound simple, Baird realizes, after more than 30 years in the heating and air conditioning business, that to achieve those simple attributes takes experience, product innovation, astute marketing, and plenty of hard work from all departments. Those are the real secrets behind Principal Heating Company, one of Metropolitan Toronto's largest and most respected designers and manufacturers of heating and air conditioning systems.

The history of Principal Heating began in 1956, when a French Canadian named Gaston Goulet and a Polish immigrant, Soloman Sporn, formed a partnership in response to the demand for warm-air heating in the many new single-family houses and apartments being constructed at the time. Working

The geriatric care facility, Baycrest Centre.

The design and manufacture of heating and air conditioning systems for some of the most prestigious buildings in the North York area originate from the 20,000-square-foot Principal Heating Company head office and factory on Penn Drive, Weston.

from experience rather than formal education, the two started work in a garage on Sable Street with six employees, each earning less than two dollars per hour. Within five years sales had increased to $3.5 million from $360,000, and the firm had moved to a sparkling new, 20,000-square-foot plant on Penn Drive, in the first industrial park built in the Weston Road and Finch Avenue area of North York.

In 1969 a corporate plan was established to expand activities in the direction of commercial and institutional

construction areas in addition to residential work. To do this, major changes in image and marketing were needed. This effort paid off handsomely, beginning in 1971 when the company was awarded a $4.5-million contract by the Metro Toronto School Board for work on 32 schools. The breakthrough was followed by several other large contracts with such major clients as Fairview Corp., Toronto Dominion Bank,

The head office of Procter & Gamble.

Commercial Union Tower, Seneca and Humber colleges, and the Constellation and Prince hotels.

Company growth continued throughout the 1970s, due in large part to several changes in operational strategy. Realizing the firm was incurring a substantial subcontract expense in the refrigeration start-up and service aspects of major contracts, it was decided to start an operating refrigeration service department to recover some of these losses. As well, a division for the manufacture of ductwork and accessories was established for sale to commercial and industrial sheet-metal contractors, including some major competitors of Principal. Both of these divisions have since become semi-autonomous profit centres, earning annual sales of $700,000 each.

In 1981, after 15 years as vice-president and general manager, Baird bought the company. Under his leadership Principal's sales have risen to $9 million annually, and it now employs more than 90 people. The firm has been ranked as high as fourth in size out of the 67 members of the Toronto Sheet Metal and Air Handling Group, the recognized labor agents for major projects in the area. The company's solid reputation has also put it on vir-

tually every invited tender list issued by major owners, architects, and engineers needing such services.

Baird is like a proud father while leading a tour of the firm's manufacturing facility. He points with satisfaction to an automated duct-line machine which, he says, is worth $750,000, was the first of its kind in Toronto, and can produce an L-shape duct for installing in a ceiling of an office building in 14 seconds. He is also proud of the fact that his factory consumes 2 million pounds of metal per year in its 10,000 square feet, whereas most factories require 25 percent more space for the same production capacity.

Principal's dedication to supplying and servicing quality heating and air conditioning systems quickly, efficiently, and at a reasonable cost has made it the preferred choice of many of Metro Toronto's premier builders. For example, in just the past two years in North York alone, Principal has undertaken projects at Baycrest Hospital, Southam Publications, Lansing Square, Procter & Gamble, Yonge & Glendora, 40 Sheppard East, and Concorde Place, to reach a total of nearly $7 million in contracts.

Obviously, Baird isn't the only one impressed by his company.

Concorde Corporate Centre.

UNISYS CANADA INC.

In 1986 two of the world's largest computer companies, Sperry and Burroughs, joined forces and became Unisys Corporation—the power of 2.

Unisys today is a $13-billion information systems firm with more than 90,000 employees and 60,000 customers in more than 100 countries. Unisys Canada Inc., with headquarters at 2001 Sheppard Avenue East in North York, has offices, service, distribution, and manufacturing facilities throughout Canada. The company is a leading manufacturer of commercial information systems, defence systems, and related services.

Unisys employs approximately 3,000 people across Canada, and has marketing and service facilities in virtually every major Canadian city from Vancouver to St. John's.

The company is divided into a number of business units:

Defence Systems provides specialized military electronics equipment to both the Canadian Armed Forces and military forces of other countries. A sophisticated defence electronics manufacturing facility employing about 500 people is located in Winnipeg.

Paramax Electronics Inc., a Unisys Canada subsidiary, is the prime subcontractor to Saint John Shipbuilding for the electronics and combat systems management required by the Canadian Patrol Frigate Program. Approximately 600 staff, two-thirds of them engineers, work at the advanced Paramax research and development complex in Montreal. A total of 12 frigates will be built as part of the program.

Both the Peripherals Group and Power Supply Operations have worldwide manufacturing mandates. The Peripherals Group supplies disk memory

Unisys Canada UNIX operating system commitment—from PC to mainframe.

units from its plant in Winnipeg and employs more than 450 people. Power Supply Operations is located in Montreal and has a staff of 300 people, designing, manufacturing, and exporting power supplies for many different Unisys products.

Information Systems, employing more than 1,000 people, is the business unit of Unisys Canada that is familiar to most customers. The Unisys strategic approach to the information systems marketplace involves concentrating on particular lines of business and serving each of them in depth. In Canada, the lines of business in which the firm concentrates include health care, finance and insurance, industrial/commercial, government, transportation, airlines, and education. The mandate of Unisys employees is to apply their experience, technology, and un-

The Canadian headquarters for Unisys Canada Inc. is at 2001 Sheppard Avenue East in North York.

derstanding of these lines of business to provide appropriate solutions to the information problems and needs of their customers.

In broad terms, the Unisys technology strategy for the 1990s includes three major themes: openness, productivity, and enterprise networking.

Unisys is committed to providing open systems solutions to the information needs of its customers. From microcomputers to mainframes, the company offers a fully integrated and connectable line of products and services. Unisys is also a leader in the development of computer systems compatible with the industry-standard UNIX operating system.

In terms of productivity, Unisys leads its competition in the development and application of fourth-generation languages and artificial intelligence. Both are key to allowing customers to streamline and expedite the process of creating computer applications software.

Unisys continues to expand and strengthen its enterprise networking capability in one of the fastest-growing areas of telecommunications—the development of open, industry-standard networks to handle the information-management needs of a total business.

F.&K. MFG. CO. LIMITED

Starting with a single 10,000-square-foot plant, operations have expanded steadily and now include the main 30,000-square-foot factory and a new 10,000-square-foot plant across the street.

F.&K. produces a wide range of metal products, including auto parts (its biggest orders), lawn mower housings, electric kettles, ovens, and even bottle openers. Facilities include a tool-and-die shop with seven tool-and-die makers, a punch press shop with up to 600-ton press capacity, and automatic tapping, welding, and riveting equipment.

But Bergmann credits people, not equipment, for F.&K. Mfg. Co. Limited's success. "We treat our people well, and, as a result, we have a very low turnover rate," he says. A good example is Juergen Walch, vice-president and general manager, who has been with the company for its full 25 years.

Metal stamping companies are not famous for the attention they pay to employee comfort. But a willingness to do things a little better, like keeping worker morale high, is just one reason why the F.&K. Mfg. Co. Limited has been so successful in this very competitive industry for 25 years.

In fact, F.&K. president and sole owner Bert Bergmann even has a policy of never closing his office door. "I have nothing to hide," explains the big, golf-loving president. "And more communication means more productivity." In addition to easy access to the boss, F.&K. employees also enjoy a profit-sharing program and full air conditioning at both company plants.

F.&K. was established in 1963 by two partners named Fischer and Kiss (hence the name, F.&K.), who did tool-and-die work out of a 3,000-square-foot basement on Bridgeland Avenue in North York. In 1968 Bergmann, who had been working for only one company since arriving in Canada from Germany in 1956, purchased 51 percent of the firm, which by then had moved into a 5,000-square-foot location on Milwick Drive, also in North

York. The property for F.&K.'s present location at 155 Turbine Drive in Steeles Avenue-Weston Road area of North York was purchased in 1973.

F.&K.'s biggest asset—its employees (left).

F.&K. manufactures a wide range of metal products on the most modern equipment in its fully air-conditioned plant (below).

APOTEX INC.
CANADA'S HEALTHCARE

Part of the challenge of starting a pharmaceutical manufacturing company is the assembly of a team of highly skilled people to operate the intricate, sophisticated equipment necessary to produce modern medicaments. In just over 12 years Apotex Inc. of North York has done this, and by reinvesting in other sectors of the health care industry, it has attained a dominant position.

Apotex (derived from the Greek word *apotheke*) is the inspiration of Dr. Barry Sherman its present owner and president. Dr. Sherman founded the company in 1974 with two employees and a 6,000-square-foot production facility on Ormont Drive in North York. Before long the firm occupied the neighboring unit, doubling its size. Business continued to outstrip the company's physical boundaries, however, and in 1985 Apotex moved to its present 73,000-square-foot facility on Signet Drive, also in the Downsview area of North York. Still experiencing growing pains, the firm has added an additional 45,000 square feet to that building and is also developing land at the south end of Signet Drive to accommodate affiliated health care facilities. Along the way Apotex has become the largest, wholly Canadian-owned, international pharmaceutical company, with 300 employees (not including subsidiaries) and annual sales of more than $60 million.

Apotex' first product was generic prescription pharmaceutical tablets, and this continues to be its mainstay. The company now makes hundreds of different medicines in an ever-

Apotex Inc., the largest wholly Canadian-owned, international pharmaceutical company, as it appeared prior to its recent expansion, is located in the Downsview section of North York.

increasing range of dosages for both the prescription and over-the-counter markets. The APO brand has become recognized as the industry leader in quality and value in generic prescription drugs, prompting thousands of Canadian pharmacies to substitute the APO alternative for many high-priced brands of medication.

From its base in pharmaceutical prescriptions, Apotex has moved into a wide variety of health care products. Through acquisitions, partnerships, and internal expansion, Apotex' interests now include X-ray equipment, veterinary pharmaceuticals, penicillins, biotechnology products, diagnostic equipment, portable medical devices, and vitamins and nutritional supplements. This diversification has helped give Apotex an international presence that now includes 53 countries.

Apotex has shared its success by generously supporting many health care organizations, such as the Canadian Foundation for the Advancement of Pharmacy and the Council on Drug Abuse. It has also donated funds toward medical research, hospital construction, and pharmaceutical faculties at various universities.

Modern laboratories with state-of-the-art equipment provide the utmost in quality control.

197

CHAPTER 9

Business
and Professions

*Greater North York's
professional community brings
a wealth of service, ability,
and insight to the area.*

NORTH YORK: THE CITY
PROPERTY & ECONOMIC DEVELOPMENT DEPARTMENT

The Property and Economic Development Department is the sales and promotional arm of the City of North York and provides three distinct functions for North York's 560,000 residents and 17,000 industries and businesses: the encouragement and promotion of and participation in the economic development of the city through a wide range of innovative programs; the management of the city's land portfolio, including buying, selling and leasing on behalf of the city; and the overseeing of municipal projects, including the Civic Centre Project (a 1.2-million-square-foot development), the Mel Lastman Square, City Hall Expansion Project, and the North York Performing Arts Centre.

Promotion of the downtown is an important aspect of the department's mandate. Only a few years ago downtown was a dream, but with direction from the city's long-standing mayor, Mel Lastman, that dream on Yonge Street has become a reality with the downtown presently containing 6,000 residents and 19,000 workers. "The department's activities have played a key role in the growth of downtown North York," says Ken Stroud, commissioner of The Property and Economic Development Department, "by creating a dynamic environment that encourages and welcomes new investment dollars to North York."

Some of the developments already completed in the downtown are the City Centre Development (1.2 million square feet), Madison Centre (421,000 square feet), the Sheppard Centre (1.4 million square feet), The North American Life Centre (first phase, 764,000 square feet), as well as many large condominium developments.

Promotion of the downtown is only part of the economic development mandate. "It is extremely important to maintain and expand North York's traditional economic base" says Larry March, director of business development. North York contains 30 percent of Metropolitan Toronto's industrial development in 18 industrial areas, and also contains five office parks outside the downtown.

Through direct mail, local media advertising, seminars, and group presentations, the department circulates information about the advantages of North York's positive business environment and about the services and assistance that the department and the city can

The downtown North York area serves as a flagship for state-of-the-art development in the city. Combined with four other office parks and 18 industrial parks, the city offers services and facilities to meet the most demanding tenant of owner requirements. This photograph, courtesy of the North York Property and Economic Development Department, shows North York looking south on Yonge. John O'Brien Photographer

provide. One of the reasons for the existence of The Property and Economic Development Department is to demonstrate to business and industry that North York cares about them, and the phenomenal growth in North York is a demonstration that the message is getting through.

The Property and Economic Development Department acts as the city's sales agent and is involved in a large number of land transactions, varying from relatively small dispositions of surplus laneways to major sales of city land in the downtown area. "The city will be selling upwards of $50 million in land over the next three years," says deputy commissioner Allan O'Neill. An important aspect of the city's property sales program in the downtown is to use the city's holding as a catalyst to development and to help complete private assemblies, thereby ensuring more comprehensive developments. The department is also involved in purchasing land on behalf of the city for such projects as park expansion, fire halls, and roads, as well as in the leasing of various premises on behalf of the city for use by other departments.

The department has successfully overseen the development of the City Centre project, whereby a city land resource was converted to a $20-million Central Library and a 1.2-million-square-foot office/retail/hotel complex was developed by the private sector on city-owned lands adjacent to city hall. The department is currently directing the expansion of city hall for a new political wing and is overseeing the development of Mel Lastman Square, a large civic open-space area in front of City Hall. "The North York Performing Arts Centre, which will consist of a 1,500-seat theatre and a 400-seat auditorium is about to move ahead," says director of civic projects, Glenn Garwood, "and the theatre should be well along the way to completion within three years."

North York's diverse and growing economy is a tribute to the many individual successes that collectively tell the story of the overall growth of the city.

COLE, SHERMAN & ASSOCIATES LTD.

The challenge of facilitating rapid yet smooth urban growth is a difficult one, but it is being met head-on and with enthusiasm by the engineers and architects of Cole, Sherman & Associates Ltd.

Since its founding in 1954 Cole, Sherman has developed the capacity to offer its clients comprehensive, one-stop shopping, providing the engineering, architectural, socio-economic, and environmental expertise necessary to take most projects from start to finish. This multidisciplined approach is applied to a wide range of assignments, particularly in the transportation and building areas.

The company's involvement in transportation is extensive. Locally Cole, Sherman was responsible for the design of Highway 404 from Highway 401 to Steeles Avenue, Sheppard Avenue from Bayview to Victoria Park, York Mills Road from Leslie Street to beyond the Don River, and Don Mills Road from York Mills to Sheppard. In 1985 the company carried out a location study for the Ontario government to determine the preferred route of an east-west rapid transit system through the city of North York north of Highway 401.

Another major transportation project is the maintenance program for VIA Rail and its $300 million worth of facilities. This job illustrates well the firm's commitment to the "soft end" of engineering and transportation planning—policy and planning programs, sophisticated modelling, demand forecasting, environmental assessments, and other aspects that complement "hard" engineering.

Other Cole, Sherman transporta-

Cole, Sherman & Associates Ltd. is extensively involved in transportation projects throughout the surrounding area such as the design of this segment of Highway 404 from Highway 401 to Steeles Avenue.

tion projects include engineering design for the TTC subway stations at Woodbine, Coxwell, Royal York, and Dupont; maintenance centres for both GO Transit and VIA Rail in Etobicoke; and many installations for CP Rail.

In the land development field, the firm has played a major role in developing several thousand acres of residential and industrial subdivisions, including more than 100 acres of the prestigious Bridle Trail in Unionville and, in a joint venture with Proctor and Redfern, the extensive Malvern development in Scarborough that will eventually house 47,000 people in 11,000 units.

Other Cole, Sherman projects include the engineering design of the University of Toronto's Scarborough Cam-

The firm provided the engineering design for the Scarborough campus at the University of Toronto.

pus, the Hyundai plant in Newmarket, and the design of two major postal plants, including the South Central Toronto Plant for which the firm received the Consulting Engineers Award of Excellence.

Cole, Sherman is also staying abreast of the industry's latest technology with extensive use of microprocessors and computer-aided design and drafting (CADD). In-house development of software programs, written specifically for clients' needs, has become an expanding part of the business. This technology is not only being applied to local operations of the company but also to a wide range of international planning and design projects in the United States and South America.

Cole, Sherman & Associates Ltd. is a Canadian company, wholly owned by its principals and associates. Led by president Ronald Cole and executive vice-presidents Jack Sherman and Derek Wicks, the firm now employs 130 people, most of them working out of its office at the corner of Highway 404 and Sheppard Avenue East in North York.

RYBKA, SMITH AND GINSLER LIMITED

Rybka, Smith and Ginsler Limited, consulting mechanical and electrical engineers, may have called the North York area home for more than 50 years, but its reputation for expertise, innovation, and reliability is remarkably international, with customers hailing from as far away as Guyana, London, Paris, Rome, and Singapore. The firm's abilities have not gone unnoticed at home either, having played an important role in much of the growth of southern Ontario. Among its projects is the spectacular $250-million City Centre development in North York's burgeoning downtown core.

One of the oldest consulting firms in Canada, the company was originally formed in 1935 by Dr. Karel Rybka and Odric Smith, who soon garnered a reputation for engineering efficiency and economic design. This kind of stability means some customers have relied on the firm for decades, such as the Ottawa Civic Hospital, which has enlisted Rybka, Smith and Ginsler for all its mechanical and electrical improvements for more than 20 years, covering some 15 projects and $70 million in expenditures.

By 1978 the firm's international market, particularly in the United Kingdom, had grown to such an extent that a new office was opened in London to accommodate the United Kingdom and European business. Since then RSG has provided services on more than 100 projects in the London area, including Cutlers Gardens, an 800,000-square-foot office development, and The Gloucester, a 600-room luxury hotel. Still, despite the global growth of RSG, its headquarters and 80 percent of its staff members remain in North York, where all the major design work is done.

Diversification and adaptability are particularly strong suits of RSG. Projects include offices, hotels, hospitals, senior citizen homes, convention centres,

The North York City Centre Development is an example of the types of projects with which RSG is involved. It houses the city's central library, a 260-room hotel, four office buildings, 230,000 square feet of retail space, and underground parking for 1,650 cars. In the foreground is the construction site of another RSG project, The Mel Lastman Square, the city's civic square in front of the North York City Hall. The square will have an ice-skating rink, wedding pavilion, rose garden, reflecting pools, decorative fountains and waterfalls, and an amphitheatre. It is scheduled for completion in late 1988. Courtesy, Toronto Photogroup Limited

This office building, the Westminister Tower, beside the Thames River in London, England, is another example of RSG's well-recognized expertise in the design of mechanical and electrical building systems.

schools, industrial plants, apartment buildings, recreation centres, museums and art galleries, shopping malls, churches, theatres, and printing plants. Services include engineering surveys, economic appraisals, project management, analyses of facilities, conceptual design analyses, contract inspections, preparation of complete working drawings and specifications, evaluation of contract tenders, and staff training in maintenance. These services can be applied to almost all technologies, including heating, ventilation, air conditioning, lighting and power, fire alarms, plumbing, sewage and drainage, communications, television reception, emergency power, computer services, audio systems, pollution control, pneumatic facilities, and X-ray units.

With such an ambitious range of services and expertise, it is obvious RSG must have a commitment to staying abreast of, and indeed playing a part in, the rapid growth of technology. This commitment has meant the adoption of computer-aided design that allows draftsmen and designers to make their plans much more quickly, in more detail, and without much of their traditional equipment. Computer-aided design is still in its formative stage, but RSG recognizes that it will someday become an industry standard

and thus is getting a head start on this technology.

RSG's list of clients over the years reads like a who's who of industrial, commercial, and institutional heavyweights in the North York area. A sampling includes the Toronto Stock Exchange, Thomson Newspapers, Stelco, Esso, Colgate-Palmolive, the University of Toronto, Maple Leaf Gardens, Holiday Inn, and Global TV. Hospital work has become almost an RSG specialty with a customer list that includes Mount Sinai, Riverdale, Queen Elizabeth, Sick Children's, and North York General. But these glittering lists do not mean RSG restricts its services to large organizations. The firm has also done work for the Boys and Girls Library and the Boy Scouts headquarters.

As part of its basic philosophy of efficiency, RSG has always been particularly concerned with energy conservation. This was true even in the days of inexpensive fuel and is particularly so today after seeing how erratic energy prices can be. To meet the challenge of inevitably rising energy costs, RSG uses advanced and developing technology to reevaluate existing building plant operation and design with a view to modifying equipment operating sequences, controls, and, in many cases, design concepts to achieve substantial operating

and energy savings. A recent example is the North York Hydro office building where, in conjunction with Hydro engineers and operators, energy savings of 40 percent annually were achieved.

RSG has also realized that energy-conserving measures need not automatically imply higher initial capital costs, and in most cases can be provided for in a normal budget if innovative mechanical and electrical designs are used. For example, at the Datacrown Computer Building heat from compression energy generated year round within packaged air conditioning unit compressors in computer spaces is reclaimed during the winter by a glycol runaround piping system that heats the remainder of the building without any additional heating equipment.

With such stability, innovation, and efficiency, it is not surprising that Rybka, Smith & Ginsler Limited is now expanding along with much of North York. Right now the firm is enlarging its North York offices to 15,000 square feet from 8,000 square feet.

DELCAN CORPORATION

Without roads, railways, airports, public transportation, water supply, and other essential services, no community can reach its full potential. Fortunately, Canada in general, and southern Ontario in particular, have been blessed with a carefully planned, dependable, and well-maintained infrastructure, due in large part to the expertise of Delcan, one of the country's foremost providers of engineering and planning services.

Delcan's history began in the late 1940s when De Leuw Cather & Company, an American firm, was retained by the Toronto Transit Commission (TTC) as general consultant on Canada's first rapid transit system, the Yonge Street subway line. In 1953, as work proceeded on this historic project, De Leuw Cather, Canada Ltd. (Delcan), was formed and assumed responsibility for the completion of the subway line.

During the 1950s and 1960s Delcan expanded its expertise to cover all the transportation disciplines. It introduced into Canada modern highway design techniques. Its staff was intimately involved in the planning, design, and implementation of Highway 401 through Metro Toronto and North York, a highway facility unique not only in North America, but also the world. Delcan also carried out all of the

CADD greatly enhances Delcan's ability to deal with the increasingly complex projects in today's environment.

North York's Highway 400/401 is just one of the many highway designs carried out by Delcan's staff.

initial studies that led to the establishment of the GO Transit commuter rail network. Delcan has been involved in every major transit project in Canada.

During those same decades Delcan expanded throughout Canada, opening offices in Ottawa, London, St. John's, Montreal, Niagara Falls, Thunder Bay, Winnipeg, Regina, Saskatoon, Edmonton, Calgary, and Vancouver. Many of these offices were opened upon invitation of the municipality, a compliment to the skills that the company exhibited. In the late 1960s the firm made its first overseas expansion and has had a significant international presence ever since. The organization's Canadian presence was further enhanced in 1979, when it acquired Willis Cunliffe Tait Ltd. of British Columbia, giving Delcan representation in more Canadian communities than any other consulting firm. That same year the corporation shortened its name to Delcan.

Delcan's geographic growth has been accompanied by discipline expansion as well. The company now has a strong municipal engineering arm that has carried out many major tunnel projects. The firm has developed the soft

sciences and has strong planning, economics, and environmental divisions. Delcan also has a certified architectural practice and has many successful building projects to its credit. More recently, the company has become heavily involved in infrastructure maintenance management, rehabilitation, and preservation. Delcan's systems engineering group has developed a strong reputation in the application of new technology.

The 1980s has seen the firm continue to forge ahead, expanding its presence into the United States, Asia, the Caribbean, South America, and Africa, enhancing Canada's reputation as an exporter of expertise. Delcan's foreign operations, conducted through Delcan International Corporation, are a growing part of the company's overall mandate. Delcan's president and chief executive officer, J.M. Main, lists as one of the company's overseas accomplishments its involvement in the planning and building of the first airport in Lesotho, a small nation in southern Africa. He is also pleased about the Caribbean airport's project in which Delcan is carrying out the rehabilitation and upgrading of 22 airports in the Caribbean.

Continuing its leadership in the transportation field is an important Delcan goal. Toward this end the company has carried out most of the computerized traffic signal work in Canada. As well, the firm was recently retained on a five-year contract to develop a freeway traffic management system for Highway 401—the same facility it helped plan and design 25 years ago. The company is also doing preliminary work on the proposed Sheppard Avenue subway line through North York. While this high-technology work may require a different breed of people than Delcan has used in the past—such as communications experts, software specialists, systems engineers, and experts in artificial intelligence—they have the same commitment to excellence.

In order to best facilitate its increasingly complex operations, Delcan has acquired and created several subsidiaries. In 1985 the firm entered the U.S. market by setting up Infrastructure Management Services (IMS), which specializes in pavement evaluation and management using laser equipment and computers. In 1986 Delcan acquired Canadian Management Systems Corporation (CMSC), which had pioneered the development of management control sytems for transportation ministries and agencies. Also that year it

formed Infrastructure Design Associates (IDA) to operate in the U.S. highway planning and design field. In 1987 two more subsidiaries were formed—Marketing Information Services of America (MISA), to service the outdoor advertising industry, and National Engineering Technology Corporation (NET), to market Delcan's systems engineering, transit, and transportation skills in the United States.

Delcan has played a major role in the development of Toronto's transit system—one of the best in the world.

The staff of Delcan's head office, located in North York for more than a quarter-century, congratulates the city on "realizing its dream."

The corporate structure and ownership of Delcan today reflects the best ideals of Canadian federalism, providing ownership and equality of both opportunity and reward to all employees, no matter where they are located. All offices are operated by resident personnel who hire and train staff, design and direct projects, and expend funds locally. Branch managers have the authority to manage their branches as independent small businesses. The company is owned 100 percent by its employees, with about one-third of the 600 employees holding shares. This system of incentive and reward has proved quite successful; revenues in 1987 reached $30 million.

Delcan has been a fixture in the Don Mills area of North York since 1968. Originally a tenant, the company now owns its 40,000-square-foot building on Wynford Drive. The building houses the firm's overall corporate affairs, the head office of Delcan International Corporation, Delcan's Toronto branch, and its Canadian Management Control Systems subsidiary.

THE MANUFACTURERS LIFE INSURANCE COMPANY

The Manufacturers Life Insurance Company began more than 100 years ago with Canada's first prime minister, Sir John A. MacDonald, as its first president. Today it is a major international financial institution.

The Manufacturers was incorporated by a Special Act of Parliament in 1887 and, as the *Toronto World* newspaper noted at the time, "no company ever came before the public under more favorable conditions." Its founders were distinguished Canadians, particularly its president, Sir John A. Macdonald; the lieutenant-governor of Ontario, Sir Alexander Campbell; and banker and distiller George Gooderham. Another important figure in the creation of the company was J.B. Carlile, an experienced and energetic insurance man who recruited many of these first participants and laid the groundwork for the firm's initial operations.

But the story of The Manufacturers certainly does not end with references

Thomas A. Di Giacomo, president and chief executive officer.

to its illustrious past. In its century thousands of men and women have endeavored to develop new profitable and responsible avenues for the firm's expansion while maintaining its reputation for service and stability, putting The Manufacturers among the top 15 life insurance companies in North America with $21.7 billion in assets. Headquartered on Bloor Street East in Toronto, the company is truly international, with sales and service offices located in major cities in Canada, the United States, the United Kingdom, Pacific Asia, and the Caribbean.

The Manufacturers designs, distributes, and administers products and services to meet the insurance, pension, and financial needs of individuals, families, and businesses. The firm's extensive investment portfolio includes

The Manufacturers Life Insurance Company headquarters is in the North Tower on Bloor Street East, Toronto.

stocks, bonds, mortgages, and real estate—all actively managed for the best relative values consistant with safety.

Under the guidance of chairman E.S. Jackson and president and chief executive officer T.A. Di Giacomo, The Manufacturers is responding to heavy competition in the insurance industry and new financial regulation by establishing a corporate position of flexibility and innovation that will allow it to react quickly to the opportunities inherent in change. One such opportunity is the current profitability of real estate development, to which The Manufacturers has responded by increasing its real estate portfolio to 20 million square feet of office, industrial, and residential space, worth more than $1.64 billion. The firm is also capitalizing on the opening of Asian markets by enhancing its presence in Hong Kong, Indonesia, Singapore, and the Philippines. Another increased area of activity is reinsurance.

As an insurance company The Manufacturers has a practical as well as moral interest in the well-being of society; it doubled its donations budget between 1985 and 1987. The firm supports a wide range of educational, health and welfare, and cultural services such as the United Way, the Red Cross, the Boston Symphony Orchestra, the Old Globe theatre in San Diego, CentreStage Company in Toronto, the McMichael Gallery in Kleinburg, and in excess of 175 educational institutions and 200 hospitals worldwide.

MANUFACTURERS REAL ESTATE

Manufacturers Real Estate, a division of The Manufacturers Life Insurance Company, approaches land development in the fullest sense, directly developing and managing its properties to ensure continuous service, stability, and sensitivity to tenants.

Manufacturers Real Estate first ventured into real estate in the 1950s with the acquisition and leasing of small commercial and industrial properties. In the 1960s, in response to high property costs, the company decided to invest through direct development, a strategy that has propelled Manufacturers Real Estate to its present status as the largest property owner in the Canadian life insurance industry and a major international owner, developer, and manager of income-producing commercial, industrial, and retail space. Operating out of 16 key metropolitan regions throughout North America, its current portfolio includes about 15.9 million square feet of office-industrial space, 4 million square feet of retail space, and 4,700 residential units, with a total value of more than $1.64 billion.

Manufacturers Real Estate uses careful market analysis, expert planning, and superior architectural design to ensure each project will satisfy the local business tenants' needs. Development experts oversee every aspect of construction, from ground breaking to the installation of lobby signage. Manufacturers' seasoned real estate investment group continually monitors its portfolio and relevant economic conditions in order to anticipate ideal opportunities as they emerge. Management involves tenant-sensitive property managers to maintain high property services

Lansing Square, Phase I and II.

and values, technical specialists to provide energy management systems, and a support staff of administration and accounting to control the continuous flow of income and operating revenues, regulatory and corporate reports, and property analysis.

When developing properties the firm strives for strategic location, efficiency, and architectural excellence. These qualities are reflected by such outstanding buildings as the ManuLife Centre in Toronto, ManuLife Place in Edmonton, Metrotown Centre in Vancouver, Cabot Place in Newfoundland, ManuLife Plaza in Los Angeles, Schaumburg Corporate Centre in Chicago, and 1850 M Street in Washington, D.C.

One of Manufacturers Real Estate's latest achievements is the comple-

Lansing Square, Phase III.

tion of Lansing Square Phase III, a 150,000-square-foot office building in North York that complements the existing 260,000 square feet of phases I and II that were built in the 1970s. Lansing Square Phase III enjoys the superb suburban location of Victoria Park Avenue and Sheppard Avenue, accessible from Sheppard, Victoria Park, the Don Valley Parkway, and Highway 401. Public transportation, already excellent along Sheppard, will be greatly enhanced with the planned subway extension along Sheppard East. The location also offers first-class accommodations at the Prince Hotel and Ramada Renaissance.

The building itself is on the leading edge of office design and technology, clad in blue reflective glass with interior and exterior finishes of natural stone and marble. Each office floor, averaging 21,000 feet, is furnished with venetian blinds and carpeted throughout, while the eight-foot six-inch ceilings feature a flat suspension ceiling system incorporating sprinklers, air conditioning, and flexible position lighting. Other important touches include a fully equipped fitness centre, restaurant, and conference facility. Integrity and commitment to quality have made Manufacturers Real Estate host to many of North America's top companies.

VALCOUSTICS CANADA LTD.

Valcoustics Canada Ltd. is a relatively small, specialized engineering firm; but companies from across the country as well as all levels of government are continually seeking its advice and services.

Valcoustics specializes in acoustics, working in the areas of architectural acoustics, noise and vibration measurement and control, environmental impact assessment and mitigation, and sound amplification, reproduction, and masking systems.

The engineering practice was founded in the early 1950s by the late University of Toronto professor V.L. Henderson, who discovered that his advice on acoustics was in such demand from his former architecture students that a profitable business could be run by dispensing it. Professor Henderson passed away in 1986, and the company is now operated by one of his former students, Alfred Lightstone, who has a Ph.D. in biomedical electronics and engineering, and by his wife, Elaine Lightstone, a former mathematics and science teacher.

Acoustics is an ancient science, but one that is increasingly in demand in a world continually sprouting more buildings, machines, and people. Thus, the role of the acoustical engineer is an interdisciplinary one, combining knowledge about modern science, in-

dustry, architecture, building science, medicine, and the entertainment industry in order to keep sound under control. Such control can mean reduction or elimination of noise sources, confinement of noise to prescribed places, or the development of effective and equitable laws to regulate the use of noisy devices. As well, it can mean enhancing sound, such as in radio, television, and recording studios, or giving it clarity for a theatre audience. In addition, the acoustical engineer may be called upon for expert testimony in noise-related disputes.

The wide-ranging need for acoustical expertise is reflected by a list of some of Valcoustics' clients. The results of its work can be seen (or rather, heard), at the Shaw Festival Theatre in Niagara Falls, the St. Lawrence Centre, the CFTO and Global television studios, numerous radio stations across Canada, Science North in Sudbury, the National Gallery and the National Museum of Civilization in Ottawa, the Ontario Legislature, the Citadel Theatre in Edmonton, and civic centres in Nepean, Scarborough, Sudbury, and elsewhere. Specialty theatre projects include such Imax theatres as Cinesphere

The late Professor George Henderson, founder of Valcoustics Canada Ltd.

at Ontario Place, Los Angeles, Kennedy Space Center in Florida, New York City, New Orleans (Expo 84), Winnipeg, Edmonton, and Vancouver (Expo '86). Other Expo '86 projects were the Teleglobe Theatre and the Ontario Pavilion.

Many prominent corporations such as Imperial Oil, IBM, Sun Life, Westinghouse, and the major banks have availed themselves of the firm's expertise in acoustics for the design of executive offices.

In the field of environmental acoustics, the company is continually involved in residential, commercial, and industrial development projects for a wide variety of developers, builders, and industries.

In North York, Valcoustics has been consulted by the designers and builders of the North York Civic Centre, Northtown Shopping Centre, the Xerox building, the Sheppard Centre, the Madison Centre, York Mills Place, Minkler Auditorium at Seneca College, the Baycrest Home for the Aged, and the Leah Posluns Theatre at the Koffler Centre for the Arts.

One of the company's most interesting challenges is the Skydome project, Toronto's new domed stadium with the openable roof.

Valcoustics Canada Ltd. welcomes the opportunity to meet new and unique challenges with its dedicated and enthusiastic staff.

Dr. Alfred Lightstone with some of the firm's computerized acoustical analysis systems.

ADAMSON ASSOCIATES

Much of the pride a city takes in itself is derived from its urban landscape—innovative mergings of glass, steel, stone, and technology acting as symbols of our culture, prosperity, and organizational prowess. In cities across Canada and around the world, much of that pride can be directly linked to the effort and inspiration of the architectural planning firm of Adamson Associates.

From a modest suite of rooms tucked away on Gloucester Street in downtown Toronto, Adamson Associates plans and designs some of the most important and technically demanding building developments being constructed today, be they in Toronto, New York, or London. The company's principals—Robert Grossmann, James Bagby, David Cody, John Bonnick, Charles Comartin, and Gar MacInnis—along with its 75 employees, carry on

a tradition of excellence that stretches back nearly 55 years.

With Adamson Associates continually at the forefront of major development, it is no surprise it is playing a major role in the building boom now occuring in North York. Just a sampling of the firm's recent projects includes the North York City Hall, North American Life Centre, *Place Nouveau*, City Centre, Kane Funeral Home, Yonge and Norton Centre, Ivan M. Nelson Fire Station No. 1, and the new corporate head office towers of Petro Canada, Procter & Gamble, and Coscan Office Tower on 100 Sheppard Avenue East.

On the international front, Adamson Associates is particularly excited about its involvement as co-

North American Life Centre—a total block development.

ordinating architect for the World Financial Centre in New York City and Canary Wharf in London, both world-class developments by Olympia & York.

Adamson Associates prides itself on its ability to respond to every client need, from such delicate aspects as site selection, economic feasibility, marketing, and image to the traditional phases of design through completion. By identifying the internal and external forces that will shape a building's form, Adamson allows the client to evaluate various design approaches in drawing and model form in order to make the appropriate response to those forces.

The firm also keeps a keen eye on budgeting. Cost benefit studies of design alternatives and value-engineering studies are provided in order to ensure the building can in fact be built, and done so within the budget.

As an architect and planner, Adamson Associates sees its role as a co-ordinator of the input provided by its clients. This co-ordination requires the ability to evaluate, recommend, and implement the integration of the highly complex interrelationship involved in creating a modern building.

With more than a half-century of experience, dozens of awards, and hundreds of satisfied customers, Adamson Associates has truly earned its reputation as a facilitator of flexible, cost-effective, and aesthetic business environments of the highest-possible quality.

North American Life Centre's Interior Atrium Court.

CHAPTER 10

Building Greater North York

From concept to completion, North York's building and energy industries shape tomorrow's skyline and keep water and power circulating inside and outside the area.

North York Hydro Commission, 212-213

Oakwood Lumber and Millwork Co. Limited, 214-216

First Professional Management Inc., 228-229

The Glen Group, 230-231

NORTH YORK HYDRO COMMISSION

Electricity is so basic to our lifestyle, available at the flip of a switch, we tend to forget that behind that switch there must be a large, sophisticated, and efficient organization such as North York Hydro.

When the fledgling council of the Township of North York approved formation of a hydro commission in 1923, electricity was still a relative newcomer to the energy scene. The population of 6,300 still lived mostly in a horse-and-buggy world, with many homes and farms relying on kerosene lamps, coal heaters, and wood-burning stoves. Those few families who could boast of electric service were supplied power by the Toronto & York Metropolitan Railway, an electrical radial line running along Yonge Street from Toronto to Lake Simcoe.

The first hydro commissioners, anticipating correctly that this area was destined for rapid growth, began a major undertaking to develop an electrical distribution network for the people of North York. In those early days telephone service cost $2.40 per month, steak sold for 28 cents a pound, and monthly rent averaged $27. Electricity was sold to North Yorkers during the

first year of operation at 5 cents per kilowatt hour for the first 60 hours and 2 cents for each additional kilowatt hour.

Over the years NYH has grown quickly to keep up with expansion as farmers' fields have changed into subdivisions and small shops into glittering skyscrapers. In the early 1920s North York had only 13 streetlights; today there are more than 31,000. The handful of staff serving 655 customers now number 430 serving more than 142,000 consumers. NYH's horse-drawn wagon and manual work methods have given way to a fleet of modern vehicles and state-of-the-art technology. North York's population of 563,000 consumes more than 4 billion kilowatt hours per year, ranking North York Hydro as the third-largest electric utility in Ontario.

As the needs and shape of the community grew, so did North York Hydro. The utility's first building, on the northeast corner of Yonge Street and Empress Avenue, was completed in 1925 at a cost of $3,650. Four years later construction began on a new $20,000 office at 5151 Yonge Street, where space was shared with the police department. Growing along with the community, NYH had, by 1956, moved its headquarters into the old Municipal Building and had established an office on Goddard Street to serve the central area. Two other work centres were then established to service the elec-

North York Hydro's innovative headquarters at 5800 Yonge Street continues to reflect a progressive utility that is keeping pace with the city's rapid development.

trical needs of the eastern and western districts. By 1965 the commission had moved into a new $1.3-million all-electric building at 5800 Yonge Street just north of Finch Avenue, and in 1986 a $2.9-million renovation project provided 15,000 square feet of additional office space and an innovative design that is convenient for all visitors.

Like the more than 300 other municipal utilities in Ontario, NYH is a publicly owned, non-profit corporation that exists to provide an essential service at the lowest feasible cost while maintaining the highest standards of safety and reliability. A financially self-sustaining corporation, it operates solely on its own revenues and is debt free. NYH buys its electricity from Ontario Hydro, which generates and sells it at cost. NYH is then responsible for building and maintaining the electrical system to deliver that power to consumers within the boundaries of North York.

As a public utility, NYH is owned by the customers it serves. And those customers choose officials to oversee their utility's operation. The North York Hydro Commission consists of three members chosen by the public during municipal elections. Two of

Hydro crews build and maintain a complex distribution system of overhead and underground circuitry to meet the changing electrical demands of North York consumers.

Technical specialists ensure that North York residents, businesses, and industries have the power they need—when they need it.

them run directly for the position of hydro commissioner, while the mayor automatically fills the third position. The commissioners, who hold office for a three-year term, supervise the retail sale of electricity within the city. At public meetings, they establish policies, set local electricity rates, monitor finances, approve spending, and guide the administrative staff in handling the system's day-to-day activities. They also act as public spokespeople on all matters affecting the utility.

It is an excellent system for public accountability. While NYH is a natural monopoly, the people it serves have direct input into how the utility is run and by whom. This system gives it special characteristics that benefit North Yorkers, such as responsiveness, lower rates, and services uniquely tailored to the community.

Electrical safety classes, for instance, are conducted in North York schools as part of the utility's community awareness program. Hydro crews are the eyes and ears of North York Hydro under a crime prevention and community assistance program called Hydro On Watch. Community enrichment is also reflected by the utility's sponsorship of a wide range of artworks for public display in its corporate headquarters. All the works—65 to date—are by contemporary Canadian artists with special emphasis placed on works by artists living and

working in North York.

North York Hydro's continuous commitment to improving customer service manifests itself in many ways. It recently tested a program in which hydro bills could be paid at 10 North York Public Library branches, giving customers a whole new dimension of convenience. As well, NYH instituted the first after-hours billing and information service for utility customers in Ontario. Seniors can now have their billing adjusted to coincide with the arrival of pension cheques, and hearing- or

speech-impaired residents can contact Hydro using a special device that converts voice messages into a printed form. All customers receive, along with their hydro bills, a newsletter, called *Hydrolines*, that provides information about everything from water heating and appliance use to billing changes and tips on avoiding fusebox problems. A popular feature of each newsletter is the section that provides a direct response to customers who voice concerns or ask questions about their utility.

North York Hydro also faces the challenge of facilitating the tremendous construction boom occurring along the North Yonge corridor. In 1986 alone, the Madison Centre, Procter & Gamble, the North York Civic Centre library and office tower, the York Mills Centre, and phase one of the Yonge Corporate Centre were all brought into full electric service. Such high-density development in downtown North York has highlighted the co-ordination between utilities, developers, and the municipality.

This utility continues to be an intricate part of the city's growth and development. There is definitely a certain electricity between the North York Hydro Commission and its customers.

The Customer Information Centre responds to calls about everything from billing inquiries and water heater service to streetlight problems and no-power calls.

OAKWOOD LUMBER AND MILLWORK CO. LIMITED

It's not easy to put a label on just what kind of business Oakwood Lumber and Millwork Co. Ltd. is. On one hand it's a factory, producing miles of wood mouldings and other accessories for builders and contractors. On the other hand it's also a retail outlet with many attractive showrooms displaying a wide variety of mouldings, doors, locks, and other home improvement products for the individual home-owner. What is for certain, though, is that the system works and has done so very successfully for decades.

Oakwood Lumber and Millwork has a long, distinguished, and interesting history, beginning in 1953 when three Italian immigrants, brothers Sam and James Corvese along with friend Carmen Tanzola, purchased a small lumber mill on Croham Road in the Eglinton Avenue West and Caledonia Road area. The newly purchased mill was meant to produce mouldings for the wood fireplace frames being manufactured by the three businessmen's other company, Canadian Mantel and Stone Co., also located on Croham.

At the time the mill consisted of a small wood-frame office and covered mill, and business was modest to say the least. It was also an entirely new kind of venture for the new owners, but

Vincent Corvese, current president.

they immediately set about tearing down the old structure and building a new large block factory and office. New, modern equipment was purchased, and production at the mill grew rapidly, along with its business.

Brothers Sam and Jim Corvese and friend Carmen Tanzola began Oakwood Lumber and Millwork Co. to produce mouldings for wood fireplace frames manufactured at their Canadian Mantel & Stone Co.

Things were going smoothly at the firm until 1963, when disaster struck. Careless smoking started a fire that raged for three days and could be seen throughout the city, completely destroying the premises. Undaunted, the owners took stock of their situation and thought about how best to rebound from this setback. They decided that since the Croham area was now largely residential, and because noise, smoke, and large trucks had become a community concern, a new location was needed. It was decided that the Downsview area of North York was ideal because land there was relatively inexpensive, zoning was industrial, and it offered accessibility to major transportation routes such as Highway 401 via arterial roads such as Keele Street. As well, rebuilding would allow Oakwood Lumber and Millwork and Cana-

and Stone and allowing Oakwood Lumber and Millwork to occupy the entire original factory.

In 1983 James Corvese passed away after nearly 50 years as a leading Italian-Canadian businessman in the area.

Through hard work, innovation, business acumen, and aided by the tremendous building boom experienced in North York in recent years, Oakwood Lumber and Millwork has developed into one of the largest producers of wood mouldings in Canada, producing more than one million feet of it a month. The many styles and woods in which the mouldings are available are attractively displayed, and customers are even encouraged to take a piece home to "see what they can do with it," says Vince Corvese.

The factory area where the mouldings are produced is a model of efficiency with wood waste being recycled to heat the entire building and excess sawdust sold to farmers as a mulch for their crops. As well, a huge 'cyclone' has been installed on the roof that removes 99 percent of all air pollutants.

dian Mantel and Stone to be combined under one roof, with many obvious advantages. Thus, within a year of the fire, the company reemerged on a four-acre site at 45 Le Page Court in the Keele and Finch Avenue area, housed in a modern, 50,000-square-foot building erected by Tancor Investments Ltd. and leased in equal portions to both companies.

At the time the firm stood alone, surrounded by fields in a still undeveloped area. But the additional space allowed Oakwood Lumber and Millwork to produce and stock new styles of mouldings using a variety of woods such as oak, pine, mahogany, and walnut. In a few years the vacant fields surrounding the factory had filled up with other businesses, and Oakwood Lumber and Millwork had become one of the largest producers of mouldings in Ontario.

In 1965, after a relationship of 30 years, the partners of this successful operation amicably terminated their long partnership. James Corvese retired, Sam Corvese assumed full control and ownership of Oakwood Lumber and Millwork, and Carmen Tanzola assumed control and ownership of Canadian Mantel and Stone. In December 1967 Sam Corvese passed away. Shortly afterward, Vince Corvese, son

Oakwood Lumber and Millwork Co. is located in this 50,000-square-foot building at 45 Le Page.

of James and nephew of Sam, took control of the company and has been at the helm ever since.

In 1973 an additional 25,000-square-foot factory was constructed behind the Le Page premises, becoming the new location for Canadian Mantel

The company's four-acre site provides adequate room for stocking a wide variety of lumber.

Moulding stock is kept neatly stacked outside, carefully separated so that air can flow between the strips to keep them dry, and the entire area is enclosed by an attractive, eight-foot wooden fence.

But Oakwood Lumber and Millwork has expanded its product line to include much more than mouldings. High-quality locks, including the finest European designs, are now a company specialty. Wood doors are also available in a myriad of designs and woods, including The Classic, which was designed and patented by Vince Corvese himself and has proved to be a top seller. As well, there are a host of other finishing work items available in almost any quantity. To keep the public aware of this fact, the company has a portable display that it can conveniently transport to trade shows.

Oakwood Lumber and Millwork Co. Ltd. has also extended care and imagination to its shipping department, which is conveniently located adjacent to the main building. Each morning empty delivery containers are replaced with preloaded containers, thus avoiding daily delays in loading trucks.

Vince Corvese and his 65 employees seem destined to continue the growth and careful craftsmanship that the company's founders established 34 years ago. In fact, Vince forsees another expansion soon. "Business keeps growing so fast, we don't know where to put everything," he says.

The business that started just to produce mouldings has diversified but still creates and stocks mouldings to suit any client's needs (above).

This classic door is just one of the many varieties of elegantly grained wood doors stocked by Oakwood Lumber and Millwork Co. (below).

YORK TRILLIUM DEVELOPMENT CORPORATION

When it comes time for a corporation to relocate, location remains an imperative; to it must be added first-class architecture, top-flight amenities, and a building design flexible enough to adapt to the continuing rush of new business technology. Combining all these elements is what has made York Mills Centre, a product of York Trillium Development Corporation, one of North York's most desirable business addresses.

York Mills Centre is a 541,000-square-foot office and retail complex at the northeast corner of Yonge Street and York Mills, perhaps the most picturesque and strategic intersection in the city. The architecturally stunning building melds perfectly into this unusually pastoral setting—a treed escarpment, winding river, and, not surprisingly, one of the nation's most prestigious residential neighborhoods. A major transportation node directly within the complex includes a subway station, bus stops, and two major private coach lines. Highway 401 and the Don Valley Parkway are but five minutes away, and Pearson International Airport a mere 15-minute drive. In fact, York Mills Centre is so centrally located that virtu-

ally all key Metro Toronto locations are within a 15-minute journey.

York Mills Centre is a building of the highest quality. Materials, fittings, and workmanship create a complex built to last well into the next century, respond easily to technological change, and maximize productivity and operating efficiency. Access flooring in all office areas puts electricity, temperature control, telephone, and other cabling closer to the people who need it, thus also allowing for quick and inexpensive reconfiguration of work stations. Smoke detection, smoke evacuation, and stair pressurization is monitored through a 24-hour central monitoring

system. Security is controlled by a customized card access system.

None of this structural efficiency, of course, precludes style. The building's exterior is mostly a sun-reflective glass skin, while the inside incorporates marble, granite, glass, and stainless steel into the lobbies and common areas that lead to the offices—each of which overlooks a six-storey glass atrium. Upon request the design team will help appoint the individual offices to reflect the corporate personality. A health club, complete with outdoor running track, continues York Mills Centre's commitment to human as well as business and technological needs.

The three phases of the seven-storey complex all have wholly separate street entrances. The 120,000-square-foot retail complex is located on the lower floors, separate from, yet still convenient to, the offices above. The retail outlets are upscale, providing such services as banking, office supplies, medical and dental clinics, fast food, catering, and four-star dining.

The York Trillium Development Corporation has created a business environment of unique design, location, quality, and amenities, a blend that has already attracted such blue-chip tenants as Sunoco/Suncor, Hartford Insurance, Cantel Inc., and Southam Publishing. Without doubt, it tops the list of many other companies ready to move up when the last phase is finished in 1989.

YORK TRILLIUM

CAMROST DEVELOPMENT CORPORATION

Camrost Development Corporation is in the impressive Madison Centre.

CAMROST

BUILDING A WORLD OF DIFFERENCE

During the past decade Camrost Development Corporation has emerged as a major force in the condominium development field, establishing a reputation for conceiving and building a number of prestigious projects.

Camrost's first major venture into commercial real estate resulted in the eye-catching, twin-peak Madison Centre in North York's downtown, a 23-storey office tower that was selected the first winner of North York's Urban Design Award.

The company, which is planning a number of condominium and office tower developments in and around the Toronto area, has achieved prominence with a quiet and low-key approach that nevertheless insists on quality and value in everything it undertakes.

The firm has also established a reputation of timing its projects so that they are always in the forefront of trends and shifts in a changing real estate market. The Madison Centre office tower, for instance, was the first new major office tower in North York to open its doors just at the time the entire North York downtown was exploding with commercial developments.

One of its earlier projects, the three-tower One ParkLane condominiums in downtown Toronto, anticipated the shift toward medium-price condominiums and sold out quickly. The project came on stream just as the condominium market began to boom, and by the time the market receded in 1981, the project was completely sold.

"I felt there was a market for the kind of condominium I wanted to build," recalls David Feldman, president of Camrost. "The industry was then catering to the upper-income buyers and the lower-income buyers.

"It was the wrong way to go in my opinion. I felt there was a market for the middle level, for the sophisticated urbanites. This was a segment that was being neglected."

The parking elevator in Madison Centre.

The lobby of One ParkLane, a three-tower, 346-suite condominium complex in downtown Toronto.

Feldman, who has the uncanny ability to anticipate market trends, was proven to be right. It was this same insight that brought Camrost into North York, where it built the prestigious Manhattan Place condominium that also was an unbridled success.

However, when the condominium market was slow, Feldman bode his time, quietly acquiring suitable parcels of land. His instincts told him in early 1985 that the market was ready for condominium buying again, and this was when the company blossomed forth with a number of successful projects.

Camrost has now established itself as a leader in condominium development, providing innovative and luxurious lifestyle projects in prime locations. Its motto is "Building A World Of Difference," and it achieves this goal by developing and building projects that are distinctive and different from each other, each designed to suit its location and type of market.

While the quality of construction and finishes are always important features, Camrost projects are never cookie-cutter versions of previously built projects. Feldman says the Camrost philosophy is quite simple—acquire only the good sites, build quality design into the structures, provide distinctive and exciting common area finishes, and make sure you offer good value for the dollar.

Before he and his associates formed Camrost, Feldman had worked for seven years at Cadillac Fairview during a period when that company was heavily involved in high-rise residential construction. He says the lessons he learned at Cadillac Fairview have stayed with him. One of them is to always be aware of the long-term image, and not to do anything for a short-term gain that will harm or impair that image. Feldman takes a personal interest in all aspects of every project, paying close attention to what buyers want.

One of the company's most ambitious projects is the World Trade Centre complex in downtown Toronto at the foot of Yonge Street at the waterfront. This is a joint venture with York-Hannover Developments Ltd. The project consists of two condominium towers with roughly 700 condominium suites and three phases of mixed-use office towers with a total of 1.7 million square feet of office and retail space. The Toronto World Trade Centre Office Towers, designed by world renowned Zeidler Roberts Partnership, will be distinctive landmark buildings that will become the new gateway to the Bay Street Financial district.

The firm, which has already been successful on the Etobicoke waterfront with its exciting Marina Del Rey condominium project, is playing a major role in the revitalization and redevelopment of the entire Etobicoke waterfront. "The potential of the Etobicoke waterfront is tremendous," says Feldman. "There's a chance here to create a people-friendly, mixed-use waterfront area that will rival any in Canada. We are planning to play the major role." The redevelopment was announced in July 1988 as "Etobicoke Harbour City."

Camrost was formed several years

Elegant penthouse living (right) in the Residences of World Trade Centre (above).

ago with Feldman and a strong group of associates. The company started as a general contractor and then later moved into condominiums and commercial and retail projects.

So far the company has built some 1,000 senior citizen suites, 2,000 condominium suites, and has current plans to market another 4,250. It is also expanding rapidly into major commercial office towers, and retail development with in excess of 2.5 million square feet of office space under various phases of development valued at more than $3 billion. Also, future projects on the drawing boards represent an additional $2 billion in development.

Here are some of Camrost Development Corporation's better-known projects:

One ParkLane, a three-tower, 346-suite condominium complex in downtown Toronto; Manhattan Place, a 227-unit condominium tower in downtown North York's Yonge and Sheppard area; Village Gate in Lower Forest Hill, a 196-suite, six-storey res-

idential building in Toronto's Lower Forest Hill; Madison Centre, a 23-storey office and retail centre, winner of the 1988 North York Best Urban Design Award, located in downtown North York on Yonge Street north of Sheppard Avenue; Residences of Madison Centre, a 28-storey, 260-unit condominium tower joining Madison Centre; Marina Del Rey I, II, and III, three phases of residential buildings comprised of approximately 820 condominium units and an office/retail building located on Etobicoke's waterfront; Canyon Springs, a 10- storey, 130-suite exclusive residential building located on the Collegeway in Mississauga; Toronto World Trade Centre office towers housing 700 condominium units, located directly south of Toronto World Trade Centre office towers at Yonge Street and Queen's Quay on Toronto's waterfront (a joint venture with York-Hannover Developments Ltd.); Granite Gates, a four-phase, 600-suite condominium complex located next to Canyon Springs, on The Collegeway in Mississauga; Hollywood Plaza, a 300,000-square-foot office tower plus a 300-suite twin-tower condominium high-rise and townhome complex located on Hollywood Avenue and Yonge Street in downtown North York; and Copperfield, a 126-unit town-house project located at King Street and Strachan Avenue, adjacent to the redevelopment lands of Massey-Ferguson in Toronto (a joint venture with Daniels Development Corporation).

The company philosophy of designing innovative and exciting quality environments has been combined with advanced marketing and sales practices to consistently provide outstanding results. Projects are initiated on the basis of Camrost's assessment of a market need and only proceed when it has been determined that a distinctive and innovatively appealing product can be developed that will attract high buyer response. Camrost's hallmark in all undertakings is "innovation and quality."

The Camrost Development Corporation is a wholly owned Canadian com-

Toronto World Trade Center

pany in its second decade of current and committed construction in luxury residential, commercial, and mixed-use projects. As such, Camrost employs a large, fully integrated staff of design, de-

David Feldman, president of Camrost Development Corporation.

velopment, financial, construction, legal, marketing, sales, and property management professionals who control projects from land acquisition through to complete occupancy and ongoing property management.

MARATHON REALTY COMPANY LIMITED

Marathon Realty Company Limited is truly a Canadian corporation. Its roots stretch back some 24 years and today it tackles the task of fitting Canadian businesses with the finest in office, retail, and industrial facilities.

Marathon's corporate history began with the expansion and diversification of Canadian Pacific, one of the nation's great railway builders.

In the late 1950s CP decided to embark on a program to maximize its natural resources, as much of its land holdings had great potential but still required imaginative development. By 1962 Canadian Pacific Investments Limited was formed to take an active interest in the companies involved in developing CP's natural resources. Among these were Canadian Pacific Oil and Gas, Pacific Logging, and Canadian Mining and Smelting Company. Thus, non-transportation interests of CP were brought under the full-time attention of CP Investments.

In 1963, as part of CP's continuing diversification program, Marathon was formed to acquire and develop those CP lands not needed for railway purposes. It was incorporated as a wholly owned subsidiary of CP Investments. Its first purchase was a number of strategic urban sites. In 1967 Marathon completed a number of transactions with CP, acquiring properties and air rights.

Since 1967 Marathon has had a policy of acquiring properties to expand its holdings of income-producing properties or to obtain more land suitable for development. In the early years operations centred mainly in the West. An important step came in 1966, however, when the company assumed responsibility for CP's commercial real estate across Canada, making Marathon a truly national organization.

In 1966 Marathon had assets of approximately $23.6 million, revenues of $4.5 million, net earnings of $600,000, and 40 employees. By the end of 1987 total assets topped $2 billion, revenues were $355.1 million, net income was $34.2 million, and the firm employed more than 700 people. Marathon's current portfolio consists of 47 office buildings, 32 shopping centres, 2.3 million square feet of leasable area in industrial buildings, 1.8 million square feet of aviation-related facilities, and 2 residential buildings containing 424 units.

Marathon Realty Company Limited is a Canadian corporation that develops, owns, and manages income-producing properties across Canada

North York Square, 45/47 Sheppard Avenue East, was purchased by Marathon as part of its $200-million acquisition of Canadian Freehold Properties in 1979.

The lush modern interior of Marathon's Atria North, Phase 1, when developed in 1979 was the first atrium-style office building in Metropolitan Toronto.

and the United States. More specifically, it has recently developed a very keen interest in the City of North York, rightfully seeing it as one of the most active growth areas in the country. That interest has translated into Marathon's holding of more than one million square feet of office space in North York.

One of Marathon's notable North York developments is 1500 Don Mills Road, a 10-storey building wrapped in silver-mirrored, heat-absorbing glass and containing 222,000 square feet of office space. It was completed in 1980 and is situated in the heart of the world-renowned suburban community of

Don Mills. The structure is extremely energy efficient with heat from machines, lights, and people recirculated to heat the building. The location is also outstanding, only a four-minute drive to the Don Valley Parkway and six minutes to Highway 401.

The organization also owns an office building at 90 Sheppard Avenue East, containing 300,000 square feet of space, which is known as CIL House (after its tenant C-I-L Inc.). As well, the firm has North York Square, also situated on strategic Sheppard Avenue, which it obtained in 1979 with the $200-million acquisition of Canadian Freehold Properties. In that same merger Marathon acquired a two-storey, 20,000-square-foot building at 4800 Yonge Street near Sheppard. Since then it has assembled land adjacent to the site and is planning a 23-storey building to provide 400,000 square feet of office space.

Marathon's most stunning contribution to North York's economic future is Atria North, a four-phase office development on Sheppard Avenue just east of the Don Valley Parkway that will set a new standard for future projects in North York. The existing Phase 1 building, completed in 1979, contains 250,000 square feet of office

1500 Don Mills, currently occupied by Rothman's of Pall Mall, was completed by Marathon in 1980 and contains 222,000 square feet of office space wrapped in silver-mirrored, heat-absorbing glass. It is situated in the world-renowned suburban community of Don Mills.

space. The Phase II building, completed in 1987, contains 310,000 square feet of office space and 30,000 square feet of retail space. Ultimately, the site will contain 1.4 million square feet of commercial space and will be the workplace for 7,000 people. Features of Atria North include plans for a landscaped promenade lined with pine, ash, linden, juniper, and honeysuckle trees; an 80-foot-long reflecting pool and classical fountain; a full-service health club; an outdoor running track; a skating rink; 3,400 outdoor and underground parking spaces; computer-controlled heating and air conditioning; high-speed elevators; total accessibility for the handicapped; and an electronic air-filtration system that will provide air three times purer than most offices. All this is encased in a riveting architectural design of solar-glazed blue and green glass. The location is outstanding as well, with easy access to Highway 401, the Don Valley Parkway, and Pearson International Airport. The proposed Sheppard Avenue subway line will reach directly into the site by 1995.

Marathon Realty Company Limited is obviously continuing the tradition of its parent company of forging boldly into the future, confident in its ability to meet the challenges ahead. This kind of stability and commitment bodes well for the future of North York.

Atria North, Phase 2 and 3, Marathon Realty Company Limited's spectacular twin-tower office project on Sheppard Avenue near the Don Valley Parkway, will contain 700,000 square feet of working environment and be the workplace for 3,250 people.

MENKES DEVELOPMENTS INC.

It does not take unusual perception to realize that there is presently a development explosion occuring in southern Ontario—with office, retail, residential, and industrial projects springing up across the region, and particularly in North York. However, such growth is not merely the result of rampant demand running headlong into supply. It takes, among other things, a sensitivity on the part of developers to the precise needs and level of quality demanded by an increasingly sophisticated business and residential market. In short, it takes companies such as Menkes Developments Inc.

Menkes Developments has been in the construction and development industry in the North York area for more than 30 years. Founded in 1956 as a family-owned and -operated firm, it began its growth cycle in the single-family housing industry and has since expanded its horizons to include industrial and office buildings, high-rise residential condominiums, and land development. Today the company owns and operates more than 6 million square feet of office, commercial, and industrial space with continuing annual development from 500,000 to one million square feet. As well, Menkes is fully integrated into the real estate industry, developing and servicing raw land with its own construction, leasing,

and property management divisions.

A building is not a success until its occupants are satisfied. Through imagination, foresight, and the ability to anticipate its clients' needs, Menkes has accumulated an impressive list of owners and tenants.

The organization currently has eight office buildings containing in excess of 1.2 million square feet of space, of which 75 percent is in North York, and another 2 million square feet is under development. Office tenants are prestigious firms, including Procter & Gamble, AT&T, and Telemedia.

Industrial buildings have been a specialty of Menkes for more than 20 years, and it currently owns 75 buildings comprising more than 5 million square feet. Annual growth in this segment is approximately 750,000 square feet per year. Tenants number more than 300 in these properties and include IBM, Toshiba, NOMA Industries, Moore Technologies, Bausch & Lomb, Bridgestone Tire, Carleton Cards, and Ivaco.

Land development is also an important aspect of Menkes. The corporation services residential lots and sells them to builders in addition to servicing industrial land for its own building pro-

Place Nouveau

Procter & Gamble Building

gram. It recently finished a 500-acre residential development comprising more than 2,000 homes in the town of Vaughan. A current project in Richmond Hill will produce another 600 single-family homes.

Menkes is successfully satisfying the tremendous demand for high-rise condominium apartment units in the North York area. Over the past 20 years it has built more than 5,000 suites and currently has 12 high-rise condominiums under way that will produce another 2,400 suites.

However, sheer numbers do not fully elaborate the efforts of Menkes Developments, which strives for the very best in architecture and quality. These efforts are perhaps best exemplified by one of its current projects, *Place Nouveau*, a spectacular residential and commercial development that will soon be

AT&T Tower

completed on Yonge Street at Finch Avenue, in the heart of North York's "new downtown." The office portion is comprised of an 18-storey tower containing 275,000 leasable square feet and encased in a reflective solar-glazed curtain wall, promising to be an architectural landmark far into the future.

The design will include many environmental and security features such as manicured landscaped grounds, high-tech central humidification, a centrally computerized electronic system linking all floors for present and future technology, its own retail concourse, and parking for 360 cars. Perhaps most important, the location is at the very hub of York Region's transit system, with tenants and employees having access to the Toronto subway station, buses, and North York's GO bus terminal—all from directly within the building. In addition, the location provides quick access to Highway 401, the Don Valley Parkway, and Lester B. Pearson International Airport.

Forest Hills, Hemispheres I and II

The residential version of *Place Nouveau* is equally impressive. The two 15-storey design buildings are each comprised of 150 units, 13 spacious suite types with many custom features, seven including private terraced gardens. On premises is the "Club Nouveau," a complete health and fitness centre with whirlpool, sauna, squash and racquetball, swimming, and exercise facilities.

Also contributing to North York's burgeoning downtown core is Menkes' recently completed Procter & Gamble corporate headquarters on Yonge Street at Sheppard Avenue. This 15-storey aluminum-clad office tower features 370,000 square feet of space and is designed with every known modern convenience, including direct access to and from the subway through the building.

Another outstanding Menkes project in North York is the nine-storey AT&T Tower, containing 150,000 square feet of quality office space strategically located at Victoria Park Avenue just south of Steeles Avenue in eastern North York. This modern design presents a very clean, sleek exterior of blue mirror glazing. The revolving door entrance opens to a two-storey atrium finished in quality marble and glass with mezzanine balconies overlooking the lobby. Sprinkler systems and computer-controlled heating and cooling also help make this suburban business environment comparable to the most sophisticated downtown.

Menkes' experience and integrity has established for it an excellent relationship among construction trades, imbuing a reputation of delivering quality products within time and financial restraints. As well, the company's asset base, due to its integrated real estate development strategy, along with excellent relationships with the banking community, provide Menkes Developments Inc. with the financial capacity to develop for the most demanding customers.

225

THE EDGECOMBE GROUP

ing projects with a value of $300 million per year.

The Edgecomb Group's network of offices.

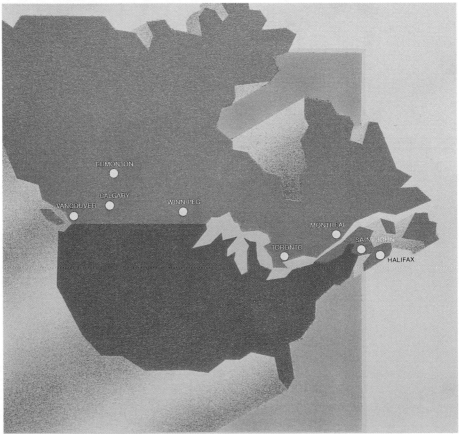

While Xerox and North American Life are the co-owners of the North American Life Centre and its major tenants, much of the credit for the project goes to The Edgecombe Group, a full-service real estate firm that took the centre all the way through from concept to completion. Led by president Kent D. Taylor, Edgecombe is an energetic team of real estate professionals who offer experienced realty, finance, development, property management, tax assessment, portfolio management, and mortgage servicing through its nationwide network of offices. Established in 1970, Edgecombe has earned a reputation for professional excellence and innovative strategies.

By bringing people and property together in a profitable way, Edgecombe has emerged on the leading edge of the real estate industry in Canada. Today The Edgecombe Group's services for corporate and private investors alike amount to more than $2 billion in realty, it manages more than 100 properties, and the firm is currently develop-

NORTH AMERICAN LIFE CENTRE

Perhaps the most graphic symbol of North York's new urban core along the north Yonge Street corridor is the North American Life Centre on the corner of Yonge Street and Finch Avenue. Developed by The Edgecombe Group for North American Life and Xerox, this stunning $200-million multiuse project has the size, design, sophistication, and amenities to rival the finest corporate addresses in the city.

Rising from a six-acre site, the North American Life Centre will reach for the sky with towers of 24 and 22 storeys, and contain more than one million square feet of prestigious office space. The centre's first phase, The Xerox Tower, with 575,000 square feet, was completed in 1986 and features a two-acre central courtyard and park, an underground concourse with 21 retail stores and a direct subway entrance, 30 condominium residential units in two low-rise buildings, 9 commercial condominiums, a sports and fitness club, a seniors' recreational centre, and 1,250 indoor parking spaces. The second tower, when constructed, will add 15 more retail stores and 500 additional parking spaces along with another 525,000 square feet of office space.

Strategic location is another critical feature of the centre. The Yonge and Finch intersection is closer to most of Metro Toronto's residential neighborhoods than is the downtown core. Highway 401 and Highway 404 are readily accessible, and transportation facilities such as TTC subways and buses as well as GO and Markham Transit bus services are virtually at the doorstep. Yet the downtown core is still only a short subway ride away, and Pearson International Airport can be reached conveniently via Highway 401. This accessibility cannot be matched by downtown Toronto.

Says David McCamus, president and chief executive officer of Xerox, "We looked at literally dozens of alternatives and concluded that the centre provides by far the best combination of advantages for our needs—uptown convenience and efficiency blended with top-quality construction and amenities."

A part of the post-modern trend in architecture toward greater freedom of form, atmosphere, and aesthetic appeal, the centre's large courtyard and plaza offers broad walkways and extensive seating areas finished in solid granite shaded by long rows of oak, locust, and birch trees surrounding a multitiered waterfall. The towers shield the inner courtyard, creating an oasis in the heart of the complex. The use of natural light is emphasized with skylights providing a major and varied part of daytime illumination. Pedestrians enter-

All the elements of the complex are dramatically integrated by the six-storey atrium, the centre's showplace.

ing from transit connections or adjacent streets have direct sightlines to central escalators and elevator banks. All the elements of the complex are dramatically integrated by the six-storey atrium—the centre's showplace—a superbly crafted environment of gleaming rose-color granite, marble, tempered glass, and stainless steel.

A full spectrum of personal retail services includes skylit restaurants for both light lunches and executive dining, and a sports and fitness club managed by the respected Racquet Sports Group, with squash, racquetball, swimming, and fitness facilities. As well, the complex is home to a major commercial banking centre, providing personal and commercial accounts.

The North American Life Centre makes full use of recent advances in computerized control technology. The building's cooling capacity leaves plenty of room for future increased use of electronic equipment. The centre's automated energy management systems can be custom-programmed to meet individual tenant needs. Equally advanced security systems include closed-circuit television surveillance, intrusion alarms, and a controlled-access card entry system. All vital systems are provided with emergency backup power. These levels of comfort, security, and cost efficiency are available to all tenants—from the largest corporate giants to the smallest professional firms and business offices.

With towers of 24 and 22 storeys and more than one million square feet of prestigious office space, the North American Life Centre is one of the most desirable corporate addresses in the city.

227

FIRST PROFESSIONAL MANAGEMENT INC.

North York Corporate Centre

Going from selling shower doors to developing land on a large scale, as Leo Goldhar has done, is not what most people would call a normal route to business success. But the founder of First Professional Management, Inc., a dynamic and rapidly growing real estate development, construction, and property management firm, has never been content with being ordinary. In fact, it is this sense of innovation, of being able to spot opportunities that others miss, that has made First Professional locations the preferred choice of so many Toronto-area business and residential tenants.

Goldhar, a Toronto native, first went into business in 1955 when he opened the Sterling Tile and Carpet Company in the Dufferin and Glencairn avenues area of North York.

Working as a contractor, installing tiling for residential and business properties, he thought there might be a market for a new product—shower doors. His hunch was dead on, and soon thousands of home builders were offering sturdy shower doors as an attractive new feature. Emboldened by this success, Goldhar turned his golden touch to real estate in the mid-1960s, developing his first property, a small industrial building, on Caledonia Road. The building was quickly filled with satisfied tenants, prompting Goldhar to move fully into the real estate business.

From its headquarters in the Consumers Road, Yorkland Boulevard area of North York, First Professional today is largely run by Goldhar's sons, Stephen and Mitchell, who studied business and political science, respectively,

before joining the family firm. First Professional owns and manages in excess of 3 million square feet of industrial, retail, and commercial space, and has another one million square feet under construction. These first-class properties are found in key locations throughout the Toronto region's prime growth sectors, including North York, Mississauga, Markham, Richmond Hill, and Scarborough.

The company has 30 full-time employees including its own architects, architectural technologists, engineers, property managers, and leasing representatives. On an equally large scale, First Professional is also involved in the housing market, both subdividing land for other builders and building residen-

tial units itself.

Typically, First Professional will purchase raw land and then go through the municipal process of gaining zoning and site plan approval. Once the designs are finalized, building permits are ascertained and construction begins. As a rule, First Professional retains ownership of the completed property, acting as landlord and property manager for its tenants. A list of First Professional's lead tenants reads like a who's who of blue-chip businesses, a tribute to the company's ability to provide first-rate accommodations. These tenants include Canadian Tire, The Brick, Consumers Distributing, Woolco, Boots Drug Stores, Toys R Us, Knob Hill Farms, and Dominion, to name a few.

Some of First Professional's newest and most exciting properties are right here in North York. The new North York Corporate Centre, for example, features the superb location of Highway 401 and Sheppard Avenue; a 100,000-square-foot, seven-storey, glass-encased office building; high-speed elevators; and heated underground parking, making it an ideal corporate head office site.

First Professional also has many impressive properties in the bustling Keele Street and Finch Avenue area—including a new 42,000-square-foot retail plaza anchored by Mother's Restaurant, and a 40,000-square-foot industrial building featuring three truck-level shipping doors and 70 parking spaces. Nearby, in the Keele and Lawrence Avenue area, First Professional is working on the second phase of its North Park Plaza, adding 40,000 square feet of office and retail space, as well as more parking to take advantage of the 100,000 cars that traverse this intersection daily.

Another outstanding First Professional property is the Crossroads Business Centre at Highway 401 and Weston Road. Tenants such as a new 17,000-square-foot full-service liquor store make up the total space of 329,000 square feet. This exceptional location includes high visibility, easy access to Highway 401 and Pearson International Airport, and plenty of parking.

It is not mere coincidence that the Goldhar family has chosen the City of North York as the location for its business, its home, and many of its properties. Stephen Goldhar, who was born in North York, says the city's municipal government is "the most cooperative in the southern Ontario area. They've been very accommodating, and they have an excellent understanding of business needs."

THE GLEN GROUP

ways be farmland in such areas as Richmond Hill, Vaughan, and Newmarket. Such forward thinking has helped establish the firm as a major supplier of quality industrial-commercial, residential, and, more recently, retail space in those regions.

Some of The Glen Group's current activities north of Metro Toronto include Keele and Seven Business Park, a 30-acre, office/commercial complex at Highway 7 and Keele Street that includes a five-storey office tower; Pine Valley Industrial Mews, a four-building project consisting of 180,000 square feet of light to medium industrial space on Highway 7 west of Weston Road; Steeles East Business Park, a 22-acre

A prime example of the impressive quality buildings erected by The Glen Group is the firm's own headquarters at 100 Scarsdale Road, Don Mills.

One of the key reasons for Metro Toronto's smooth transition to a world-class city over the past three decades has been the ability of land developers, in concert with governments, to correctly anticipate and provide for the needs of new businesses and residents, particularly in the suburban areas and beyond. One excellent example of such a developer is The Glen Group.

The founders of The Glen Group, Jack Rose and Dr. Ralph Halbert, first teamed up in 1963 when they developed a 300-acre residential project of single-family, semi-detached, town house and high-rise homes on the northeast corner of Jane Street and Finch Avenue in North York. This project satisfied an important need for housing in Metro Toronto at the time.

Another major project for The Glen Group began in 1967, when the company started developing a 225-acre business park on the southwest corner of Dufferin Street and Steeles Avenue in North York. Today this total development encompasses more than 3 million square feet of prime industrial and commercial space and represents an important business base in the northwestern section of North York, housing such important companies as Bell, Alcan, and Extendicare. More firms will

be able to capitalize on the strategic location and exceptional workmanship of this site shortly as The Glen Group develops the final 24 acres.

Foresight has always been a trademark of The Glen Group, an attribute evident by the fact that it anticipated the present explosion of growth north of Toronto as early as the 1960s, acquiring what others thought would al-

project that will include four industrial/commercial buildings, from 70,000 square feet, each of which can be built and finished to suit tenants' needs; Whitmore Commercial Centre, a 37,000-square-foot commercial complex at Highway 7 and Whitmore Road in Vaughan that will feature units available from 975 square feet and a 4,000-square-foot freestanding restau-

rant; and Granton Corporate Centre, a 120,000-square-foot combined office and industrial facility on Leslie Street near 16th Avenue in Richmond Hill that offers a range of tenant units from 2,613 to 40,000 square feet.

While its development of commercial and industrial space has been extremely successful, The Glen Group is still actively involved in residential development. The company is particularly proud of its elegant subdivision, The Bayview Hill, developed in conjunction with Metrus Management-Land Development in Richmond Hill. This exclusive 1,000-acre residential community combines modern convenience with traditional craftsmanship and grandeur, featuring individually stylized homes of no less than 3,000 square feet on properties averaging 70 feet wide and 140 feet deep. Not surprisingly, the first phase of this prestigious community has been sold out, but potential home buyers can take solace in knowing Phase 2 is coming soon. Another outstanding residential development by The Glen Group is Promenade Towers, three buildings totalling 600 condominium units, in Vaughan that the firm is building along with Menkes Developments.

As the economy of southern Ontario shifts from an industrial to an increasingly commercial and service-oriented base, The Glen Group is mov-

This office/industrial complex at 1111 Flint Road is just one of the many such projects constructed by The Glen Group.

ing with it, taking what vice-president Samuel Lepek calls a "more well-rounded approach" to land development by placing more emphasis on shopping centres. One stunning example of this change in direction is The Promenade at Highway 7 and Bathurst Street. Developed along with Cadillac Fairview and completed in 1986, The Promenade is by far the dominant shopping centre in the region and easily rivals the finest mid-town centres in size and sophistication. Set on 48.7 acres, The Promenade enjoys a superb location amidst the thriving new communities north of Toronto and yet is still just minutes from such major transportation routes as Highway 401 and Yonge Street.

The structure itself is a re-creation of a fine Italian palace set in the countryside, with walls of brick and terra cotta clay, a canopied entrance, and windows that rise from floor to ceiling. Inside, a total gross floor area of 903,000 square feet is spread over two architecturally striking levels, each linked by a spectacular central courtyard rising three storeys to a domed skylight. The retail mix, anchored by Eaton's, Sears, and Brettons, is designed to offer the widest-possible variety, with emphasis on fashion and food. Other features of this exceptional project are 3,500 parking spaces, public transit that stops at the site, a 20,000-square-foot cinema, and 48,000 square feet of office space.

The Glen Group is a privately owned, closely knit enterprise that employs 35 people. In total, the organization owns and manages in excess of 2 million square feet of industrial and commercial space at 31 properties, as well as 747 residential units at eight locations. The firm has been headquartered in North York for 11 years but only recently moved into its present location at 100 Scarsdale Road—a beautiful 19,000-square-foot building that proudly expounds the type of quality The Glen Group stands for. In fact, Jack Rose sees quality workmanship and design as cornerstones of the company's success. "We build buildings to keep," he says. "And if you want a good building 20 years down the road, you have to spend more than someone who is building to sell. That's why we exceed parking, building, and environmental standards on every project."

Landscaped courtyards provide a pleasant work environment in the office/industrial complex located on Dufferin Street.

TRIDEL ENTERPRISES INC.

Leo. Sensing a shrinkage in family sizes, a rise in land costs, and a growing affinity for luxury, the four men then developed the concept of adult lifestyle condominiums. Forty thousand customers later, their hunch is still paying off.

Today Tridel's residential real estate division is producing between 1,500 and 2,000 units per year, almost exclusively in the Metropolitan Toronto area. Its operations are completely integrated, with in-house expertise in land assembly, zoning, design, marketing, finance, and construction management. Real estate division assets in 1986 were $262.9 million, and sales

Construction gets under way on Tridel's flagship project, Governor's Hill (left).

Rodéo Walk provides a select group of residents with an exclusive lifestyle in an exciting condominium complex (below).

Few companies become symbolic with the products they provide, but such is the case with Tridel Enterprises Inc., the truly legendary North York firm that anticipated, pioneered, and built a lifestyle phenomenon in becoming North America's leading developer of high-rise condominium projects.

The Tridel story stretches back over a half-century, to 1934, when the late Jack DelZotto, a bricklayer from Fruili, Italy, built his first house in Toronto. He continued to build single-family homes in the Toronto area until the late 1960s, when he was joined by his three sons—Angelo, Elvio, and

Flags fly over another project by Tridel, one of North America's leading developers of high-rise condominium projects.

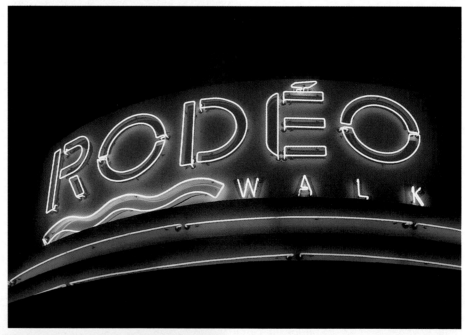

reached $122.1 million. The division directly employs 350 people and, through subtrades and suppliers, generates an additional 5,000 jobs.

Tridel Enterprises also includes a large construction technology division, operated by Aluma Systems Corp. Distinct yet complementary to the real estate side, Aluma Systems is North America's largest supplier of shoring, forming, scaffolding, concrete accesso-

The DelZotto presence at Tridel is still strong, with Angelo serving as chairman and chief executive officer, Elvio as president and chief operating officer, and Leo as executive vice-president. In addition, Tridel has attracted a blue-chip board of directors that includes Conrad Black, chairman and chief executive officer of Argus Corporation.

Tridel projects have been successful across southern Ontario, but nowhere more so than in its home base of North York. Three outstanding examples of Tridel craftsmanship in North York are The Savoy, Rodéo Walk, and the company's flagship development, Governor's Hill.

Towering over the wooded ravines and glistening water of Ross Lord Park in the Finch Avenue and Bathurst Street area, The Savoy enjoys one of the most sought-after locations in all the Metro Toronto area. And, in keeping with such a superb setting, this single condominium high rise features extensive landscaping, including a garden gazebo, private tennis courts, and a picnic and barbecue area. Luxury continues inside, with special guest suites and an exclusive social, health, and recreation centre. The Savoy offers a glittering array of spacious, extra-large suites,

This painting by Gordon Grice captures the idyllic setting at Governor's Hill (left).

Tridel's finest effort, Governor's Hill overlooks Hogg's Hollow and is central to fine shopping, restaurants, and public transportation (below).

ries, and other products related to the construction industry. In Canada it carries on business as Umacs of Canada Inc. In the United States it operates as The Burke Company, and internationally as Aluma International. In 15 years Aluma Systems has grown from an in-house experiment to a thriving company with 1,400 employees and estimated 1987 sales of $175 million.

In 1986 Tridel issued public shares for the first time, and is now listed on both the Toronto and Montreal stock exchanges. Investors enjoyed an immediate return when profits hit a record $8.5 million.

accented by superlative hardware and finishes as well as open balconies, marble ensuites, European designer cabinetry, and dozens of other features. Security is impeccably assured, with ensuite alarms, electronic TV surveillance, perimeter security for ground-floor suites, and a 24-hour concierge. In short, The Savoy is a symphony of classic elegance, lavish decor, and comprehensive recreational amenities.

Conveniently located at Yonge Street and Sheppard Avenue in the heart of North York's exciting new downtown, 23-storey Rodéo Walk provides its select group of residents with a truly exclusive lifestyle. The building incorporates such luxurious amenities as The Springs, a lavish hideaway dedicated to providing all the facilities necessary for both physical and personal renewal, such as squash courts, whirlpool, saunas, and a glass-enclosed pool.

Billiards, exercise rooms, a tanning deck, meeting rooms, overnight guest suites, and craft rooms are also nearby. Imaginatively designed and superbly appointed, the living quarters are luxurious one- and two-bedroom suites that redefine the concept of style. Each is replete with the fine features that have become Tridel hallmarks, such as recessed lighting, contemporary cabinetry, plush broadloom, and fine ceramic tile. And, depending on the suite, breakfast rooms, glass-enclosed sun rooms, and ensuite master bathrooms are also available. From the aesthetically pleasing expanse of the lobby to the uncompromising attention to the smallest details, it is obvious that Tridel has made Rodéo Walk one of the most exciting condominium projects in all Metro Toronto.

Undoubtedly Tridel's finest effort, and perhaps the most gracious condominium project ever developed in Canada is presently taking shape in the prestigious Yonge Street and York Mills Road area of North York. Governor's Hill, set on a ravine overlooking historic Hogg's Hollow, is central to everything that matters—fine shopping, restaurants, services, and public transportation. And yet, an almost endless

array of amenities is available without ever setting foot outside the stone-post gatehouse entrance. Fabulously landscaped grounds and a woodland garden with a waterfall is visible from both the guest suites and recreation centre. Inside, a country club atmosphere prevails, with a sparkling indoor pool, whirlpool, saunas, squash courts, an exercise gym, hobby rooms, and a party lounge. This exclusive condominium project offers a stunning selection of one-, two-, and three-bedroom residences, each rich in fine detail. Spacious living rooms opening onto beautiful sun rooms, gourmet kitchens with greenhouse-style breakfast areas, magnificent master retreats with walk-in closets, and ensuite baths are exquisitely appointed. At Governor's Hill, Tridel has taken luxury to new heights with the kind of detailed planning, design, and craftsmanship that is simply not available anywhere else.

While these three projects are symbolic of the firm's newest and most exciting efforts, the unmatched Tridel level of excellence can be found across Metro Toronto at such prestigious addresses as Gibraltar in Richmond Hill, Gates of Guildwood in Scarborough, the Polo Club in downtown Toronto, Discovery Place in Pickering, and The Towne in Mississauga.

The secret to Tridel's tremendous success over the years is perhaps so simple that its competitors have overlooked it. Explains Tridel's vice-president/sales, John McDonald: "The Tridel philosophy is clear. Buildings are merely inanimate objects. It's people who build them, and Tridel's people build them for other people." Building buildings for people, says McDonald, involves first finding out what they want—a step again so obvious that others may have forgotten it.

"We've had some 40,000 happy customers, so we go to them and ask, 'Where do you want to live? How much do you want to pay?' And then we act on it. Listening to those men and women is a way of life for Tridel," he says.

The name Tridel ("tri" from the three DelZotto sons and "del" from the family surname) has come to truly embody luxury adult condominium living in Metro Toronto. With more than 50 years in the construction business, the people of Tridel know exactly what today's modern home-buyers demand of such an important investment. And they give it to them.

CONCORDE PARK

In the 1950s a group of investors, planners, and builders with unique and fearless vision carved from several thousand farm acres something the world had never seen on such a scale before. It was a totally integrated community, complete with schools, roads, government services, housing of various kinds, and commercial, industrial, and retail facilities. It was, and still is, known as Don Mills, and it was hailed as the future of modern urban planning, attracting admirers and imitators from around the globe. Today, in that same historic area, a new vision is taking shape: Now the future is Concorde Park.

When Don Mills was first created it was considered the boondocks of Metro Toronto, somewhat off the beaten path. But today, as anyone familiar with booming Toronto knows, it is one of the most desirable midtown locations there is. And Concorde Park, the superbly appointed residential and commercial project now under development, is particularly well situated, just east of the Don Valley Parkway north of Eglinton Avenue East. Much more than convenient, the site also benefits from magnificent sightlines to the downtown Toronto skyline and the Don Valley ravine system.

Concorde Park represents the com-

A view of the entire Concorde Park project.

pletion of a 33-acre development in the valley that began in 1980 and already includes several residential buildings and prestigious corporate addresses, including the head office of McDonald's of Canada. Concorde Park consists of 1.5 million square feet of residential condominium space (to be completed in three phases and incorporated into

the two largest towers ever built in North York) and 750,000 square feet of commercial space (to be completed in two phases and known as the Concorde Corporate Centre).

Concorde as a corporate entity is a subsidiary of Bell Canada Enterprises, which represents the pension funds of Bell Canada and Northern Telecom employees. Concorde is in turn managed by Bimcor Inc., another BCE subsidiary. Project manager for Concorde Park is the well-known Teron International.

The Concorde Park residences, situated against a wooded ravine and overlooking the scenic Don Valley ravine, represent simply the finest in condominium living and feature every conceivable amenity—and more. The main level, for example, features an indoor swimming pool, two theatres, a hairdresser and massage room, a fully equipped fitness centre, a residents' lounge with outside barbeque area, a billiard room, a whirlpool, and a large party room with kitchen and bar. In the centre of each building there is also a 'great room' where residents can relax under a skylight dome amidst land-

The Phase I office buildings from across the Don Valley Parkway.

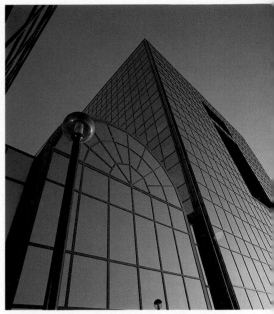

The large atrium joins the 12-storey office building to the four-storey office building (above).

The impressive front entrance to the Phase I office building (left).

scaped greenery.

The units themselves come in a variety of sizes and configurations, yet all are uniform in their quality and value. Among the luxury standard finishes are an extra-large floor-to-ceiling glass solarium; an energy-saving heat pump system providing year-round individually controlled air conditioning and heating; washer, dryer, range, refrigerator, and dishwasher; a Florida sunshine ceiling in the kitchen; ceramic tile kitchen floors; mirrored closet doors in the front entry; and an elegant marble bathroom. Concorde Park residents also enjoy underground parking, ground-level storage space, concierge service, state-of-the-art electronic security, and individual suite entry lobbies on each floor.

The Concorde Corporate Centre's first phase is now nearly completed and consists of one 12-storey office tower and one four-storey tower, linked by a gorgeous glass-vaulted atrium. Phase II will be its mirror image. These imposing all-glass structures are already the cause of much "rubber necking" along the Don Valley Parkway from their location on Concorde Place just north of the Eglinton interchange.

They are built with Teron technology, a pre-cast structural framing system integrated with a unique mechanical and electrical distribution system, thus affording economies that can be passed on to the end user. The unique building system also results in space with 11-foot ceilings and indirect cove lighting, creating a spacious and airy effect. Other outstanding features include elevator lobbies with elegant polished travertine walls, high-quality carpeting along common corridors, marble washrooms, and underground parking. Retail services, including a restaurant, will be located on the ground floor.

The developers of Concorde Park have taken special heed of the needs of its commercial and residential clients by creating a multimillion-dollar, award-winning Presentation Centre. Rather than standing on a wind-swept half-built site imagining what the finished product will be like, potential tenants and investors can make their important decisions from the comfort of the Presentation Centre, which features an audio-visual room, detailed scale models of the entire project, three fully decorated model residential suites, and a fully furnished model office suite.

The Don Mills area of North York has always been a model for modern residential and business accommodations. Concorde Place has just upped the standard.

PENTA STOLP CORPORATION

It started with three friends investing $5,000 in an option on 28 Scarborough lots. It was 1982, and the housing market was slow. Henry Stolp wound up selling 177 homes that first year in business. It was an auspiscious start to Stolp Homes. Two years later Penta Group was launched to handle the company's growing portfolio. The two now go by the name Penta Stolp Corporation, which has expanded into high-rise condominium development, office towers, industrial buildings, and land assembly.

It was the quality extras that Stolp, John B. Overzet, and Chris Mullin offered customers in their new homes that gave the firm its early business edge. Those extras are now a Penta Stolp trademark in all its projects—commercial or residential.

Since its inception Penta Stolp has gone on to build 22 residential projects in the Toronto and Ottawa areas, selling more than 600 homes per year. The company has also become a major player in the condominium and commercial markets, with joint ventures in such prestigious North York buildings as the 400,000-square-foot Madison Centre, the 220-suite Manhattan Place, and the 383-unit Vogue Condominiums now under construction. Recently it was given the go-ahead on two large innovative projects in downtown

Seneca Square—a unique association. Penta Stolp creates an office/retail centre and new Seneca College head office/campus, all in one complex.

North York.

In the fall of 1987 plans were announced for Gibson Square, a huge commercial complex to be built on the northwest corner of Park Home Avenue and Yonge Street. The $200-million tower will be located at the present site of a half-acre rose garden. Penta Stolp will preserve this parkland by creating a beautiful glass-enclosed rose garden on the ground floor of Gibson Square. Penta Stolp will also develop a three-acre public park beside the tower on land where houses now sit.

In the spring of 1988 Seneca College announced Penta Stolp Corporation had been selected to build a $100-million educational and business centre in downtown North York. Seneca Square will incorporate the college's head office and an educational centre as well as a day-care facility, a 23-storey office tower, and a retail concourse. Seneca Square will replace the college's Sheppard campus—a single-storey renovated factory—tripling campus space.

Gibson Square—Penta Stolp's commercial complex atop a glass-enclosed rose garden opposite city hall.

J.J. BARNICKE LIMITED,
REAL ESTATE

The real estate market in Metro Toronto indicates the region's economic health. Climbing residential values are now legendary, and nonresidential space is also in soaring demand. The keen competition means investors, developers, landlords, and tenants need a reliable and resourceful real estate firm. That is where J.J. Barnicke Limited comes in—and has been coming in for nearly 30 years.

In commercial, investment, retail, and industrial real estate, J.J. Barnicke is the largest independent, internally controlled real estate firm in Toronto, and one of the largest in Canada, with connections worldwide. Led by founder and chairman Joseph J. Barnicke, each member of the team brings a wealth of experience and expertise, providing personal and creative service to every client, whether they be a multinational corporation or a one-man shop. The chairman claims, "Our success can be attributed to three things: We work hard, give good service, and we know what we are doing."

J.J. Barnicke's Office Leasing Division is widely respected in the industry and, as a result, is offered the leasing assignments for many of the prime new office developments. In the major bank tower of Commerce Court West, the firm was responsible for leasing more space than all other brokers combined. Other top-flight developments in the core area utilizing J.J. Barnicke's services include WaterPark Place, 30 St. Clair West, and 95 Wellington West.

J.J. Barnicke's retail leasing team has leased more than 10 million square feet in more than 30 retail projects across Canada. Recognition of its retail

leasing abilities is so high that developers often ask J.J. Barnicke to handle their anchor department store lease negotiations. In 1971 the firm pioneered the concept of grouping food outlets in one convenient spot in retail centres, an innovation that has spread across North America. J.J. Barnicke's retail clients include Lime Ridge Mall in Hamilton, Square One in Mississauga, and South Common Mall in Mississauga.

The company's strong identification with the corporate marketplace has also made it one of the most reliable and efficient movers of industrial space. Knowledge is critical to these transactions—company representatives are in constant contact with devel-

Atria North, Phase II, is just one of the prime new office developments for which J.J. Barnicke is offering leasing arrangements.

The key to the company's success is its ability to combine the right information about the market with the needs of its clients. An example is the Xerox Tower in the North American Life Centre (shown here).

opers and municipalities. Knowledge of market trends and when new properties will be available and serviced are also company trademarks. Build-to-suit arrangements are expertly handled as well.

J.J. Barnicke also provides a wide variety of investment consultation, feasibility studies, financing advice, and market research. The firm has a special commitment to urban redevelopment, helping all levels of government nationwide achieve the right mix of uses in their downtown cores.

J.J. Barnicke is the sole Canadian affiliate of The Office Network, an organization of 3,000 real estate professionals across North America and Europe. It is also a founding member of the Canadian Commercial Real Estate Network, which represents and integrates real estate people in 11 major markets across Canada.

J.J. Barnicke Limited is fully aware of the rosy economic prospects for North York, handling the leasing arrangements for the stunning Atria North and the equally impressive North American Life Centre.

COUNSEL PROPERTY CORPORATION

Counsel Property Corporation, a full-service organization, has established itself as a leader in the field of commercial property investment, development, and property management across Canada. And not surprisingly, this successful company has seen fit to participate in the growth of North York, acquiring part ownership in 1987 of The Yonge-Sheppard Centre, one of the city's most prestigious developments.

"We have the finest location in North York," says Counsel vice-president Denis Beneteau proudly. "Now we want to make sure it remains compatible with the new development in the area."

The centre was built a decade ago as an office-residential complex featuring direct access to the Sheppard subway station. Shopping, while of high quality, was seen as a complement to these main functions, and, as a result, the building's design somewhat disguised the shopping available inside. Now, with thousands of people strolling through the booming downtown North York area, Counsel plans to increase walk-in traffic at the centre with extensive renovations to the building. As financial, development, and property manager of the centre on behalf of all investors, Counsel hopes to give Yonge-Sheppard shopping a higher out-

side profile and greater streetscape, and thus create a more humanizing effect for the whole building.

The Yonge-Sheppard Centre is just one of 50 properties from Fredricton, New Brunswick, to Vancouver, British Columbia, owned or managed by Counsel Property Corporation. The company handles projects of all sizes, from 20,000-square-foot convenience plazas

Victoria Park Mall

The Yonge-Sheppard Centre

to the likes of Yonge-Sheppard, with its 560,000 square feet of office-retail space and 1,000 apartment units.

Counsel's office, industrial, and commercial space adds up to more than 5 million square feet and includes properties in most major cities across Canada. In Ottawa there is the 129,000-square-foot Gateway Business Park, in Calgary both the Franklin Mall and the Glenmore Landing Shopping Centre, and in Toronto Counsel is part owner of the 400,000-square-foot Canadian General Electric Building. With owned and managed assets of $700 million, Counsel Property Corporation is at the leading edge of development, renovation, and remerchandising of commercial property in Canada.

Dealing primarily in shopping centres and office buildings, with a minor interest in industrial buildings, Counsel invests in property on behalf of pension funds and other financial institutions. Counsel, however, treats all of its properties as if it owned them. In fact, in many cases Counsel does take a financial interest in the properties it administers, which ensures investors that maximum effort is being made on their behalf.

Counsel Trust headquarters at 36 Toronto Street

Counsel's team of highly skilled professionals perform a number of functions in the development, renovation, management, investment, and re-merchandising areas. On a typical project Counsel will acquire a property, identify its best use, and then work closely with architects and planners to design the most efficient building possible. In renovation, Counsel will upgrade existing properties to maximize space and its potential uses.

An outstanding example of Counsel's skills in renovating is located near Lawrence Avenue and Don Mills Road in North York. In 1984 Counsel bought what was an old bowling alley, gutted it, and converted it into an attractive and profitable strip plaza.

In re-merchandising, Counsel's experienced team of real estate and marketing analysts work hand in hand with existing shopping centres. After identifying and creating a new merchandising philosophy, Counsel then sets out to attract the right retail tenants for the desired merchandising mix.

Counsel Property Corporation is a subsidiary of Counsel Corporation, a company involved in the financial services, health care, and real estate industries. Counsel Corporation began in 1979 with assets of $3.6 million. Just eight years later Counsel's growth has proven exponential, with assets now totalling just more than one billion dollars and the company administering a further $1.7 billion.

Counsel Corporation's main financial service subsidiary is Counsel Trust Company, which is registered to do business in all provinces except Quebec and the Northwest Territories. In 1986 Counsel Trust launched DirecTrust, the first phone-in savings, investment, and mortgage service in Canada. Short-term deposits, guaranteed investment certificates, RRSPs, and residential mortgages are available by telephone, 24 hours a day, seven days a week.

Diversicare Incorporated, Counsel Corporation's health care division, bought 3 nursing centres in Texas, and 11 nursing homes and 2 retirement centres in Arkansas in 1986. This will likely double Diversicare profits for 1987. Of the more than 4,000 beds under Diversicare's management, half are owned by Counsel and the rest managed for other investors.

Hard work, expertise, and a knack for identifying quality investment opportunities are what have brought Counsel Property Corporation to the forefront of its field. And as partners in the progress of North York, the firm's future and that of the city look even brighter.

895 Lawrence Avenue East

TRILEA CENTRES INC.

It is hard to believe that it was a full 24 years ago when one of Canada's largest and most fashionable retail centres, Yorkdale Shopping Centre, first opened its doors to the public. Equally difficult to imagine is the centre sitting amidst acres of farmers' fields, as it did in 1964. Today it is nestled in the thriving and heavily populated Allen Road and Highway 401 area of North York, and linked directly to the Metro Toronto subway. That Yorkdale has enjoyed such prosperity over the years and has always belied its age are tributes to the foresight and ongoing management of its owner, Trilea Centres Inc.

Trilea is a Canadian shopping centre company devoted to the ownership, development, and management of commercial retail properties. Its assets, valued at $1.6 billion, include shopping centres and other commercial properties totalling approximately 13 million square feet of rentable space in urban and suburban markets nationwide.

Trilea is a relatively new corporate entity, but much of its management and direction are drawn from two well-known and established companies. It was formed in 1986, when Bramalea Limited of Toronto and Trizec Corporation Ltd. of Calgary amalgamated their Canadian shopping centre assets. As a result, Trilea Centres Inc. was created as a wholly owned subsidiary of Bramalea Limited. The parent com-

Yorkdale Shopping Centre is just one of the retail complexes in the Toronto area owned by Trilea Centres Inc. Trilea's marketing and management staff strive to make shopping an unparalleled experience (above and opposite page).

pany, Bramalea, has a $4-billion portfolio of properties, including office buildings, business parks, hotels, apartment buildings, and shopping centres, as well as a large home-building division. Bramalea's chairman is former Ontario Premier William Davis.

One of Trilea's flagship properties, Yorkdale Shopping Centre has always been an innovative facility. When it first opened, it was the largest of its kind in the world, offering its customers one million square feet of shopping

pleasure. It was also the first shopping centre in Canada to feature two major department stores—Eaton's and Simpsons—together under one roof.

Other important conveniences included a unique underground delivery system for retailers and ample free parking for shoppers. The year 1986 was particularly exciting for Yorkdale; it saw the connection completed to the Yorkdale subway station, which links the centre to all of Metro Toronto. This $11-million expansion added 30 new stores and brought total retail space to more than 1.5 million square feet. Another expansion has added The Bay to Yorkdale's fold of prestigious tenants.

Style, convenience, quality, and selection—and lots of them—have always been hallmarks of the Yorkdale Shopping Centre. The result is that shoppers can enjoy the ambience of extra-wide malls and elegant marble finishings while choosing from 215 (and counting) stores and services that offer

everything from stereos and steaks to haircuts and haute couture. Yorkdale puts particular emphasis on its fashion retailing, and is a leading fashion centre in Canada.

In addition to unparalleled shopping, Yorkdale's 74-acre site also features 126,000 square feet of office space, including the five-storey Yorkdale Place office building, constructed in 1979, which houses Trilea's operations office as well as a bus terminal for regional and national carriers.

But despite its impressive numbers, it is the people of Trilea, led by president and chief executive officer Gordon Arnell, who have made it one of the most dynamic retail property operations in Canada. To keep pace with the changing demands of the marketplace, Trilea brings innovative forms of merchandising and marketing to its centres. Close attention is paid to selecting the right merchants for each market, and to providing enjoyable shopping forums

for tenants and shoppers alike. To promote merchant sales productivity, continued advertising and promotional programs are maintained by the company's marketing and management staff. And, of course, Trilea keeps its centres in first-class condition to create an outstanding shopping experience in an attractive and stimulating setting.

Trilea's presence in the Toronto-area market is far from limited to Yorkdale. The company also owns and manages Scarborough Town Centre, The Shops on Steeles and 404, Shoppers World Albion, Bramalea City Centre, Shoppers World Brampton, and Shoppers World Danforth, all of which are major retail centres in their respective communities. As well, Trilea Centres Inc. is embarking on comprehensive remerchandising and upgrading programs in its more mature centres in order to maintain its leadership position in the Canadian shopping centre industry.

FALCO PROPERTIES

In 1955 professional engineer Joseph Fialkov and master electrician Roman Abraham Blankenstein combined to form Falco Electric, an industrial and commercial electrical contracting firm. From this base, the founding company has grown to include not only contracting, but land development, construction, and property management, and has become one of Canada's largest private real estate organizations.

Falco Electric has been recognized for the past 32 years as one of the leaders in electrical design and contracting. Projects have included many of Toronto's famous residential landmarks such as the exclusive 40 Rosehill and the waterfront project known as King's Landing. Most of Ontario's largest developers call on Falco Electric for their high-rise projects.

From the knowledge and experience gained in the electrical contracting field, Falco Properties was created. The company began with construction of apartment buildings, then progressed to industrial-commercial projects and residential housing. Today apartment towers built, owned, and managed by Falco Properties are located throughout the Metropolitan Toronto area as well as in the United States.

Commercial structures are also built and managed by Falco Properties. The buildings, numbering more than 75, are located in prime industrial parks ranging from Whitby to Oakville.

The construction of residential housing began under the name Marble

Arch Homes. Today this company is recognized as a leader in the construction of quality homes in the Metropolitan Toronto area.

To continue this growth pattern and maintain its existing buildings, Falco has assembled a team of experts to design, construct, and maintain buildings of every description and use. The principals of Falco fully expect the

Falco Properties is renowned throughout the area for retail/commercial/industrial developments such as this complex at 1070 Lorimar Drive, Mississauga.

This elegant Heritage Estates home in Richmond Hill was created by the firm's Marble Arch Homes Division.

growth in the next period to far exceed the first 30 years.

Falco is committed to helping the communities in which its properties are located. For example, the company has its head offices and 23 buildings in North York. Locally, Falco Properties has sponsored sporting and cultural events, as well as participated in many community affairs.

BRAMALEA LIMITED

Bramalea Limited is one of North America's largest and most diversified real estate companies. It is involved in all categories of real estate—from housing, shopping centres, and business parks to hotels and office complexes. The firm, however, started out as a builder of communities.

Its history, spanning 30 years, begins with the vision of creating a "new town" in the township of Chinguacousy. That dream exists today as the Bramalea community in the city of Brampton. It is a full-service community created by Bramalea Limited. It provides its 100,000 inhabitants with everything they need and expect—a wide choice of single-family housing, rental apartments, and high-rise condominium suites; a thriving business park producing thousands of local jobs; shopping ranging from neighborhood malls to regional centres; a resort-style hotel; government and business offices; and acres of sweeping parkland and recreational facilities.

Today, while the size and scope of the company have changed significantly, Bramalea remains a significant builder of communities, with assets in some 40 cities and towns throughout North America. Bramalea has a large Residental Group producing new housing product in numerous communities in southern Ontario. It also has a rapidly expanding community development and housing business in Southern California.

One of the communities where Bramalea is increasingly applying its diverse property development and property management expertise is the city of North York. In particular the company has been developing a presence in the design and construction of family housing—first in single-family housing, then rental apartments, and more recently condominium residences.

In North York, Bramalea was an innovator in the condominium market, beginning with the Atrium I complex at Yonge and Sheppard. More recent condominium projects include the Atrium II and Windfield Terrace complexes. In addition, Bramalea developed and owns the award-winning Galleria rental apartment complex on Finch Avenue East.

In 1987 Bramalea Limited was selected by York University as the preferred developer of a new residential community on a 20-acre site at the southwest sector of the campus. The firm is currently seeking the necessary approvals to proceed with this signature housing development, which will create a community of 1,600 luxurious adult-oriented condominiums linked by a central parkland complete with its own man-made lake.

In the years to come Bramalea expects to play a growing role in meeting the housing needs of North York. Bramalea also plans to build Balmoral, a superior new community of 195 luxury single-family homes in North York.

Another aspect of the firm's contribution to community life is in the shopping centre field. The contemporary shopping centre is very much a climate-controlled village where people congregate to dine, chat, plan, and browse as well as shop. Bramalea develops, manages, and redevelops "retailing communities," with 42 centres throughout North America, from Florida to California, and from British Columbia to Nova Scotia.

Bramalea's Canadian shopping centres are owned and managed through a subsidiary company, Trilea Centres Inc. This is one of the most important shopping centre portfolios in Canada. Among the more than 30 malls is Yorkdale Shopping Centre, the jewel of the Bramalea retailing portfolio, the pride of North York shopping.

The diversity of Bramalea also embraces the development and management of office complexes. Here again, many modern office complexes are self-sustaining working communities with recreational, dining, and shopping elements. Bramalea's largest urban project is a 72-storey office tower that dominates the skyline of Dallas (home of J.R. Ewing in the TV series, "Dallas"). Other major urban complexes are in San Diego, Los Angeles, Denver, Oakland, Edmonton, and Toronto.

Many of Bramalea's projects are scaled to the intimate needs of the community, including the company's first office building in North York on Sheppard West near Yonge Street. The firm is developing new office buildings in Metropolitan Toronto and is seeking further commercial development opportunities in North York.

Bramalea's diversity extends to other aspects of the property business. The company's hotels, for example, include the world-famous Four Seasons Hotel in Yorkville. Business parks in Brampton and Pickering, Ontario, also reflect Bramalea's ingenuity in creating design-controlled industrial properties in parkland settings to produce new jobs in the Toronto region.

Bramalea Limited is a publicly traded Canadian company with more than 3,000 individual and institutional shareholders and 2,500 employees. The firm is active in some 40 markets throughout North America and controls assets, as of 1987, of $3.8 billion.

But most of all, Bramalea Limited is a company committed to meeting community needs through the development and management of housing, shopping, office, and other commercial real estate projects.

Bramalea has been a major developer of high-rise condominiums and rental apartments in North York. The company is also seeking commercial development opportunities in the city.

OLYMPIA & YORK DEVELOPMENTS

Over the years Olympia & York has achieved a harmony between corporate idealism and the public interest, between building as a family legacy and earning the esteem of the urban communities on which it leaves its imprint.

The company's rise to the pinnacle of international real estate development is enshrined at Battery Park City, in the foreground of lower Manhattan. It is universally admired for its powerful architecture and graceful style, for the balance between state and city aspirations and commercial viability, and for the rebirth of downtown Manhattan and the extension of its streets to the Hudson River.

World Financial Center, the commercial capital of that new city, is the very model of an astoundingly productive partnership between the public and private sectors.

In Toronto, Olympia & York has recreated a piece of the city's history with the largest renovation in North America. Queen's Quay Terminal, which once languished as a decaying marine terminal on the docks of the central waterfront, has been reborn as a glittering mix of retail, office, and condominium uses. The site is owned by Harbourfront Corporation, in-

World Financial Centre, New York City (right).

Canary Wharf, London, England (below).

First Canadian Place, Toronto, Ontario (right).

Aetna Canada Centre, Toronto, Ontario (above).

itiated by the federal government.

A few blocks away First Canadian Place, the centre of Canada's financial universe, was developed by Olympia & York in a spirit of cooperation with municipal officials that has always characterized the company's philosophy. It was the firm's springboard to a development trail of 50 million square feet that winds through the major urban markets of North America.

On the other side of the continent, in San Francisco, work is under way on Olympia & York's 25-acre Yerba Buena Gardens development in a neglected part of the city's downtown. The project is the vision of a mixed-use community for the 1990s.

All of these projects are pivotal developments that create new spheres of urban influence. They are designed to attract and sustain the best of tenants—to satisfy the most demanding standards. They are the largest of their kind. They have replaced decrepitude or stagnation, or barren landfill, with award-winning, signature developments.

CHAPTER 11

Quality of Life

Medical and education institutions, contribute to the quality of life of North York area residents.

Sunnybrook Medical Centre, 250-251

York-Finch General Hospital, 252-253

Université York University, 254-255

Baycrest Centre for Geriatric Care, 256

Seneca College of Applied Arts and Technology, 257

North York Branson Hospital, 258

North York General Hospital, 259

Northwestern General Hospital, 260-261

The North York Board of Education, 262

SUNNYBROOK MEDICAL CENTRE

Created in response to the country's greatest crisis, World War II, Sunnybrook Medical Centre's first challenge was to care for those who fought to protect the future. Today, while continuing to care for veterans, the hospital faces new challenges, such as cancer and an aging population, and is meeting them with the vigor, expertise, and compassion that have become Sunnybrook traditions.

Prime Minister William Lyon Mackenzie King officially opened Sunnybrook Hospital in 1948, dedicating it to "the gallant men and women of the Armed Forces of the Dominion of Canada who have suffered in her wars for freedom, and to the doctors, nurses, and staff whose services are devoted to their healing, comfort, and welfare." The hospital was administered by the Department of Veterans Affairs of the federal government, offering a wide range of veterans' services. The approximately 100 acres on Bayview Avenue where the hospital was built was given to the City of Toronto in 1928 by Alice Kilgour, widow of Joseph Kilgour, for use as a park. When the city decided to give the land to the federal government in 1942 for use as a hospital, the Kilgour heirs gladly consented.

In 1966, in response to a dire need for additional acute care beds and more hospital teaching programs, the federal government transferred ownership of Sunnybrook to the University of Toronto. While maintaining and improving veteran care, Sunnybrook has become one of the country's leading hospitals with major teaching and re-

search responsibilities. Now known as Sunnybrook Medical Centre, it has 1,200 beds and provides multidisciplinary care for more than 2,000 patients each day. The 15,000 patients admitted annually and average of 100 emergency patients treated daily make Sunnybrook the most utilized health care facility in Canada. Sunnybrook has 250 physicians on its medical/dental staff and employs 3,500 personnel.

In the past few years the hospital has instituted a master plan that will ensure programs are multidisciplinary, a regional resource, have established expertise, provide academic excellence,

In 1988 more than 2,400 participants took part in Sunnybrook's Run for Research, which in seven years has raised close to one million dollars for medical research. The Run for Research is Ontario's largest charitable run.

One of Canada's largest hospitals, Sunnybrook Medical Centre is located on more than 100 acres of beautiful land—a calm setting for an active centre.

meet community needs, and provide a unique service. Based on these criteria, Sunnybrook has identified its major roles as care of the elderly, cardiovascular disease (including stroke), rehabilitation, mental health, cancer, and trauma (including spinal cord injury).

Sunnybrook has already earned a reputation as a centre for excellence and an innovator in program planning for the elderly. Inpatient services include assessment, long-term care, rehabilitation, and psycho-geriatrics. The new 270-bed Geriatric Centre, due for completion in mid-1989, will include 100 community chronic care beds and has been architecturally designed specifically for the elderly to focus on a home-like environment.

Treatment of cardiovascular disease at Sunnybrook includes such well-established services as a sophisticated stroke unit, the Regional Pacemaker Unit, non-invasive diagnostic procedures, the hypertension unit, exercise and stress testing, and various clinics for patients who need special care. In this area Sunnybrook researchers lead the way in such studies as the effects of caffeine and smoking on the heart, and new approaches to the management of high blood pressure.

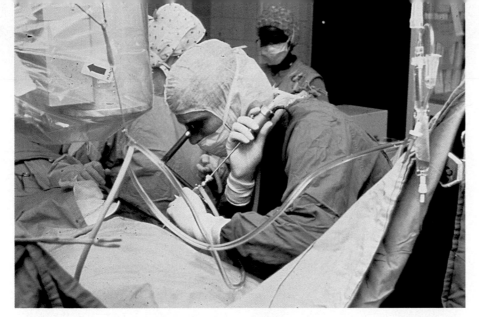

The relaxing and contemporary environment of Sunnybrook's Aids-For-Living Centre is evidence of its commitment to helping people with physical disabilities live to their fullest potential. Clients who come to the centre, which is the largest of its kind in Canada, are fitted with specially designed orthotic and prosthetic devices, and then participate in a rehabilitation program under the guidance of a multidisciplinary team of health care professionals. The centre has also developed a unique expertise in the area of facial prosthetics—artificial ears, eyes, noses, and other features help to restore clients to their normal appearance, and in the process contribute to improving their sense of social and emotional well-being.

Sunnybrook's psychiatry department has the largest and most comprehensive program of its kind in Metro Toronto teaching hospitals. Distinct inpatient units investigate and treat problems of adult and geriatric age groups, while a special unit treats disorders of adolescents. Day treatment, outpatient, and aftercare divisions deal with virtually all emotional disorders, including schizophrenia, depression, alcoholism, sexual dysfunction, and psychosomatic and sleep disorders in a variety of ways, including drug treatment and therapy.

In fighting that most feared disease, cancer, Sunnybrook researchers labor to find causes, innovative treatments, and cures, while a comprehensive inpatient and outpatient program provides chemotherapy, radiation, and surgical treatment with compassionate care.

Sunnybrook's Regional Trauma Unit for the care of the multiply injured patient is Canada's first and foremost trauma centre, and among the best in the world. Built around the golden hour theme of immediate and

Since its sale to the University of Toronto in 1966, Sunnybrook has evolved from a veterans' hospital into a sophisticated tertiary hospital with a major academic focus. Resources and programs are now designed to serve the needs of both acute- and extended-care patients.

concurrent surgical treatment, the program follows severely injured patients from the time of injury to their reestablishment in a rehabilitation centre or at work or home. Sunnybrook staff were also instrumental in the development of the Ontario Ministry of Health's Air Ambulance Program. Sunnybrook's Acute Spinal Cord Injury Unit is Canada's leading centre for the treatment and management of spinal cord injury patients.

High-quality teaching is another important aspect of Sunnybrook's mandate. It trains more than 1,400 medical, nursing, and other students each year, building on a history of education that includes the training of Ontario's first paramedic team and the opening of the first Family Practice Department in a Canadian teaching hospital.

Sunnybrook offers its patients aesthetic enjoyment as well as top-flight care. On its picturesque grounds is the historic McLean House, one of Ontario's most magnificent Georgian-style mansions, exquisitely refurbished to serve as a conference, social, and meeting facility.

Sunnybrook is continually looking for better and more efficient ways to deliver health care. One example is the hospital's proposal to convert a vacant police station in North York into a community health centre for seniors, women, and teens. Over the next five years Sunnybrook plans to renovate accommodation for 225 acute care patients, centralize laboratory services, replace its 40-year-old operating rooms and critical care beds, and acquire new equipment. The extent of this expansion has necessitated that Sunnybrook look, for the first time, to the community it serves to provide financial help. Strong support of The First Sunnybrook Fund by corporations, members of the community, associations, and service clubs has brought the campaign close to its target of $29 million.

As a teaching hospital Sunnybrook seeks to ensure that nurses have access to continuing educational opportunities. Flexible work schedules permit staff to attend classes, and the University of Toronto has recently named four nursing units for special teaching and research endeavors.

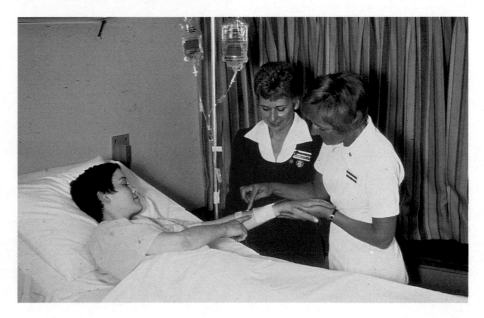

YORK-FINCH GENERAL HOSPITAL

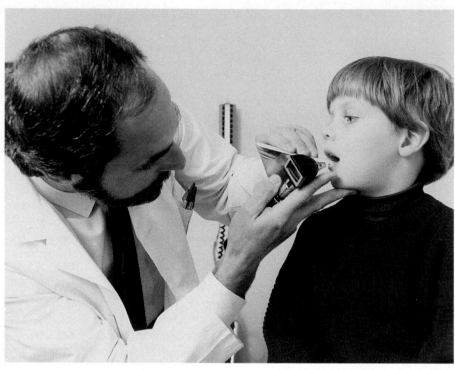

A family practice physician checks out a young patient.

A hospital is by definition the kind of place where most people would rather not be. But since its opening in 1970 York-Finch General Hospital has seen as one of its prime objectives to make the hospital as responsive and accessible to the community as possible. The strategy has been more than successful, with York-Finch becoming one of North York's busiest health care facilities.

York-Finch General Hospital is a fully accredited, 303-bed acute care facility located at 2111 Finch Avenue West, serving the area bounded by the Humber River to the west, Dufferin Street to the east, Rutherford Road to the north, and Highway 401 to the south. The hospital also continues to expand its services to the new growth areas north of Steeles Avenue in the Town of Vaughan. Commensurate with its commitment to serve the health care requirements of this community, York-Finch has tailored its services in recognition of the heavily ethnic and industrialized nature of the area. The imperative role York-Finch plays in its community is reflected by the fact that 70 percent of its patients live in North York.

York-Finch is dedicated to the provision of high-quality, inpatient and outpatient services at a level in keeping with its role as a major acute care community hospital. And as the community has burgeoned around it, so has York-Finch's workload. In 1986 the hospital handled more than 13,000 admissions, logged in excess of 100,000 patient days, delivered 2,000 babies, and treated 75,000 people in an emergency department originally designed to handle just 25,000.

York-Finch functions under legislation contained in the Ontario Public Hospitals Act and other appropriate provincial and federal regulations. In 1985 the hospital was awarded three-year accreditation status by the Canadian Council on Hospital Accreditation. This body has established national standards that all hospitals must attain in order to receive accreditation status. In the case of York-Finch General Hospital, the council concluded that in most areas the hospital goes beyond the standards, and the three-year status is the maximum that can be awarded.

Meeting these many challenges for York-Finch is a staff of 1,000 full- and part-time employees, 220 medical staff, and 16 interns. The hospital provides a comprehensive range of specialty and subspecialty services in surgery, medicine, obstetrics and gynecology, pediatrics, and psychiatry. The hospital board has made significant investments over the past five years in providing state-of-

More than 74,000 people visited York-Finch General Hospital's Emergency Services Department in 1987.

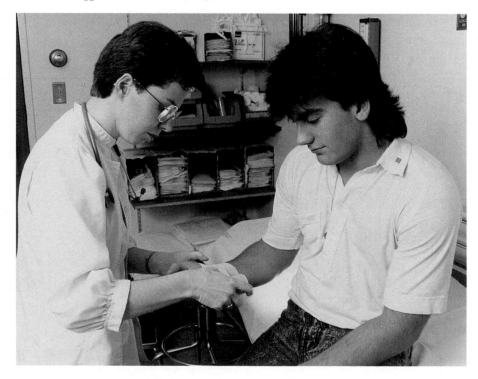

An artist's conception of the future expansion of York-Finch General Hospital.

the-art medical technology, including one of the finest C.T. Scanner suites in Canada and a YAG laser for delicate eye surgery.

York-Finch General plans to intensify its support of clinical experience to medical, nursing, and other paramedical students through its affiliation with the University of Toronto, the Toronto Institute of Medical Technology, and the community college system. The hospital is also committed to the support and provision of patient and community education programs geared to promoting the individual's continuous well-being. In addition, the hospital will continue its participation in and support of clinical research programs.

Volunteers are often the backbone of a thriving community hospital, and York-Finch's Volunteer Services Organization is no exception. More than 100 adult volunteers work at many services throughout the hospital, while youth volunteers, numbering in excess of 90, cover the in-hospital programs in the evening. These young people not only provide an important immediate service, but their exposure to the disciplines required in a hospital helps continue the flow of young talent into the health care system. Thirty York-Finch volunteers also turn their much-needed attention outside the hospital, visiting patients at the nearby Arleta Manor, the Shoreham Clinic, and the Glaucoma Screening Clinic. The Volunteer Services Organization also raises money for the hospital, contributing

$87,000 in 1986.

The York-Finch General Hospital Foundation was created as a non-profit, charitable organization committed to maintaining and enhancing the hospital's level of excellence and high standard of providing sophisticated care. The foundation is playing an increasingly important role for the hospital as it is providing leadership to the $5-million Facing The Future Together capital campaign.

The governing board of York-Finch General Hospital has taken action to ensure that community needs will be met in the future. This includes plans for expanded diagnostic, treatment, and support facilities to be added to the present building. This major redevelopment will include a new emergency department; a new and expanded laboratory; expansions to the surgical suite, labor and delivery suite, and recovery rooms; provision for a number of specialty clinics; an expanded medical imaging department; additional space for staff development and education; and a new ambulatory care unit to accommodate a variety of outpatient services.

York-Finch General Hospital has a tremendous responsibility to meet as the major health care facility in one of the fastest growing, and changing areas of Metro Toronto. The board, medical staff, hospital personnel, and volunteer organization are highly committed, and if the community responds to calls for support as it always has, York-Finch General Hospital's future will remain a bright one.

A special care-giver cares for one of the 2,000 babies who enter the world each year at York-Finch General Hospital.

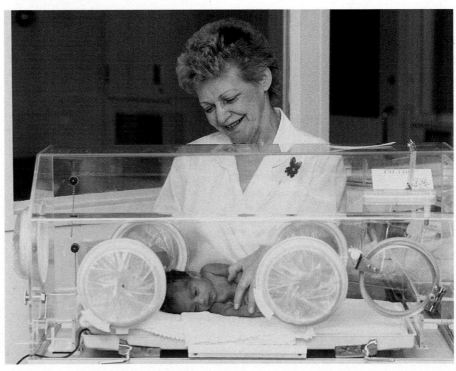

UNIVERSITÉ YORK UNIVERSITY

The dream of York began in the late 1950s, the era of Sputnik and the early days of the space race when baby boomers were still babies. It was a time when the impact of technology on everyday life was just beginning, when people feared universities might become the exclusive domain of the rich, and when the exponential growth of the Metro region, with its influx of new Canadians, threatened to overwhelm the city's capacity to accommodate a new generation of students. A quarter-century later, defying tremendous odds and shortages of funds, York has emerged as a dynamic institution, recognized for opening doors to students from every background as well as for its dedication to excellence in high technology and the liberal arts.

The move to establish a new university in Toronto started when the North Toronto YMCA began considering how it could play a role in developing adult education. The idea found strong support among leaders in government and industry, with Premier Leslie Frost agreeing to bring a bill to incorporate York University before the legislature. By the time the act received royal assent in March 1959, the school had cut its ties with the YMCA and affiliated with the University of Toronto for a short time.

In September 1960, with 76 students and nine full-time and part-time faculty, York held its first classes in a borrowed downtown lecture hall. The next year it moved to small but stately Glendon Hall, now known as Glendon College, on a beautiful ravine site at Bayview and Lawrence. York opened its second campus, at Keele Street and Steeles Avenue, in 1965.

Today, with 40,000 students, York is the third-largest university in Canada and the second largest in Ontario. Its 5,500 staff members, including 1,200 full-time and 1,100 part-time faculty, also make the university the largest employer in North York and among the top 10 employers in Metropolitan Toronto.

From the beginning, York sought to be an accessible, multidisciplinary school with special strength in the liberal arts through the Faculty of Arts, and a concentration on bilingual studies at Glendon College. Other faculties are equally prominent: Administrative Studies, Fine Arts, and Education rank among the largest and best in Canada; the Faculty of Science is widely recognized for research in molecular biology,

Artstart programs and minicamps bring children from local neighborhoods to York for summer fun and learning.

Student residences overlook the panorama of the York campus.

atmospheric chemistry, and space science; while the Faculty of Environmental Studies is the largest school in Canada for self-directed interdisciplinary study in environmental systems. Osgoode Hall Law School, affiliated with York since 1969, is the country's largest common law school and among its most eminent. The Faculty of Graduate Studies also enjoys a strong international reputation. Atkinson College focuses on part-time and mature students, those who missed the chance earlier in life for higher education.

York has attracted and produced some of Canada's brightest academic stars, who continue to build the university's reputation through their publications and participation in academic conferences around the world. More than 35 faculty have been named Fellows of the Royal Society of Canada. And in recent years York has taken nearly one-third of the awards presented by the Ontario Confederation of University Faculty Associations to faculty nominated by colleagues and students for teaching excellence.

York researchers are also renowned. Their rate of success in obtaining research fellowships, such as those offered by the Social Sciences and Humanities Research Council of Canada,

is consistently higher than that of other Canadian universities. York also boasts nine research centres, including the Centre for Research in Experimental Space Science, the Centre for the Study of Computers in Education, and the Centre for International and Strategic Studies.

York's strength in research and teaching continues to attract top faculty and students. To support its innovative, multidisciplinary programs, York offers a rich array of resource materials collected in five libraries, and provides a centralized computer service with access to networks across North America.

Since 1969, when the first international project linked York with Kenya in a training program for civil servants, faculty have continued to share their skills and knowledge around the globe. A special office, York International, coordinates overseas projects and acts as a liaison with embassies, international groups, and the federal govern-

Professor Elaine Newton explains puritanism, Greek fate, and Freud to help students understand the work of playwright Eugene O'Neill. Professor Newton is among the many York faculty who have won awards for teaching excellence.

ment. York has joint programs or exchanges with Brazil, Great Britain, China, France, Japan, Mexico, Qatar, the Soviet Union, Sweden, Thailand, and Uganda.

York University president Harry Arthurs, a former dean of the law school, has ambitious plans for the university. Convinced that close links to the business community are essential, he formed the York University Development Corporation (YUDC), offering private-sector interests the chance to be involved in developing York's considerable land assets. Arthurs hopes to bring in the capital needed to provide the academic space and student services York is determined to offer. The YUDC's current plan integrates the needs of prospective tenants with those of the university community.

Innovation York is another solid link to business: a service offering companies working with emerging technologies the chance to consult with researchers in the Faculty of Science, and to tap the management expertise of the Faculty of Administrative Studies.

York can offer no better example of its links to the community and the quality of its product than the new Institute for Space and Terrestrial Science, a provincial government Centre of Excellence established at York in 1987. As well, the Ontario Centre of International Business, headquartered at York in 1988, will focus on multilin-

Graduate student Brian McKenzie adjusts the autoscan ring dye laser in York's Laser Processing Laboratory. The transfer of discoveries in basic science from university to business takes place in research and development facilities such as these.

gual and multinational programs in business, trade, marketing, and cultural and legal systems.

York's contribution to North York's community life is a special one. Its camps and art programs are a summer highlight for many local children. International calibre sport facilities, such as the Metropolitan Toronto Track and Field Centre, training ground for world champion sprinter Ben Johnson, are open to the public. Each summer the National Tennis Centre plays host to the Canadian Open Championships. Law school students run legal aid clinics for low-income groups on campus, downtown, and in the neighboring areas. The university also welcomes the public to view its superb art collection and special exhibits at seven campus galleries, and to enjoy lectures and performing arts events throughout the year.

York's flexibility and creative spirit have made it one of Canada's most impressive young universities. Fueled by steadily increasing academic grants and teaching awards, and at the centre of North York's thriving business and residential community, York's future looks brighter still.

BAYCREST CENTRE FOR GERIATRIC CARE

From a house in downtown Toronto where a group of neighborhood women cared for 20 elderly residents, Baycrest Centre for Geriatric Care has grown into a five-facility campus of care, serving more than 2,000 people on 19 acres on Bathurst Street in North York.

The pioneering group of women of the Ezras Noshim Society who raised the funds to buy the original house on Cecil Street would be overwhelmed to see that there are now 1,500 staff members and 900 volunteers working at Baycrest Centre, a 1,800-member Men's Service Group and a 3,400-strong Women's Auxiliary. They would also be proud to learn that Baycrest Centre has earned a worldwide reputation for excellence and leadership in meeting the social, emotional, and medical needs of elderly persons.

In keeping with its mission, Baycrest Centre has grown to meet the increasing needs of the community it serves. It is now comprised of the 376-bed Jewish Home for the Aged; the 204-unit Baycrest Terrace, a seniors' apartment building providing minimal care; the Joseph E. and Minnie Wagman Centre, a cultural, social, and recreational community centre for persons 55 and over; the Baycrest Day Care Service for the Elderly; and the Baycrest Hospital, also known as the Ben and Hilda Katz Building, a 300-bed geriatric hospital.

Along with its world-class facilities and personnel, Baycrest Centre is still keenly aware that community members are the foundation of its success. In addition to their hands-on work, many volunteers also sit on the board of governors, board of directors, and a number of advisory committees to ensure that the Centre is responsive to the needs of the community.

With the opening of the Baycrest Hospital in May 1986, the Centre realized the culmination of a dream. It is the first medical facility in Canada to bring together a comprehensive range of inpatient, outpatient, and assessment services specifically for the elderly.

Hundreds of visitors from around the world tour the institution each year to see the facilities and benefit from the experience of Baycrest's seniors' specialists. Annual medical, nursing, and social work clinic days provide a forum for the Centre's professional staff to share their knowledge of aging with others in the field. As well, students, interns, and residents from many disciplines train at the hospital's facilities, as do visiting doctors from across North America and as far away as Israel.

Perhaps most important, the Centre continues to provide leadership in the delivery and development of high-quality services to the elderly by striving to make breakthroughs in research

Many activities, such as this garden sale, keep Baycrest residents and visitors active. Courtesy, Gary Beechey

A group of seniors enjoy the sun filtering through the trees and unique architecture of the Saul A. and Isabel Silverman Garden Court. Courtesy, Gary Beechey

on aging. In recognition of these efforts, the board of directors has established a formal research program in order to continue the institution's leadership position in the provision of quality care and services to the elderly.

Although the number of services at the Baycrest Centre for Geriatric Care has increased enormously since 1918, the women of the Ezras Noshim Society would be pleased to know that the development of programs for a growing and changing elderly population is still based on the respect for the individual and high standards for quality of life and quality of care.

SENECA COLLEGE OF APPLIED ARTS AND TECHNOLOGY

Seneca College has been a progressive and innovative institution since it opened in 1967 out of a small, one-storey renovated factory operation at Sheppard Avenue and Yonge Street in North York. Seneca has grown from an initial enrollment of 852 full-time and 1,067 part-time students to one of the largest community colleges in North America, with 20 campuses and locations providing educational and training services to more than 95,000 registrants annually. Seneca graduates enjoy an average placement rate of 98 percent.

Seneca has always taken pride in its ability to provide high-quality programs taught by skilled professionals aimed directly at specific career fields. School officials continually monitor and communicate with the country's various economic sectors and tailor programs to fit future needs. The result is a wide range of programs under the divisions of Allied Health, Applied Arts, Business, Computer Studies, Health Science, Office Administration, and Technology. Within these divisions are practical programs running the gamut from word processing to early childhood education, business administration to fashion, and executive secretary to civil and resources engineering technology.

Seneca's excellent record of preparing people for the work force has also

Graduates of Seneca College find relevant employment with the average placement rate at 98 percent.

Seneca's Minkler Auditorium, located at the college's Newnham Campus, is home for many community-based events, including concerts, films, and children's shows.

been achieved through the cultivation of extensive networks in the business and industrial communities and through its strong reputation as an institution that delivers quality programming utilizing industry-standard equipment. These networks have been developed through many avenues, including the Business and Industrial Division, in which the school provides consulting and educational services to the local business community; the Friends of Seneca Association, a group of 120 leaders of the local business, political, and educational communities who meet four times per year to gain an understanding of the educational services of the college; *Senescan*, a magazine featuring articles on many areas of technology and entrepreneurship designed to encourage communication among industry, government, and education; and international programs in which the college exchanges faculty and students with countries such as Singapore, Japan, China, Kenya, Syria, and the United States.

In 1968 Seneca opened Phase 1 of the then Finch Campus (now Newnham Campus) and introduced its Aviation and Flight Technology program; the 1,100-seat Minkler Auditorium opened at the Finch site, the home of the North York Symphony and many other community activities; in 1974 the college opened the Equestrian Centre; and 1986 was highlighted by the op-

ening of the first Ontario Skills Development Office in the province and an ACCC National Spotlight Award presented to Seneca College and Ford Electronics for partnership and innovation in their delivery of employee training. In April 1988 Seneca announced the expansion of its Sheppard Campus. The new $100-million complex, located at Sheppard and Yonge, will house an education centre, an office tower, and a shopping complex.

Seneca recognizes that there is more to college life than studying, and offers a wide range of extra-curricular activities. In athletics, students can compete at either the intra-college or varsity level. Students can also participate in student government, campus clubs, the campus newspaper, or special events of a cultural or artistic nature. Seneca awards scholarships to students who make outstanding contributions to these aspects of student life.

Of Seneca's 20 campuses and locations, 12 are in North York, including Newnham, the main campus, located at the intersection of Finch Avenue East and Don Mills Road. The other North York locations are the Dufferin, Leslie, Sheppard, Jane, Yorkdale, Glen Park, Fairmeadow, Spring Garden, Caledonia, Lawrence, and the School of Communication Arts.

NORTH YORK BRANSON HOSPITAL

The North York Branson Hospital was established in 1957 as an 80-bed community hospital located on Finch Avenue West, at that time a concession road in the Township of North York. The township is now one of Canada's largest cities, Finch Avenue a major traffic thoroughfare, and Branson Hospital a full-service 374-bed active treatment general hospital with a reputation for clinical expertise rendered in an atmosphere of genuine concern and compassion.

Branson functions under the sponsorship of the Seventh Day Adventist Church, from which it derives its philosophy of achieving health by treating the total person—body, mind, and spirit. The hospital derives its name from William Henry Branson, a humanitarian known for his work on four continents—North America, Africa, Europe, and Asia. A strong administrator and aggressive builder with a passion for excellence, Branson used his influence and skills to encourage the healing work of hospitals worldwide.

The hospital features many primary services that support the practice of family medicine in the community: general medicine, general surgery, gynecology, obstetrics, pediatrics, pathology, psychiatry, radiology, and anaesthesia, as well as 24-hour emergency care. Among its secondary services are cardiology, dermatology, gastroenterology, neurology, neurosurgery, nuclear medicine, ophthalmology, oral surgery, orthopedic surgery, otolaryngology, plastic surgery, respirology, ultrasound, urology, and vascular surgery. Outpatient services include a broad range of ambulatory care clinics. A 10-bed coronary care unit features the latest technology.

The hospital serves on an annual basis well in excess of 100,000 patients, of whom approximately 14,000 are provided inpatient care, the balance being treated in the Emergency Department and provided diagnostic and therapeutic services in numerous departments. These services are provided by approximately 1,000 employees, in excess of 250 physicians, and scores of active volunteers.

Located on Finch Avenue just west of Bathurst Street, Branson's primary patient-referral area encompasses the central third of the city of North York along with a portion of York Region, being bounded by Highway 7 on the north, Highway 401 on the south, and from Bayview Avenue on the east to Keele Street on the west.

Of particular significance is Branson's Centre for Health Promotion, which offers programming designed to help participants to identify and reduce the risk of heart disease, cancer, and stroke—the three leading causes of premature death. The centre's computer-assisted programming includes lifestyle risk assessment and the following results-oriented classes in health behavior change: smoking cessation, weight control, personal fitness, sensible nutrition, eating disorders, childbirth preparation, and healthy aging.

In keeping with its tradition of excellence, Branson is currently involved in a $12-million capital project, of which $4 million must be achieved through a fund-raising campaign for the replacement and expansion of its clinical laboratory, operating suite, and obstetrical facilities with new and expanded facilities.

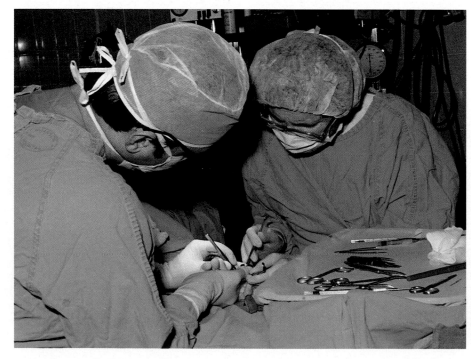

NORTH YORK GENERAL HOSPITAL

The miracle of birth, the crises of emergency, the fear of disease, the despair of death, and the complexities of diagnostic work are regular occurrences and require extremely high levels of efficiency, expertise, and technology. That it has been able to maintain such standards and still provide an atmosphere of accessibility and warmth is a tribute to the people of North York General Hospital.

North York General Hospital began as a vision by a group of concerned citizens in the early 1960s for a small hospital to serve the North York area north of Eglinton and east of Yonge Street. Discouraged at first by the prohibitive cost, the group was soon joined by the Missionary Health Institute and the Imperial Order of the Daughters of the Empire Children's Hospital, both of which were planning their own expansions, and Canadian Mothercraft, a nursing school that was looking for an institution to help train its students. The four groups decided an amalgamation of their resources and services would best serve the public, and thus a hope for a 70-bed hospital became solid plans for a full-blown 600-bed medical facility. On March 15, 1968, John Robarts, then premier of Ontario, officially dedicated the new hospital on Leslie Street north of Highway 401, built at a cost of $8.3 million, almost half of which was raised by a dynamic fund-raising campaign.

Today North York General Hospital is a fully accredited, community-oriented hospital with 541 beds, 1,978 employees, and 450 physicians. The emergency department is one of the busiest in the province with nearly 100,000 visits per year. The hospital also has the largest inpatient psychiatric unit in the Metropolitan Toronto area for a general hospital.

With 4,000 births annually, North

North York General Hospital is a fully accredited, community-oriented facility with 541 beds served by 1,978 employees and 450 physicians.

York General Hospital is a major obstetrical centre and offers a full-scale genetic counselling program. Ambulatory care programs include a diabetic education program, a child development and counselling service, a hearing testing centre, and speech therapy and audiology programs for children.

In 1985 North York General Hospital opened its new Seniors' Health Centre, a multilevel care facility that includes 120 nursing home beds, a Day Centre, a chiropody clinic, and a Seniors Assessment Service. In 1987, 60 additional chronic care beds were approved for the facility. The Seniors' Health Centre reflects the hospital's desire to accommodate the needs of North York's growing seniors population and to keep them as comfortable and independent as possible.

From the beginning the hospital has been associated with education.

With a growing senior citizen population in the community, North York General Hospital established the Seniors' Health Centre, which offers a full range of health services.

North York General Hospital trains interns and residents from the University of Toronto's Faculty of Medicine, nursing students from Seneca College, and technical students from the Toronto Institute of Medical Technology.

Volunteers play a critical role at the hospital. They provide a vital supply of compassion and caring that cannot be duplicated by all the sophisticated technology in the world.

North York General Hospital sits in the centre of one of the fastest-growing areas in Canada, and facilities are becoming strained under increased public demand. The Hospital Foundation plays an important role in raising funds necessary for the ongoing development of hospital facilities and programs.

Many people have contributed to what the North York General Hospital has become, from the busy mother who finds a few hours to volunteer to the wealthy couple who recently set up a $2-million endowment fund for the Seniors' Health Centre. With friends like these, and some government help, North York General Hospital will continue to provide an excellent level of health care to the community it serves.

NORTHWESTERN GENERAL HOSPITAL

Northwestern General Hospital is a case of something positive resulting from tragedy.

In May 1949 at St. Hilda's Anglican Church Canon Albert Jackson was summoned by the leader of the church's Teenaged Girls Group, who was frantic because a 16-year-old member was seriously ill. Jackson immediately saw that the girl's life was in danger, but all the city hospitals could not admit her because they were filled to capacity. Jackson called an ambulance anyway, and when she arrived at the hospital, the girl was given a bed in a corridor, where she died a few hours later.

Soon others were inspired by Jackson's determination to prevent others from suffering the same fate, notably Dr. Darby Philp, Dr. Sam Rowley, and Ralph Cowan. Later the group was joined by, among others, Father Francis Gallagher and Rabbi David Monson, who, along with Canon Jackson, exemplified the moral and spiritual convictions of the hospital's founders.

After creating an executive commit-

tee, a powerful address by Rowley convinced York Township council to put a plebiscite to the people in the next municipal election, asking if they approved of a new hospital being built in their community, to be partly financed by government aid. The result was a resounding 'yes,' with 80 percent approving the plan. Shortly afterward, the hospital's first board of governors was established.

The group began organizing for the long road that still lay ahead. Alternatives such as affiliating the hospital with an existing one, or using prefabricated war emergency buildings were considered but rejected in favor of building a fully modern active-treatment general hospital. In choosing a name, 'York' already existed in two other Ontario hospital names, so Northwestern was chosen because it denoted York Township's position within the City of Toronto and also because Dr. Rowley, the board's chairman, had attended Northwestern University in Chicago.

Land and financing were the next major hurdles. A 15-acre site on Keele Street, owned by the township, was deemed appropriate, but the $15,000 price was prohibitive to a board with no financing. Cowan was able to interest Dominion Stores Limited in the project, and the company financially assisted the board in buying the land. Paying for the facility, at a time when government grants accounted for only

Ground was broken at 2175 Keele Street for Northwestern General Hospital in 1952. Two years later the four-storey, 104-bed facility was officially opened.

one-quarter of the cost of financing a hospital, posed even greater problems. But again Cowan came to the rescue, proposing that the municipality provide a large portion of the funds through a specified local property taxation, a means of financing a hospital that had never been used before. Once more the people responded 'yes,' agreeing by a 3-to-one majority to provide $750,000 through the special tax.

Community support for the new hospital did not end with the vote but swelled, with several voluntary organizations taking shape. Not surprisingly, the medical fraternity joined in quickly, and in 1951 the Medical Society was formed under the leadership of Dr. Henry Kingstone, Dr. Vernon Malowney, and Dr. Luke Teskey, Sr. Alice Bickerton, a charter member of the board, soon organized the Northwestern General Hospital Auxiliary and mounted a membership drive. The auxiliary then proceeded to raise funds, as well as sewing thousands of yards of material into sheets, pillow cases, and other linen supplies.

With funds provided by York Township, the provincial and federal governments, and many private individuals, the board appointed the architec-

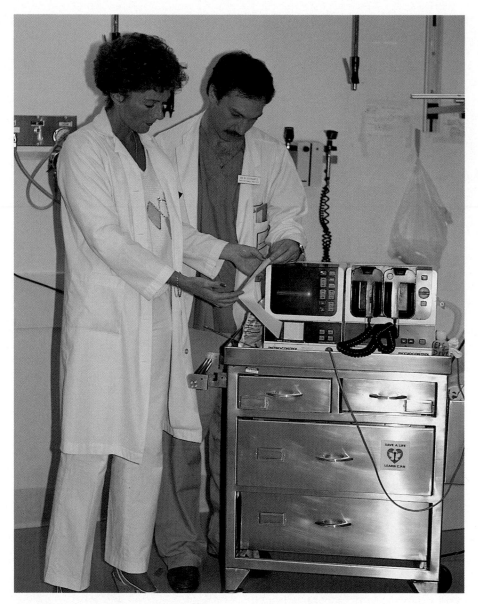

The emergency department at Northwestern General is one of the busiest in Metro Toronto with more than 60,000 visitors per year. Here Brian Schwartz, M.D., head of emergency, and Susan Ogilvie, R.N., nursing unit manager, check a printout on the Life Pak 8 defibrillator in Room One, the department's resuscitation room.

tural firm of John B. Parkin Associates in December 1951. A year later the cornerstone was laid on a four-storey, 104-bed hospital of the latest design. On August 10, 1954, Northwestern General Hospital was officially opened. On September 4 of that year the first patient was admitted, and four months later all the patient beds were fully utilized.

It was apparent from the outset that Northwestern was desperately needed by the community. Within two years the emergency department was treating 12,500 patients per year, and it was common to find occupied beds in the corridors. The incoming Ontario Hospital Insurance Plan (OHIP) further increased demand for the hospital.

It was clear that expansion was needed, and in February 1960 construction began on an additional four floors.

In the baby booming 1960s Canada's population grew tremendously, particularly in the areas served by York Township and the Borough of North York. The hospital again strained under increased demand, and further expansion became imperative. In 1973, despite financial austerity on all levels of government, plans for a new East

Building were approved. Completed in 1975, it officially opened in June 1976 by then-Premier William Davis.

Today Northwestern is a 268-bed, acute care general hospital with a full range of medical, surgical, and diagnostic services, including emergency, obstetrics, pediatrics, psychiatry, surgery, radiology, nuclear medicine, echocardiography, pulmonary function, and physiotherapy. In 1984 the Harold and Grace Baker Centre, a 240-bed nursing home and retirement residence, opened. Included in this building is the Ernie Boccia Creative Child Day Care Centre.

Located at 2175 Keele Street, Northwestern serves an area housing some 100,000 people in the cities of York and North York. The hospital employs approximately 800 staff members working in a variety of areas, including nursing, dietary services, physiotherapy, housekeeping, technology, and administration. Roughly 160 physicians are associated with the hospital and are divided into departments of anesthesia, dentistry, medicine, obstetrics and gynecology, otolaryngology, pediatrics, psychiatry, radiology, surgery, and family practice. The institution's current chairman is Murray Makin, a vice-president of Bell Canada, who has been involved with Northwestern since 1978.

Northwestern General Hospital operates on an annual budget of $35 million, of which $29 million is provided through Ministry of Health operating grants, while the rest is raised from other sources. As the southern Ontario region has continued to grow rapidly, Northwestern is again in need of expansion, particularly its emergency department, one of the busiest in Metro Toronto, with more than 60,000 visits per year. The hospital is presently in the midst of a $15-million fund-raising drive to enlarge its emergency department and to create an ambulatory care centre for health promotion and disease prevention programs. Given the local community's history of helping to turn visions into reality, these much-needed new services should not be long in coming.

THE NORTH YORK BOARD OF EDUCATION

By urging them to become active learners, North York Schools' teachers foster students' self-esteem and personal, social, and academic growth.

Size alone makes The North York Board of Education one of the city's biggest corporations. One hundred and thirty-four schools, more than 110,000 day- and night-school students, and an annual budget of $300 million command the attention of 5,600 employees.

The board may be big, but its chief focus is on providing exemplary service.

Since its inception the board has believed in two things: one, that its foremost goal be student achievement—academic, personal, social, and vocational—and two, that partnerships—parents and children, students and teachers, trustees and electors, schools and communities, staff members and volunteers—form the backbone of the education/learning process.

In recent years the board has formed additional partnerships with seniors, child care providers, linguistic groups, cultural organizations, and businesses. While maintaining excellence in traditional programs, the board seeks to identify and satisfy new community needs.

Fourteen publicly elected trustees meet regularly to set policy and to ensure that North York Schools' students have opportunities to develop the necessary skills, knowledge, attitudes, and values to live in and contribute to Canadian society.

Students are encouraged to aspire to any career goal. Programs and services stress the development of self-worth and self-discipline. Courses are structured to ensure equality of the sexes and freedom from racial, ethnic, or religious bias.

North York Schools are accountable as well as accessible. The board freely reports to the local taxpayers who finance 90 percent of its operation (government grants and board revenues account for the remaining funds). In turn, the community actively supports the schools.

More than 2,680 volunteers contribute more than 100,000 hours per year to assist students in classrooms, libraries, on field trips, and in countless other ways. The board's Adopt-A-School program is rapidly expanding, too. Seventeen companies have adopted schools, exposing students to the world of work and to different careers. In return, businesses are invited to use school facilities and examine first hand how schools are managed.

Increasingly, North York Schools themselves are adopting an entrepreneurial spirit. A business approach to education governance has resulted in the creation of several management models to ensure excellence in academic programming. Schools have written and annually review strategic five-year plans. They also involve community residents in financial decision-making at the local level. The board continually conducts reviews of curriculum to maintain quality assurance and sees that teachers receive evaluation and assistance to achieve top performance through a Supervision for Growth program.

The board takes pride in living up to its Champion in Education identity. It launches new programs and forms associations with community organizations with realistic expectations. A supportive administration of strong, committed, and respected leaders champion new programs. Talented teachers and support staff put them into action.

The North York Board of Education has a proven record of responding to community needs quickly and of demonstrating energy and educational leadership. North York residents have every right to expect the tradition to continue.

North York Schools teach students to think for themselves. Libraries provide a quiet study environment for individuals or small groups, and offer a wide assortment of written, visual, and computer-generated information to augment classroom studies.

CHAPTER 12

The
Marketplace

*North York's retail
establishments, service
industries, and products are
enjoyed by residents and visitors
to the area.*

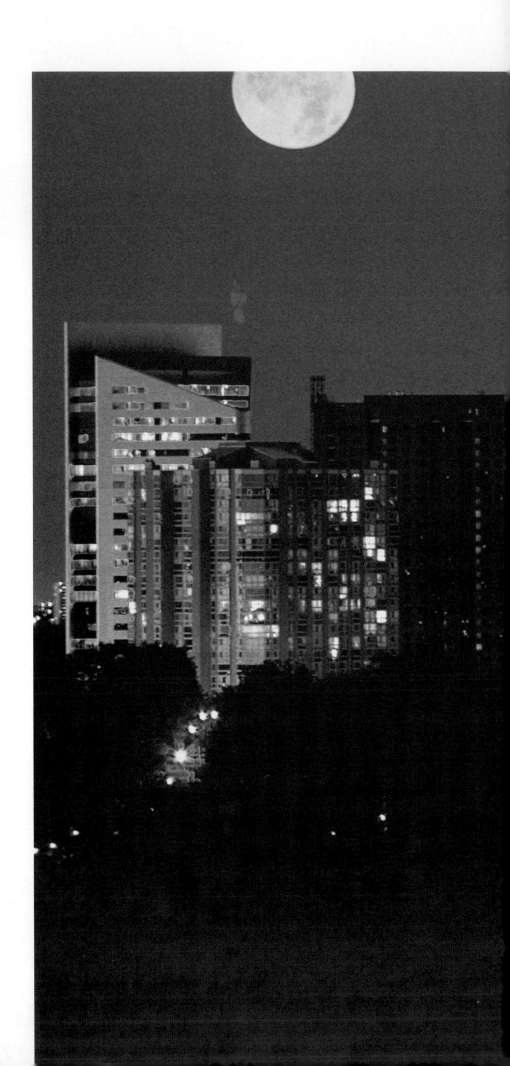

XEROX CANADA INC.

It is not a street address, a secret radio code, or the name of a new automobile.

It is the text of the first legend ever fashioned by the process of xerography, invented in a makeshift laboratory in Astoria, Long Island, on October 22, 1938, and named for the Greek "xeros," or "dry," and graphein, "to write." The inventor of the xerographic process was a patent attorney named Chester Carlson, who believed that the world was ready for an easier and less costly way to make copies. He was right.

The Haloid Company of Rochester, New York, took up the challenge of developing Carlson's invention into a useful product, and in doing so the giant multinational company now known worldwide as Xerox Corporation.

In 1953 the Haloid Company established The Haloid Company of Canada Limited as a wholly owned subsidiary to market its products in Canada. The name was changed to Xerox of Canada Limited in 1961 and to Xerox Canada Inc. in 1980. Xerox Canada was a part of U.S. operations until 1972, when it became a member of the international group within Xerox Corporation, a wholly owned subsidiary of the parent

While "Xerox" means photocopying to the world, Xerox Canada is a leading supplier of business products and systems that facilitate all facets of document processing: the creation, reproduction, distribution, and storage of documents.

company in Stamford, Connecticut. In 1984 Xerox Canada issued shares to the public, and is now 21-percent publicly owned with common shares listed on the Toronto and Montreal stock exchanges. Total revenue in 1986 was $865 million.

Xerox Canada has come a long way from the early days when 118 employees operated what was part of Xerox Corporation's Northern Region. Today the firm employs 4,700 people across the country, with its new corporate head office—the Xerox Tower—located in North York. The Xerox Tower, officially opened in December 1986, stands in the heart of downtown North York as a symbol of community and corporate growth, a landmark not only for the company but for the city itself.

As a community, North York has witnessed rapid economic development in the 1980s; as a corporation, Xerox Canada is continuing to expand its leadership position across the

The management group at Xerox Canada Inc.

nation—carrying on the tradition of growth and excellence started by Chester Carlson.

"The move to the Xerox Tower is symbolic of our confidence in our future as a company," says David R. McCamus, president and chief executive officer. "We're proud of what we've accomplished since our establishment in Canada three decades ago and excited about being part of the growing spirit of North York."

The 24-storey tower accommodates 650 people employed at the firm's corporate head office. In addition, the company operates the Xerox Research Centre of Canada in the Sheridan Park Research Community in Mis-

Xerox Tower, the corporate head office of Xerox Canada Inc., opened in December 1986 as one of the newest landmarks in downtown North York.

sissauga, which has a worldwide mandate for original and long-range scientific investigation of materials that affect the xerographic process. Also in Mississauga is the Canadian Manufacturing Centre-Toronto, which has a world product mandate from Xerox Corporation to manufacture copier paper-handling devices. Toner and developer for the Canadian and export markets are produced by the company's Oakville Toner Plant.

The name Xerox is synonymous with photocopying to business people worldwide, but Xerox Canada actually has two major enterprises. It is a leading supplier of business products and systems and, as one of Canada's largest equipment leasing companies, operates a rapidly expanding financial services division.

Xerox Canada supplies office technology, equipment, and services that facilitate the creation, reproduction, distribution, and storage of documents. Its range of products includes xerographic copiers and duplicators, electronic printers, Memorywriter electronic typewriters, facsimile equipment, and indus-

267

every employee strives: a dedication to understanding customers' requirements and solving their problems, a work culture and ethic in which every employee assumes personal responsibility for continuous quality improvement, and a management style that encourages each employee to reach his or her maximum potential."

If customer satisfaction is the cornerstone of Xerox Canada's marketing strategy, the basis of its identity as a good corporate citizen—of Canada as well as North York—is its corporate contributions program. "Community support is a way for a company to make

The Xerox Research Centre of Canada in Mississauga is one of three Xerox Corporation research centres in North America and has a world mandate for materials research.

try standard networks. All products are supported by a well-established service force.

In 1987 the company formed the Xerox Financial Services Division to assume responsibility for its expansion into the financial services business. In addition to financing Xerox products and services, the division offers long-term leasing services for capital equipment not manufactured by Xerox—primarily in the manufacturing, resource, transportation, construction, and utility sectors.

McCamus says the firm's primary objective is to be the preferred vendor in its two major businesses—business products and systems, and financial services. "These two businesses operate in very competitive markets," McCamus notes. "We're convinced that the only way to achieve a competitive advantage in today's tough marketplace is through superior customer satisfaction—understanding and meeting customer needs."

To achieve customer satisfaction the firm has developed and implemented a process it calls Leadership Through Quality, which has become not just a campaign but the basis for the company's entire corporate culture.

"A customer-oriented organization has three key attributes," says McCamus. "It provides innovative products and services, it is responsive to customer needs and concerns, and it is easy to do business with.

"In the Leadership Through Quality process we have set three broad goals for our company, goals for which a public statement about its own identity," explains McCamus. "As a member of the business community, we believe it is important to be a responsible corporate citizen, and to support programs and activities consistent with this objective."

The organization's community involvement program has three principal elements: educational support, United

Way and Junior Achievement programs, and employee and local community involvement.

Xerox supports higher education through awards granted to students at universities and community colleges, and has supported co-operative research projects in materials sciences and computer sciences at several Canadian universities.

In August 1987 Xerox and the National Science Engineering Research Council teamed up to form the Industrial Research Chair at McGill University in Montreal, headed by Dr. Robert Marchessault, Xerox Canada's vice-president of research. Partnerships such as this confirm Xerox Canada's support for excellence in education in Canada.

The company also supports various cultural activities and participates in other major events in the commu-

Xerography has come a long way since its invention in 1938, and Xerox is still a pioneer in the copier/ duplicator market. Leading-edge products range from the 1012 desktop copier to the high-end 1090 Marathon that produces 92 copies per minute (right), to the 1005 color copier (below) that copies in 12 colors and can produce prints or transparencies from 35-millimeter slides.

nity. Xerox was a sponsor of Expo '86 and is a major sponsor of the annual professional squash tour in Canada. This sponsorship includes the Xerox Canadian Open tournament, which attracts the world's best squash players to compete for the richest purse ever offered in the sport.

Xerox was an official sponsor and supplier of the XV Olympic Winter Games in Calgary in 1988, a sponsor of a major exhibition of Leonardo da Vinci's works in Montreal, a corporate participant in Toronto's Skydome sta-

dium, and a sponsor of the Ontario Games for the Physically Disabled.

On a more local level, Xerox takes its role as a North York citizen very seriously. As part of its broader commitment to improving the quality of education in Canada, the company participates in the North York Adopt-a-School program in which corporations become "partners" with schools in a co-operative educational relationship. Xerox has adopted Northview Heights Secondary School in North York.

Xerox is also a corporate sponsor of the North York Senior Citizens' Centre, the North York Arts Council, and the North York Winter Carnival.

"I'm very proud of the people that make up Xerox Canada," says McCamus. "Together we've brought the company a long way from its beginnings as a Xerox Corporation branch office in 1953.

"The Xerox Tower stands as a beacon to all we've accomplished and as a reflection of the efforts and initiative of all employees who have contributed to Xerox' success over the years. The enthusiasm they've shown in striving for excellence and superior customer satisfaction is our most valuable asset."

Chester Carlson would be proud.

FOUR SEASONS HOTELS

Many people thought that Isadore Sharp was, to put it mildly, misguided when he and a couple of friends pooled their resources in 1960 to build a luxury hotel on one of the raunchier streets of Toronto's east side. Similar sentiments were expressed by the hotel establishment in 1963 when Sharp and company purchased 16 acres in a semirural setting in the Borough of North York with a vision of creating Canada's finest suburban hotel. Since then Toronto has emerged as one of the world's great business centres; North York has become a thriving city and a favored corporate location; the Inn on the Park bustles amidst the well-manicured landscape of many commercial parks; and Four Seasons Hotels is the undisputed leader among Canadian hotel chains. Strangely, those early skeptics aren't so easy to find these days.

"Issy" Sharp and his associates had a theory that if a hotel chain were to put a premium on quality without being excessive, make that quality dependably uniform across the chain, pay painstaking attention to detail to the point of recording even the smallest requests of individual customers, and carefully select locations in areas destined for growth, then the world would literally beat a path to its doors—even at a premium price. Twenty-seven years after that theory was formulated few can argue with the logic. Four Seasons now owns or operates 23 hotels in Canada, the United States, and England, containing 7,250 rooms. Gross revenues in 1986 surpassed $500 million and profits rose to $9.5 million, more than double that of 1985, earning shareholders a hefty 21-percent return on investment.

In 18 months alone, from 1986 to 1987, the company has opened four new hotels—the Four Seasons Newport Beach in California; the Four Seasons Hotel and Resort in Dallas at Las Colinas; the Four Seasons Austin, Texas; and the Four Seasons Hotel, Los Angeles. In the same time period the company acquired the historic Biltmore resort hotel in Santa Barbara, California, and announced plans for a 14-acre beachfront resort hotel on the

Hawaiian island of Maui. The firm employs more than 9,000 people and, because it is so protective of their privacy, counts Prince Charles, Bob Hope, Michael Jackson, and Tina Turner among its guests.

Born in Toronto, Sharp studied architecture at Ryerson Polytechnical Institute, graduating with honors in 1952. He then joined the housebuilding business of his father, a Polish immigrant, but soon dreamed of forging out on his own. For five years he knocked on doors, fruitlessly trying to convince investors of the validity of a luxury hotel in downtown Toronto. Finally his brother-in-law, Eddie Creed,

Courtesy, quality, and attention to detail are all trademarks of the Four Seasons Hotels chain (above and opposite page).

then and now a well-known Toronto furrier, and friend Murray Koffler, who would go on to build the Shoppers Drug Mart chain, chipped in $100,000 each. They opened the Four Seasons Motor Hotel on Jarvis Street—an area considered by many to be too rough to attract an upscale clientele—in 1961, boldly using elements of modernist architecture such as interior courtyards to control the environment.

In 1963, with only parkland animals and a garbage dump for neighbors,

Inn on the Park, Toronto, opened in North York. Today the 569-room complex thrives amid the dozens of corporate offices that soon sprouted up around it. In 1970 the company opened Inn on the Park, London, that remains to this day its pride and joy. Located next to Hyde Park, the inn enjoys a remarkably high 95-percent occupancy rate in one of the toughest hotel markets in the world.

Other landmark achievements for the firm include the opening in 1976 of Four Seasons Hotel, Vancouver, which despite a stagnant local economy was booked solid for six months during Expo '86; the opening in 1978 of the company's finest Canadian effort, Four Seasons Hotel, Toronto, in the heart of Yorkville (which spends $60,000 on cut flowers annually and is the favored

stayover of Elizabeth Taylor and Peter Ustinov); the opening in 1979 of the first U.S. hotel to bear the company name, Four Seasons, Washington, which has been rated by influential *Institutional Investor* magazine as the best in North America and is also praised by Thomas Peters and Robert Waterman in their book *In Search of Excellence*; the acquisition and sensitive restoration in 1981 of The Pierre in New York, often cited as the best hotel in the Big Apple; and the opening in 1986 of the Four Seasons Hotel and Resort in Dallas, at Las Colinas, the world's first luxury conference centre and reflective of the company's new emphasis on resorts and specialty properties.

Four Seasons Hotels has created a market niche for itself in the hotel industry by specializing, operating only

medium-size hotels of exceptional quality. Without going overboard, fine appointments such as antique furnishings, Royal Doulton china, and fresh-cut flowers give Four Seasons Hotels a decidedly luxurious atmosphere. Each hotel has a concierge, 24-hour room service, free use of bathrobes and hair dryers, and possibly the softest toilet paper available. There is twice-daily maid service during which clothes are hung and beds turned down. There is also a keen awareness of changing lifestyles reflected by special health-conscious menus and luxurious fitness clubs. None of these features is unique of itself, but the combination of all of them, and their availability without exception across the chain, is one of the key reasons for Four Seasons' success.

In 1986 Four Seasons Hotels went public, with investors, mostly Canadian and European, purchasing 44.4 percent of the company, although Sharp remains controlling shareholder and chief executive officer. The firm is headquartered at 1165 Leslie Street in North York, a quarter-mile from the Inn on the Park and in the heart of the 'wasteland' they once said couldn't support a luxury hotel.

TEXACO CANADA INC.

In the competitive and often volatile oil and gas industry, a firm with a history that stretches back more than 110 years and yet which still aggressively plans for the future is certainly the exception. However, no one ever said Texaco Canada Inc. was an ordinary company.

Texaco Canada's earliest ancestor was McColl and Anderson Ltd., founded by John McColl and William Anderson, which began selling lubricating and illuminating oils in Toronto in 1873—when Canada was but six years old. By serving the needs of the burgeoning railway industry, the venture soon had a nationwide distribution network. An even larger market emerged with the advent of the automobile, prompting McColl Brothers and Company Ltd., as it was now known, to build its first gasoline manufacturing refinery in 1925, in Toronto. It was not long before the demand for fuel was more than McColl Brothers could handle, and, as a result, it merged with Frontenac Oil Refineries Limited (a similar company with a Montreal refinery among its assets) and became McColl-Frontenac Ltd. in 1927.

The next few years were marked by tremendous growth. Through several acquisitions and its own expansion program, the firm's assets grew to include several hundred service stations, three lake tankers, a pipeline company, and

an exploration and drilling operation in Trinidad. Sales of gasoline boomed from 29 million gallons in 1928 to 122 million gallons by 1935.

To finance the organization's continuing growth, McColl-Frontenac then encouraged the purchase of its common shares by The Texas Company of the United States, using the fresh capital to acquire new subsidiaries

Texaco's Canadian corporate headquarters on Wynford Drive.

and increase refinery capacity. By 1941 the firm had a network of 4,000 retail outlets (85 percent independently owned) and product sales of 226 million gallons.

By 1947 the company had generally adopted the Texaco signs, brand names, and product identification—replacing earlier product names such as Red Indian with more internationally recognized names such as Sky Chief. That same year the discovery of oil in Alberta prompted the corporation to pursue its own aggressive exploration program in the West. To finance the project 900,000 new shares were issued, most of which were purchased by Texaco—which then became the controlling shareholder. In 1959 McColl-Frontenac shareholders approved the name change to Texaco Canada Ltd., aligning the firm with the world-spanning Texaco organization and its familiar red star and green "T."

In the ensuing years there have been many other Texaco Canada milestones, including the purchase in 1963 of Elias Rogers Company, the largest fuel marketer in Toronto; the launching in 1968 at Collingwood of the 53,000-barrel tanker Texaco Chief; the start of construction in 1974 of the $480-million Nanticoke refinery on

Texaco Canada operates refineries at Nanticoke, Ontario, and Dartmouth, Nova Scotia. A major $80-million capital project to expand and upgrade the Nanticoke Refinery was completed in 1987, resulting in higher product yields, greater efficiency, and improved energy conservation.

include a food store, car wash, and service bays in addition to gasoline pumps. The success of the System 2000 program reflects the rising number of motorists who want more than just gasoline from their service station.

Texaco Canada is also a sound corporate citizen, contributing toward a wide variety of educational, medical and health, welfare, community, and cultural causes. Of particular note are the company's 46-year sponsorship of the Metropolitan Opera on CBC Radio; its Drive to Survive program, in which parents are encouraged to seek professional driving instruction for

Lake Erie; Texaco's commitment in 1976 to a 40-percent interest in a $20-million deepwater drilling project off Newfoundland; and the formation in 1983 of AT&S Exploration Ltd., with Texaco as a 25-percent partner, which has commenced on a $250- million exploration program in the Arctic and off the East Coast.

In 1987 Texaco Canada ranked third among Canada's integrated oil companies based on net income of $320 million—giving shareholders a healthy 12.8-percent return on equity.

Texaco Canada has principal investments and percentage interests in Federated Pipe Lines Ltd., Manito Pipelines Ltd., Trans-Northern Pipelines Inc., Alberta Products Pipe Line Ltd., and Montreal Pipe Line Ltd.

Recognizing that customers want more than just gasoline from their service station, Texaco adopted a System 2000 program, adding food stores, car washes, and service bays.

The company's revenues were $2.8 billion. Assets totalled $3.9 billion.

Texaco is an industry leader in maximizing recovery from established oil reserves, and it has frontier holdings in the Beaufort Sea and off the East Coast.

In the downstream, Texaco has reduced its number of retail service stations in recent years (from 2,769 in 1982 to more than 1,800 by the end of 1987) but is selling more gasoline, thanks largely to its expanded System 2000 program. System 2000 stations are efficient, high-volume outlets comprised of a family of buildings that may

Texaco Canada has frontier holdings in the the Beaufort Sea and off the East Coast.

their children; and the Texaco Mile, an annual world-class run around Queen's Park to raise money for charity.

In the Toronto area, Texaco has a terminal on Keele Street, its computer centre on Sheppard Avenue, a Home Comfort Centre on Wilson Avenue, and its Canadian corporate headquarters on Wynford Drive. The latter, occupied by the firm in 1970, is the workplace of 600 people, including its president and chief executive officer, Peter I. Bijur.

Texaco Canada customers, employees, and shareholders take comfort in knowing the firm is part of the international Texaco Inc. organization, which has $35 billion in assets and a global network of research, exploration, production, refining, and retail facilities.

DEBOER'S

Entrepreneurs frequently point out that their expertise and success are a result of having spent many long years learning the ins and outs of a particular business. Precious few, however, can match the claim of Anne DeBoer, founder of the prestigious DeBoer furniture chain, of having actually been born aboard a floating furniture store.

This floating enterprise was better known as a potship, a common means of merchandising along the many canals that traverse the country of Holland. For years the DeBoer family potship navigated those waters, selling its wares at each village along its well-travelled route. Later an on-land operation was opened in the town of Hoogeveen, Holland, where Anne worked for several years with his brother, Hans.

However, the mental scars of war and the adventurous spirit overtook Anne, and in 1951 he and his young family moved to Canada.

Things were not easy in the New World at first, and there were years of struggle, but DeBoer was insistent in his belief that there must be a need in Canada for excellent design and value. His first store sold furniture from Holland and the Scandinavian countries, as well as appliances and home entertainment products. Canadians, who had previously been quite traditional in their decorating tastes, eventually responded to the clean lines of European-designed furniture. Thus, by combining a commitment to product value with a keen eye for quality and design, DeBoer's furniture found a firm position in the Metropolitan Toronto marketplace.

Today, after 35 years of experience in international buying, DeBoer's is solidly established with five locations in the Metro Toronto area: 5051 Yonge Street in the heart of North York, in the Scarborough Town Centre, on Dundas Street West in Mississauga in Pickering's Design Centre, and in the fashionable College Park complex in downtown Toronto. As well, DeBoer's recently moved its warehousing, distribution, and head office operations into a beautiful new 40,000-square-foot facility on Drumlin Circle in Concord, Ontario, just north of Steeles Avenue and west of Dufferin Street.

While Anne DeBoer still keeps his hand in the business, most operations of the family-owned company are now handled by his son, John. Like his father, the younger DeBoer sees the success of the firm as rooted in its ability to offer varied and unusual furniture styles at reasonable prices. "We wander," he says, "literally all over the world to buy our furniture. The bulk of it is Canadian, but we supplement it with products from the United States, Europe, South America, and the Far East." John DeBoer also shares his father's belief that Canadians are appreciative of contemporary furniture styles, if they are exposed to them. "Being in the forefront of the business, we try to be innovative. I wouldn't use the word

'educate,' but we try to make people aware of what's out there."

In order to maintain a full line of contemporary and often unique furniture, DeBoer's is continually scanning the design horizons for the latest trends in color, style, texture, and materials. In 1987, for example, the rough-hewn yet chic southwest style was in vogue, and DeBoer's showrooms emphasized natural colors, hand-crafted accents, and much use of glass and stone in pieces such as the Madera Armoire, Pueblo Sofa Suite, and Ynez Cocktail Table. For the less fashion-driven, DeBoer's also offers many classic, timeless items.

Another DeBoer's constant is its superb leather galleries, in recognition of the wonderful adaptability and gra-

cious comfort of that material. Also, DeBoer's showrooms give customers a fuller appreciation of the furniture by presenting concepts rather than individual pieces. This is particularly useful in an age of shrinking living quarters, when the most must be made of available space.

DeBoer's stands apart from any other furniture dealer in that it offers full service—delivering, assembling, and even arranging furniture for its customers. As well, the company boasts some of the best salesmen in the business, seeking out people with a strong furniture sales background and continually helping them upgrade their knowledge and skill. Although not given to flashy gimmicks, DeBoer's does con-

duct two major in-store sales and one warehouse clearance sale per year. Because the quality is very high, DeBoer's furniture does not come cheap. But for the same reason it is worth it.

DeBoer's has been in North York since its founding, and the Willowdale outlet, at 5051 Yonge Street in the centre of the city's burgeoning downtown core, is one of the company's largest, encompassing 40,000 square feet and employing 12 of DeBoer's 100-member staff. "When we first moved here, it was on the edge of the centre of Toronto," says John DeBoer. "But it has grown into an excellent location because we can draw from all areas of Metro Toronto."

CORO CANADA INC.

No longer does the attractiveness of a piece of jewellery hinge solely on the value of the precious metals and stones it contains. Today's fashion-conscious consumer wants style, co-ordination, and the ability to adapt to the latest trends without having to adapt to poverty at the same time. These are some of the reasons for the tremendous boom recently in the popularity of fashion jewellery (no longer, for the above reasons, called costume jewellery), and for the soaring success of an old hand at the business, Coro Canada Inc.

Coro began way back in 1903 in New York (getting its name from its founders, Cohn and Rosenberger) and opened its Canadian division in 1922. Despite its longevity, however, Coro Canada's business has never been as prolific as in the past 17 years, when sales have blossomed to $40 million from a previous $5 million annually. Its manufacturing headquarters on Bartley Drive in North York employs 450 people in a myriad of functions. The company also maintains a showroom in Toronto's Eaton Centre and offices in Vancouver, Calgary, Edmonton, London, Ottawa, Montreal, Halifax, and Quebec City. No Canadian firm produces more of this unique and increasingly popular product than Coro.

The popularity of fashion jewellery of late has not only emerged from public demand but also from the effective marketing and design of innovative companies such as Coro. Coro has successfully penetrated department, jewellery, boutique, and specialty stores, giving its jewellery a new, wider, and more prestigious sales forum. Upscale outlets realize fashion jewellery is now a desirable accessory item for consumers of all incomes. Coro has struck a deal with international designer Oscar de la Renta to produce a new and exclusive line that ranges as high as $200 per piece. Coro covers the mid-price range with its Vendome line, from $10 to $40, and the modest range with its traditional Coro line, which sells from $4 to $10.

The trend-oriented nature of fashion jewellery has created some difficult technological challenges. The firm must adapt virtually overnight to new styles, switching over its design, moulding, assembly, and cutting operations to meet the latest whims of the public. To this end Coro employs a team of designers to come up with new, appealing pieces.

Coro's manufacturing cycle is complex and labor intensive, demanding exceptional interdepartmental teamwork. Base metals such as tin and brass are cast or stamped by precision moulds and dyes. Pieces must be soldered, polished, plated, and stoneset by skilled workers. Much of the assembly work is done by hand because the rapidly changing fashion trends preclude a large volume of individual items. Packaging, warehousing, and shipping are also complex operations owing to the variability in size and content of orders and the delicate nature of the products.

Coro's ability to blend up-to-the-minute creativity with mass production is a result of dedication, experience, and hard work, according to William Landy, company president since 1969. At last count there were 37 members in the firm's 25-Year Club. All this adds up to a lot of employment for North York residents, an exciting future for Coro Canada Inc., and a continuing supply of stylish, affordable fashion jewellery for consumers.

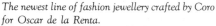

The newest line of fashion jewellery crafted by Coro for Oscar de la Renta.

PATRONS

The following individuals, companies, and organizations have made a valuable commitment to the quality of this publication. Windsor Publications and the City of North York, Property & Economic Development Department, gratefully acknowledge their participation in *North York: Realizing the Dream.*

Adamson Associates*
Apotex Inc.
  Canada's Health Care*
J.J. Barnicke Limited*
Baycrest Centre for Geriatric Care*
Board of Trade of Metropolitan
  Toronto
Bramalea Limited*
Browning Business Equipment Inc.
Camrost Development Corporation*
Canada Cup Inc.*
Canada Dry Bottling Company Ltd.*
Cole, Sherman & Associates, Ltd.*
R.H. Collins Insurance Brokers Ltd.
Concorde Park*
Coro Canada Inc.*
A. Costantino Real Estate Ltd.
Counsel Property Corporation*
Crown Food Service Equipment
  Limited*
DeBoer's*
Delcan Corporation*
The Edgecombe Group*
Falco Properties*
F.&K. Mfg. Co. Limited*
Fiberglas Canada Inc.*
Financial Solutions Inc.
First Professional Management Inc.*
Four Seasons Hotels*
The Glen Group*
Grafco Enterprises
Inducon*
Inland Projects Corporation
Jones, McKittrick, Somer Limited
  Real Estate Appraisers and
  Consultants
The Manufacturers Life Insurance
  Company*
Manufacturers Real Estate*
Marathon Realty Company Limited*
Menkes Developments Inc.*
Morguard Investments Limited
Motorola Canada Ltd.*
North American Life Centre*
Northway Map Technology Limited
Northwestern General Hospital*
The North York Board of Education*
North York Branson Hospital*
North York General Hospital*
North York Hydro Commission*

Oakwood Lumber and Millwork Co.
  Limited*
Olympia & York Developments*
Penta Stolp Corporation*
Petro-Canada*
Principal Heating Company*
Protran Limited
Reff Incorporated*
Royal Plastics Limited*
Rybka, Smith and Ginsler Limited*
Seneca College of Applied Arts and
  Technology*
Joseph D. Sorbara
Sunnybrook Medical Centre*
Texaco Canada Inc.*
Tridel Enterprises Inc.*
Trilea Centres Inc.*
Unisys Canada Inc.*
Universitè York University*
The Upjohn Company of Canada*
Valcoustics Canada Ltd.*
Xerox Canada Inc.*
York Cemetery
York-Finch General Hospital*
York-Trillium Development
  Corporation*

*Participants in Part II: "North York's Enterprises." The stories of these companies and organizations appear in chapters 8 through 12, beginning on page 172.

SELECTED BIBLIOGRAPHY

BOOKS

Armstrong, Frederick H. *Toronto: The Place of Meeting.* Burlington: Windsor Publications Canada, 1983.

Berchem, F.R. *The Yonge Street Story 1793-1860.* Toronto: McGraw-Hill Ryerson, 1966.

Brown, Craig, ed. *The Illustrated History of Canada.* Toronto: Lester & Orpen Dennys, 1987.

de Reus, Mary. *Metropolitan Toronto Business and Market Guide, 1988.* Toronto: The Board of Trade of Metropolitan Toronto, 1988.

Gerard, Fred, ed. *City of North York 1988-89 Business Directory.* Richmond Hill: Alcoma Communications, 1988.

Graham, M. Audrey. *150 Years at St. John's, York Mills.* Toronto: General Publishing Co., 1966.

Guillet, Edwin C. *Early Life in Upper Canada.* Toronto: University of Toronto Press, 1933.

Hart, Patricia. *Pioneering in North York.* Toronto: General Publishing, 1968.

Hathaway, E.J. *Jesse Ketchum and His Times.* Toronto: McClelland and Stewart, 1929.

Hotson, Fred. *The De Havilland Canada Story, 1928-1978.* Toronto: de Havilland Aircraft of Canada, 1978.

Jenness, Diamond. *The Indians of Canada.* Toronto: University of Toronto Press, 1977.

McNaught, Kenneth. *The Pelican History of Canada.* Harmondsworth, Middlesex, England: Penguin Books, 1969.

Myers, Jay. *The Great Canadian Road.* Toronto: Red Rock Publishing Co., 1977.

Sauriol, Charles. *Tales of the Don.* Toronto: Natural Heritage/Natural History, Inc., 1984.

Scadding, Henry. *Toronto of Old.* Toronto: Oxford University Press, 1966.

Township of North York Industrial Committee. *Industrial North York.* City of North York, 1986.

West, Bruce. *Toronto.* Toronto: Doubleday Canada, 1967.

OTHER SOURCES

The Enterprise

Ethnocultural Data Base. Province of Ontario, Ministry of Citizenship and Culture, 1986.

Facility and Street Guide. City of North York Parks and Recreation Department, 1984.

Historical Outline of the Administration of the Borough of North York. Borough of North York, Public Information Office, 1978.

List of Service Clubs and Religious Institutions. City of North York, April 1988.

Living in North York, 1988-89. City of North York, Public Information Office.

Look Out World! We're North York. City of North York, Department of Economic Development (undated).

The Mirror

1988 Summer Services Guide. City of North York Parks and Recreation Department.

1988 Winter Services Guide. City of North York Parks and Recreation Department.

Office of the Mayor, City of North York

Office Space Statistical Summary as of December 31, 1987. Toronto: A.E. Lepage Ltd., 1988.

150 Years of Progress—Education of North York. North York: Board of Education: 1975.

Ontario Ethnocultural Profiles. Province of Ontario, Ministry of Culture and Recreation, 1981.

Ontario Hydro News

Ontario Science Centre

Planning Department, City of North York

Property and Economic Development Department, City of North York

Report on Business Magazine

Toronto Life

Toronto Star

Toronto Sun

The York Pioneer

INDEX

THIS BOOK WAS SET IN GOUDY TYPE

PRINTED ON 70 LB. BASKERVILLE GLOSS

AND BOUND BY

FRIESEN PRINTERS